Tangerines and Pies

The Story of the 2015/16 Football Season for Blackpool and Wigan

Steve Leach

BENNION KEARNY

TABLE OF CONTENTS

PREFACE

In 2014, my book *Conference Season* was published. It described my visits during the 2012-13 season to the 24 towns in which a current Conference team was located, and the games I saw there. It proved a thoroughly enjoyable experience, but by its very nature covered at most three or four games played by any given team, and in some cases only one. As a follow-up, my plan was to cover one or perhaps two clubs throughout the 2015-16 season, so that a sense of their changing fortunes over the whole of the season could be captured.

But which club or clubs should I choose? Much as I would have liked to have picked Stockport County, whom I've supported for nearly sixty years (and whose relegation from the Conference was tearfully chronicled in *Conference Season*), I had to recognise that an account of a club in the Conference (now National League) North would have limited appeal. Also, it so happens that many of the clubs in the National League North are currently located in the Midlands. The prospect of long trips to Brackley, Gloucester, Hednesford, Boston and Lowestoft was not inviting.

I was not interested in writing about Premier League or Championship clubs; my current enthusiasm for professional football covers Divisions One and Two (and the upper levels of the non-league pyramid). The problem was that there was no particular club – within these divisions – that I felt strongly enough about to want to spend a whole season following them (and what if, by January, the club selected was becalmed in mid-table?)

Then I had the bright idea of following the fortunes of two contrasting clubs in either Division One or Two. The clubs would have to be located in the North-West to enable me to avoid the long trips and overnight stops which would be too disruptive to family life. After trying a range of permutations, I came to the conclusion that Blackpool and Wigan Athletic would provide a fascinating, contrasting pair of choices.

There are a number of similarities in the recent histories of the two clubs, but also some striking differences. Both clubs were in the Premier League as recently as 2011 (Wigan until 2013). Both have since experienced spectacular falls from grace, culminating in relegation from the Championship to Division One in 2015. But whereas Blackpool's descent was predictable (and widely predicted) – they started the 2014-15 season with a squad of fifteen (mainly free transfers and loanees) – Wigan's was totally unexpected. The previous season they'd reached the play-off final, where they'd been beaten, arguably unluckily, by Queens Park Rangers, and also the FA Cup semi-final, where they'd lost to Arsenal on penalties. The club was being tipped for promotion rather than relegation, but finished next-to-bottom and went down with Blackpool. Something had gone badly wrong in 2014-15.

Both clubs have long-term wealthy owners; in the case of Blackpool the Oyston dynasty, who purchased the club in 1987, and in the case of Wigan, David Whelan (who took over in 1993) and his family. But whereas David Whelan is still regarded with affection and gratitude at Wigan, despite a series of costly misjudgements in 2014-15, the Oystons are loathed by many of the Blackpool supporters, who accuse them of putting their business interests before those of the club and allowing it to fall into a (possibly terminal) decline. In March 2015, David Whelan handed over the chairmanship of the club to his 23-year-old grandson David. Owen Oyston's son Karl became chairman in 1999, but his 82-year-old dad remains on the board. It is likely that both octogenarians remain influential.

Both clubs appointed new managers towards or at the end of the 2014-15 season. Wigan went for Gary Caldwell, a highly-regarded former club captain (at the time still on the playing staff, though with a long-term injury), but with no managerial experience. He replaced Malky Mackay a few games before the season's end.

Blackpool's Lee Clark, after a dismal five months in charge, resigned at the end of the season and was replaced by Neil McDonald, who had been Sam Allardyce's assistant at West Ham for the previous few years.

Both teams had retained relatively few of the previous season's playing staff, but at least this year Blackpool had assembled enough players to field a team and fill the substitutes bench for the first match of the season (which they'd failed to do in August 2014). Both teams had recruited players with reasonable track records, at least by the standards of Divisions One and Two. As was the case the previous year, the pundits in the football press expected Blackpool to be relegated, and Wigan to at least make the playoffs. I wasn't so sure. Wigan had a new and inexperienced manager, and a squad dominated by newcomers, who might (or might not) prove capable of gelling into a cohesive unit. Blackpool had acquired an experienced (at assistant level) manager, who had been allowed to bring in credible new players, to a greater extent than had his predecessors.

Although I'd seen both clubs in action from time to time over the past few decades, I felt no sense of identity with, or commitment to, either of them. I would be able to sit back as an objective observer and make dispassionate judgements about their progress (or lack of it). Had I decided on Stockport County, such objectivity would have been much more difficult.

The plan was that I would seek to watch each club in action in around a third of their season's fixtures, including the two games when they played each other and provide detailed reports of these matches. Brief summaries of all the other fixtures would also be included, drawing on video footage of the highlights (now widely available on the net and *The Football League Show*), press reports, and comments on social media.

In covering each of the two clubs' 46 league matches (plus the Cup games), I felt that it would be important to describe (briefly) most or all of the goals scored by my chosen clubs. For spectators and (in particular) supporters, goals are the memory-triggers in recalling games, the focal points around which the shape of each game can be remembered, and enjoyed (or otherwise) in retrospect. But therein lies a problem. There are only so many ways of describing how a goal has been scored and all of them have been used ad nauseam by football writers throughout the country. 'Brown towered above the defenders to power home a header' ...... 'Smith neatly side-footed the ball past the advancing keeper into the corner of the net' ...... 'Jones hit a thunderous volley from the edge of the area into the roof of the net' and so on. I have no magic formula for finding new ways of describing such things! Readers will just have to put up with these (and many other) familiar phrases. Okay, they are clichés, but – as far as I'm concerned – unavoidable ones, and at least clichés have the advantage that everyone knows what you mean by them and can picture them! Have you tried to find convincing alternatives to 'defence-splitting through balls,' 'shots finding their way through forests of legs,' or 'headers cannoning back off the bar'? No, I thought not!

The book is intended as a portrayal of football, as it is experienced below the top two tiers, and as a testament to the significance the game has in the lives of many thousands of residents of the two towns concerned. It chronicles the journeys of Wigan and Blackpool over the nine months of the season, starting in August, and ending in early May (or later if a play-off place is achieved), the highs and lows, the joy, despair, tragedy, humour and farce. It seeks to explore the relationship between the history of each club, and their current circumstances and aspirations; and the relationship between the towns themselves and the clubs who are so important a part of their cultural heritage.

Both clubs hit the headlines in the 2014-15 season: Blackpool as a result of the poisonous relationship between owners (the Oystons) and the fans, which culminated in a pitch invasion and protest at Bloomfield Road on the final day of the season, causing the game to be abandoned: and at Wigan the controversial appointment of a manager with racist and sexist views (to name but two), and the suspension of the club's owner (David Whelan) by the FA for a series of subsequent remarks, made in support of the manager. Both sequences of events had repercussions well into the 2015-16 season. I endeavoured to understand the dynamics of these two problematic situations and their continuing impact on the fortunes and public perceptions of the clubs. An aim greatly facilitated by insights gained from interviews with key figures in the supporters' organisations of both clubs (see below). In essence, I wanted to embark and report on two contrasting journeys into the (then) unknown, which I hope readers will enjoy sharing with me.

The structure of the book is as follows. The first two chapters are portraits of the towns of Blackpool and Wigan respectively, drawing on what has been written about them by authors as diverse as George Orwell, J.B.Priestley, Bill Bryson, and Stuart Maconie, and on my own knowledge and experience of them. In each case, I also provide a brief history of the football club up to the start of the 2015-16 season and make connections between the town and the club. The fortunes of the two clubs are then described and analysed on a month-by-month basis. There is one interruption to this pattern between November and October, when, three months into the season, I seek to provide interpretations of the current state of play of each club, and how this has been influenced by events on and off the field over the previous year or so. This chapter draws heavily on interviews carried out with Christine Seddon, William Watt and Phil Hartley regarding Blackpool, and Martin Tarbuck and Jonathan Jackson regarding Wigan. The book ends with a retrospective chapter, which looks back over the 2015-16 season and speculates on the prospects for both clubs.

The book has benefitted greatly from the help I received from the following people. Martin Tarbuck, the editor of the Wigan Athletic fanzine *The Mudhutter*, has been an invaluable source of information and insight regarding the recent history of the club, and the problems encountered in the 2014-15 season. We discussed the progress of the 'Latics' (as they are widely-known) throughout the season, and he kindly read through and commented on all my draft chapters. In addition, he was instrumental in enabling me to obtain a ticket for Wigan's crucial away fixture at Burton, late in the season, through his contact with Jonathan Jackson, the club's chief executive. Many thanks, Martin, the book owes a great deal to your involvement. Jonathan Jackson not only agreed to provide me with a ticket, when officially the ticket office had sold out, he also spent an hour with me at the end of the season, answering my questions with a refreshing openness, and providing me with helpful insights into the financial and recruitment policies of the club, as well as the problems of the 2014-15 season, and how they had been overcome.

Christine Seddon, vice-chair of Blackpool Supporters Trust (BST) kindly agreed to be interviewed and provided me with a clear and comprehensive account of the origins, history and recent initiatives of BST, plus a critical appraisal of the way in which the Oystons have run the club, and their impact on the recent decline in the club's fortunes. William Watt, the Blackpool FC correspondent of *The Blackpool Gazette* since 2011 was also kind enough to share with me his take on the recent history of the club, and the deteriorating relationship between owners and fans. His regular columns in *The Gazette* proved an invaluable source of information throughout the season. Phil Hartley has supported Blackpool since the 1960s. Along with around two thousand other season-ticket holders he and his family made no use of their two season tickets throughout 2015-16, as a protest at the way the club was being run. We discussed Blackpool's progress at regular intervals throughout the season, and he provided many valuable insights, not only on the club, but also on the town, as well as commenting on several draft chapters, and loaning me one of his season tickets.

I approached Karl Oyston with a request for an interview with himself or failing that with someone else on the club's staff who could provide me with an insider's perspective. The request was politely declined.

James Lumsden-Cook of Bennion Kearny again played a supportive and proactive role in the book's progress, making numerous helpful suggestions regarding textual changes in all the draft chapters.

Finally, grateful thanks to my wife Karen Lloyd (now herself a published author; check out *The Gathering Tide; A Journey round the Edgelands of Morecambe Bay*; Saraband Press 2016) and to our sons Callum and Fergus, for providing a wonderfully supportive family environment, which made the project so much easier to carry out. The book is lovingly dedicated to them.

CHAPTER 1
WIGAN: THE TOWN AND THE FOOTBALL CLUB

Blackpool and Wigan; two Lancashire towns. One is a seaside resort, still the most popular in Britain, although struggling, as are all British resorts, to cope with the competition from continental destinations where the weather is more reliable. The other is a relic of the industrial revolution, when it served as the administrative centre to a large number of surrounding coal mining settlements, as well as a prime location for the cotton industry. Both coal and cotton have long since departed, but Wigan survives, despite the loss of its economic base (as such places always do), as the home of Uncle Joe's Mint Balls ('keep you all aglow'), and Heinz, of the 57 varieties fame (but who can name more than a dozen of them?)

However much they may be loved by their residents (and in Blackpool's case, its tourists), neither town has enjoyed a good press from those who have chosen to write about them. Wigan's most famous chronicler is George Orwell, who went to stay there to research his study of the plight of the working class in the Great Depression of the mid-1930s. *The Road to Wigan Pier* (which he never managed to find) records in detail the appalling living conditions of the miners, mill workers, and large numbers of unemployed people who lived in and around the town. He lived (briefly) in a common lodging house which doubled as a tripe shop, although the tripe business was struggling. "We don't seem to get no customers nowadays," the proprietor is quoted as saying. "I don't know 'ow it is. The tripe's just a-laying there, day after day – such beautiful tripe it is too." So tripe, which was still widely available in Manchester in the 1950s when I was a lad (and apparently still is in Wigan), is one of the many unflattering images associated with the town. Orwell was angry about the plight of the town and sympathetic to the efforts made by its working-class inhabitants to keep going in extremely difficult circumstances,but his book has unwittingly contributed to the unflattering present day popular image of Wigan.

Some 50 years later, in 1982, Paul Theroux (father of the better-known Louis, who has featured in numerous TV programmes in recent years, typically interviewing nutters of various descriptions) visited Wigan in *The Kingdom by the Sea*, his 'candid and compulsive account of a journey round the coast of Britain.' Quite how that brought him to Wigan, which is over 20 miles from the nearest bit of sea, is by no means clear, but visit Wigan he did. He thought it had a somewhat countrified look, with "its winding main street on a little hill, with red-brick hotels and two railway stations, and many public houses fitted with bright mirrors and brass-work." But the town was now lifeless; "the town had once been a centre of coal mining and cotton mills; both had now gone." Wigan was "as bereft of energy and as empty a ruin as Stonehenge," And this was in 1982, before the ravages of Thatcherism had yet to make their full impact.

Twelve years later, Bill Bryson visited Wigan and recorded his impressions in *Notes from a Small Island* the first of a series of travel books which have made him famous. He was more impressed than he expected to be. He managed to find Wigan Pier without any difficulty…"you can hardly miss it now, there are cast-iron signposts pointing the way to it on almost every street corner." Having wandered around the site, noting that the pier was really an old coal shed on the side of the Liverpool-to Leeds Canal, and having failed to get into the tourist attraction, which comprised a museum, gift shop, snack bar and pub (The Orwell), all closed on Friday, he walked up the hill to Wigan town centre, which he was "truly astonished to find that it was handsome and well-maintained." He was particularly impressed by the way in which "some talented architect had managed to incorporate a new shopping arcade into the existing fabric of the buildings, in a simple but deceptively clever and effective way." Bryson had been very critical of ill-designed town centre developments elsewhere in the book, and was "delighted to think that if this sort of thing was going to happen just once in Britain, it should be in poor beleaguered Wigan."

More recently, Mathew Engel in *Engel's England*, his excellent record of a tour around the 39 traditional counties of England, was unimpressed by what he found, when following the brown tourist attraction signs to Wigan Pier in 2013. "The 'Wigan Pier Experience', a 'heritage attraction', was closed in 2007," he reports. "The museum had gone. The Pier Nightclub the other side of the canal had gone. Even the Tourist Information Office had gone."

Wigan Pier had gained fame (or perhaps notoriety) in the music hall performances of George Formby Senior (father of the rather more famous singer and ukulele player) in the 1920s. It was in reality, claimed Engel, a small jetty, rather than a pier (so not the coal-shed that Bryson thought it was? Please can we have a definitive answer). Engel shared Bryson's enthusiasm for the town centre, which he thought had "an unexpected air of prosperity and charm." I agree. The centre is on top of a small hill and has a lively feel to it, aided by the fact that there is no large concrete-and-glass retail monstrosity dominating it. So credit is due to the council for their good judgement in turning away the Arndale Centres of this world, even if they've failed to keep the Wigan Pier Heritage Centre going (an outcome for which the coalition's government's imposed cuts on local council expenditure may well be responsible).

Pies are another element of the mental picture outsiders have of Wigan. As Stuart Maconie notes in *Pies and Prejudice*, his affectionate portrait of the North of England, the town's enthusiasm for pies has been immortalised in many a joke, although he omits my favourite; What do you call a balanced meal in in Wigan? A pie in one hand and a pie in the other. It's never been clear to me why it's Wigan with which pies should be associated in the popular mind, rather than several other

Lancashire towns with an equivalent enthusiasm for this delicacy (Preston North End used to have a fanzine called *The Pie-Muncher*). One theory, I was told, is that the pie association dates back to the 1920s, when after an unsuccessful strike, the miners in the plethora of pits close to Wigan 'were forced to eat humble pie'.

George Orwell, Wigan Pier, pies and the town's lead role in the Northern Soul phenomena of the 1970s just about sum up the popular image of Wigan, with its trophy-rich rugby league history often thrown in for good measure. This amalgam of images greatly annoyed the writers of the excellent *Pies and Prejudice* (not Stuart Maconie's book, but a chronicle of Wigan Athletic's 2004-05 season, when they won promotion to the Premiership). Reacting against the kind of coverage their team had been receiving in *The Guardian*, they identified "twenty clichés that you must get into each match report featuring Wigan Athletic. Just insert these, join the letters up and hey presto you have an article."

"Mention that 'it's grim up north'… refer to Wigan Pier… refer to George Orwell… refer to pies… mention all the kids you saw throwing a rugby ball around on the way to the ground… and don't forget to mention that IT'S A RUGBY TOWN."

The authors Martin Tarbuck and Andrew Vaughan are by no means happy about the fact that Stuart Maconie pinched the title of their book, published two years before his (can you take out patents on book titles, I wonder?).

Wigan has always felt like a Lancashire town; it is right in the middle of the red-rose county. So it may come as a surprise to discover that it is now located in Greater Manchester, or at least the council is. This is clearly a nonsense as far as community identity is concerned. Big and sprawling though Greater Manchester is, its far-reaching tentacles don't extend as far as Wigan, though they arguably do to the other main centre of population in the borough – the adjacent townships of Leigh, Atherton, and Tyldesley. There was just as strong (or weak) a case for making Wigan part of Merseyside. In reality, it is and always has been a Lancashire town.

Due to its fringe location in the conurbation, Wigan has ended up playing the role of honest broker in the convoluted affairs of the Association of Greater Manchester Authorities (or AGMA), which was set up following the abolition of the Greater Manchester Metropolitan County Council (or GMC) by Margaret Thatcher in 1986, to oversee those activities which still had to be planned and delivered on a conurbation-wide basis, such as public transport, police and waste disposal. Because none of the City of Manchester's satellites (Bury, Bolton, Oldham, Rochdale, etc.) trusted Manchester City Council to play the lead role in this conglomerate, they looked to Wigan (which isn't really part of Greater Manchester, and so could be relied on to operate in an objective fashion) to do so, which it has done very effectively since 1986, with the council leader Peter Smith (now Lord Smith of Wigan) operating as AGMA's de facto leader. His role has grown in importance since George Osborne launched the Northern Powerhouse initiative late in 2014, which has involved the devolution of a number of responsibilities (previously within the domain of central government) to AGMA (which is now called the Greater Manchester Combined Authority (or GMCA), but don't worry too much about that, no-one's going to ask you!). So whatever Wigan's reputation as a 'hick town' (Stuart Maconie's characterisation), it has a high profile in the government of Greater Manchester.

Both Wigan Athletic and Blackpool can be seen as 'big clubs' who have fallen on hard times. As recently as 2010-11 both were in the Premier League, attracting crowds of over 15,000. By the start of the 2015-16 season, both had dropped into Division One, which is largely populated by small-town clubs such as Crewe Alexandra, Burton Albion, Scunthorpe United and Fleetwood Town. Only Sheffield United and Coventry City are comparable with Wigan and Blackpool in terms of former status. But if you delve back into the history of both clubs, you will find (in common with most Football League teams) a chequered past, punctuated with low points as well as highlights.

Wigan Borough were formed in 1921, and entered the newly-formed Division Three North the same year, together with a host of clubs from medium-sized towns throughout the north. They finished fifth in 1923 and fourth in 1929, but otherwise had a relatively undistinguished record, before resigning and folding in 1931. A new club, Wigan Athletic, was established the following year and joined the Lancashire Combination. For almost 50 years after that Wigan Athletic were one of the best-known of the non-league clubs, alternating between the Lancashire Combination and the Cheshire County League (where there was clearly a relaxed view about the definition of the boundaries of Cheshire!) and later the Northern Premier League when it was founded in 1969. Their high profile was the result of epic performances in the FA Cup, most memorably a 2-2 draw at Newcastle United in 1954 (followed by a gallant 2-3 defeat at Springfield Park) and a 0-1 defeat in 1971 at Maine Road, against a high-flying Manchester City.

Wigan's ambitions to return to the Football League were never in doubt. In their period in the wilderness, they made 35 applications (which must constitute an all-time record). In frustration at their repeated lack of success, they made a headline-catching (but unsuccessful) application to join the Scottish League Division Two in 1972, evoking some interesting possibilities – Forfar versus Wigan, the battle of the 'Latics'! They finally made it back in 1978, at the expense of nearby Southport although it has to be said there was some controversy about the manner of their doing so. On the first ballot, the two clubs each received 26 votes, with Rochdale, who finished in 24th position no doubt relieved (and surprised) to survive, having emerged from the ballot ahead of both. In the second ballot, Wigan's 'superior canvassing' won the day; there are reports of some very up-market pens being gifted to the delegates!

Wigan coped well with the demands of league football, finishing sixth in both of their first two seasons. The next season they were eleventh, but in 1982, they were promoted, after finishing third in what was then Division Four. They struggled for a while in the lofty heights of Division Three, but gradually improved and finished fourth in 1986 and again in 1987, which was the year in which the play-off system was first introduced (Wigan failed to negotiate their way past Swindon Town in the semi-finals). That was as good as it got. After a series of finishes in the lower reaches of the table, the club returned to Division Four in 1992, having finished next to bottom, and ended up as low as 19th in their first season back there.

But salvation was on the way in the form of local millionaire businessman David Whelan, who purchased the club in 1995. Whelan, although born in Bradford, grew up in Wigan, where in his early adulthood he ran a market stall. He moved on to running a grocery business, which expanded into a supermarket chain, and which was sold profitably to Morrisons in 1992, by which time he had built up the JJB sportswear stores into a national chain. He was every small-time league club's dream, a local benefactor who wanted to deploy a large chunk of his accumulated fortune in putting his local club on the map. A recent precedent had been the role of Jack Walker at nearby Blackburn Rovers. His millions had transformed a run of the mill second-tier club into Premiership champions in less than a dozen seasons. David Whelan made it clear that he had a similar objective: reaching the Premier League from Wigan's current fourth-tier position, within the same kind of timeframe. It was fortunate for the football club that Whelan's enthusiasm was for soccer rather than rugby league, although the formidable rugby league side did, in due course, benefit from Whelan's largesse.

When Whelan bought the club, Wigan were still playing at Springfield Park, an atmospheric but antiquated ground, where the club had played ever since its foundation in 1921. It was clearly not fit-for-purpose when the purpose was a speedy rise to the Premiership. So plans were soon drawn up for a new state-of-the-art stadium a mile or so to the west of the town centre. The JJB Stadium (which later came to be known as the DW Stadium when

Whelan sold his sportswear business) was ready for the start of the 1999-2000 season and has since been used by the rugby club as well as by Wigan Athletic. In its early years, its 25,000 capacity was rarely tested; the average gate in 1999-2000 was just over 7,000.

One of Whelan's first innovations was to use his business connections to recruit a trio of Spanish players: Isidro Diaz, Jesus Seba and Roberto Martinez (later to become Wigan's manager). They became known as 'The Three Amigos'. To have three Spaniards in a fourth-tier team was then unprecedented (and indeed still is) and was a potent symbol of Whelan's ambitions for the club. The Wigan fans must have thought they were in dreamland!

Although interest and attendances unsurprisingly increased, progress on the field was slower than Whelan (and the supporters) would have liked. Wigan finished tenth at the end of Whelan's first year of ownership. The following season they were promoted, as champions, with John Deehan as manager, but back in Division 2 (as it now was) progress was unimpressive, at least by the exacting standards of the new owner. The playoffs were reached in three successive seasons (1998-2001) but each time Wigan failed to come through, although they did make it to the final in 2000. Managers came and went in quick succession: Graham Barrow, John Deehan, Ray Mathias, Bruce Rioch, Colin Greenall and Steve Bruce arrived and departed within the space of seven seasons, a measure of Dave Whelan's impatience and frustration. Then at last, in 2003, under the managership of Paul Jewell, Wigan made it to the second tier for the first time in their history. And they did it in style, accumulating 100 points, suffering only four defeats, and with the meanest defence in the whole of the Football League (25 goals conceded in 46 matches). The golden years had begun.

In their first season in the Championship, Wigan narrowly missed out on a play-off place. Had West Ham's Brian Deane not scored an equaliser at the JJB Stadium seconds from the end of the final game of the season, Wigan would have secured the coveted sixth place on goal difference from Crystal Palace (who went on to win promotion). But the next year, at the end of the 2004-05 season, they finally made it to the Premier League, under the inspired managership of Paul Jewell, without having to cope with the uncertainties of the playoffs. Wigan finished runners-up to Sunderland, securing an impressive 25 wins, and owing much to the goal-scoring achievements of Nathan Ellington (24 goals) and Jason Roberts (21).

Ten years previously, Wigan Athletic had finished 14th in Division Four, and their average attendance at down-at-heel Springfield Park had been a paltry 1,832. For the regulars who'd witnessed defeats there to the likes of Barnet, Mansfield Town and Lincoln City, the idea that ten years later they would be facing the prospects of visits from Arsenal, Liverpool and Manchester United would have invoked incredulity. But that's part of the magic of football isn't it, that such transformations can and occasionally do happen. I experienced a similar 'can this really be happening?' feeling in 1996, when Stockport County emerged from obscurity to reach the lofty heights of the Championship (then Division One), where they proceeded to defeat Manchester City, Wolves, West Bromwich Albion and Stoke City.

For eight seasons, Wigan competed with the elite in the Premiership. They never finished higher than tenth, but that was probably the limit of their ambitions; a top four position was never really a plausible outcome, nor had David Whelan ever set his sights that high. But Wigan survived season after season, sometimes by the skin of their teeth (just two points clear of the drop in 2007; three in 2011). Managers came and went, some highly-regarded by the supporters (Paul Jewell, Steve Bruce (although he didn't stay long)), others less so (Chris Hutchings). Similarly with the players; some made a big impact (Antonio Valencia, Pascal Chimbonda); others proved a disappointment (Ronnie Stam, Mauro Boselli). In 2009, Roberto Martinez was appointed as manager, and soon endeared himself to the supporters when Wigan, for the first time since they were promoted, won games in the Premiership against the elite clubs; Arsenal, Chelsea and Liverpool were all defeated at the JJB Stadium in the 2009-10 season.

Then in 2012-13 came the turning point. It was a remarkable season in many ways. For the first (and possibly last) time in their history, Wigan won the FA Cup. Not only did they win it, but they defeated the formidable bank-rolled Manchester City in the final. With extra time looming, substitute Ben Watson scored with a far post header, which will be etched forever in the memories of all the Wigan fans who witnessed it (and which caused great delight to many of the TV audience, including me, who relished the fact that it was still possible, on such an occasion, for a small club to defeat one of the Premiership giants). But the joy turned to despair a few days later, when a defeat at Arsenal condemned Wigan to relegation. Their eight-year spell in the Premier League had come to an end. Martinez left for Everton, and Owen Coyle was appointed as his replacement.

The first season back in the Championship was by no means a disaster, although things hadn't looked good half-way through the season, when after three successive home defeats, Wigan had dropped into the lower half of the table. Owen Coyle was sacked, a move popular with many Wigan fans, including the editors of the excellent fanzine *Mudhutter*, who had not warmed to the more 'direct' style of play favoured by Coyle, after four seasons in which Martinez had persevered with a more attractive 'build it up from the back' approach. Coyle's replacement was the former Manchester City player Uwe Rosler, who had taken Brentford to within a whisker of promotion the previous season (a missed penalty in the play-off final had made all the difference).

Rosler reverted to the more free-flowing inter-passing system of the Martinez era, which quickly began to pay off. Wigan soared up the table, finally making it to the top six on the back of six successive league wins. If that wasn't enough, they very nearly made it back to

Wembley, losing on penalties to Arsenal in the FA Cup semi-final, after leading 1-0 until the 83rd minute. Their brief encounter with Europe, however, did not go so well. They finished bottom of their group, but no doubt it was fun while it lasted!

Wigan's marathon season – 62 games in total – came to a disappointing end when they were defeated in the playoff semi-final by Queens Park Rangers. Leading one-nil on aggregate half an hour from the end of the second leg at Loftus Road, they were undone by two goals from Charlie Austin, the second in extra time. Devastating though this must have felt at the time, it didn't detract from the reality that Wigan had enjoyed another eventful and largely successful season. The golden years, which had commenced in 2002 still seemed to be in operation in 2014. Indeed, with Uwe Rosler firmly established as manager and an excellent playing record in the second half of the season, Wigan were widely predicted to be promotion candidates in 2014-15. There remained an air of optimism in and around the club.

But soon it all went horribly wrong. Wigan had a reasonable-enough start; at the end of September, they were a respectable ninth in the table. But after a run of 12 games which included only one victory, David Whelan lost patience and dismissed Rosler, less than six months after he'd come close to securing an immediate return to the Premiership. It may be that the manager had 'lost the dressing-room'; in the aftermath of his last game in charge, a 1-3 defeat at Bolton, he accused his players of 'giving up' when conceding three goals in 11 second-half minutes. But there were many who felt he should have been given more time to sort things out.

But worse was to follow. Rosler's appointed successor, Malky Mackay had a reasonable track record as a manager; he had taken Cardiff City to the Premiership in 2013, although he was sacked by Cardiff's unpredictable owner Vincent Tan, allegedly for 'overspending' halfway through what turned out to be the club's only season at the top level. But at the time of his appointment by Wigan, he was involved in a controversy, widely featured in the tabloids, regarding the publication of an exchange of texts with his assistant at Cardiff the previous season. The texts provided evidence that Mackay's repertoire of attitudes embraced racism, sexism, homophobia and anti-Semitism (amongst others), and that there was a distinct possibility of him being disciplined by the FA. It looked like a high-risk (to say the least) appointment, at a time when the club needed a period of calm and stability.

When challenged in a *Guardian* interview about the wisdom of appointing Mackay in these circumstances, Whelan did himself and the club no favours and raised the level of controversy surrounding the appointment to heightened levels. The club chairman went out of his way to defend both the appointment, and Mackay personally, and in the process made remarks about Jewish and Chinese people which were deemed 'offensive' by the FA, who fined him £50,000 and banned him from all football-related activities for six weeks. Shortly afterwards, he stepped down as chairman in favour of his 23-year-old grandson David Sharpe.

If Mackay had managed to halt Wigan's decline, and steer the club back up the table, then maybe the supporters would have been prepared to overlook his array of prejudices. Indeed, it's not unlikely that there was a sizeable group of fans who weren't too bothered by them anyway. But, as it turned out, Mackay proved unable to turn things round. I saw his 13th game in charge, a 1-3 home defeat to a Bournemouth side who were in a different class, at the end of which his record read 'Played 13, Won 1, Drawn 3, Lost 9'. In comparison, Uwe Rosler's record earlier in the season didn't look too bad! Mackay initiated a major turnover of the playing staff. In the week before the Bournemouth game, six new players had been signed (three of them on loan), and several well-established players allowed to leave, which introduced a degree of upheaval and instability not conducive to success on the field (but it's striking how many new managers feel the need to operate in this way).

To add insult to injury, Mackay was an adherent of the Owen Coyle school of football strategy. Out went the patient inter-passing approach favoured by Rosler (and Martinez before him), and in came the much less attractive long-ball game. Again the Wigan fans might have put up with it if it had worked, but it didn't. Having failed to inspire a single home win (and only a couple of away victories), Mackay was sacked in April, and replaced by the popular former club captain Gary Caldwell (who was still on the playing staff). By this time, relegation was almost inevitable, and whilst Caldwell supervised the first home win for seven months (against Brighton), and did oversee an improvement in form, it was all too late. Wigan finished on 39 points, eight below the number which would have ensured survival. They managed only three home wins all season (even Blackpool beat that!). Wigan's annus horribilis had come to a merciful end.

Not surprisingly, there was a further upheaval in the playing staff over the close season. The players Mackay had brought in had proved (with only one or two exceptions) ineffective (fortunately many of them were loanees). Of the players registered at the start of the 2014-15 season, only a handful were retained. Of the close season signings, Will Grigg, who had scored 20 league goals for MK Dons on their way to the Championship, stood out. Craig Morgan had been recruited from Rotherham United, Craig Davies from Bolton Wanderers, Max Power from Tranmere Rovers, and David Perkins (who I remember well from his time at Morecambe) from Blackpool. It was certain that the team that kicked off against Coventry City would be unrecognisable from the one which completed their disastrous 2014-15 season at Brentford.

Despite the uncertainty surrounding a largely new playing staff and a new inexperienced manager, those in the football media who chose to make pre-season predictions expected Wigan to be, at the very least, playoff candidates. The predictions made by the representatives of the supporters of the 24 clubs in Division One, when averaged out, put Wigan in second place. Ian Aspinall of Wigan wasn't so confident. "Very difficult to predict as there's been a huge turnover in playing staff while we have a new untried manager in Gary Caldwell and the youngest league chairman in David Sharpe," he wrote. "I'll be pleasantly surprised if we make the playoffs". Certainly the young chairman's statement to the press that he didn't just want to win the league, "I want to smash it and get 100 points" sounded like a hostage to fortune, which he may well be regretting come May 2016!

CHAPTER 2
BLACKPOOL: THE TOWN AND THE FOOTBALL CLUB

Whilst George Orwell was experiencing the delights of tripe and pigs' trotters in Wigan, another famous chronicler of the condition of England in the mid-1930s – J.B. Priestley – was casting his eye on Blackpool. He went in November (when the illuminations season was over), and found the town to be "deserted or asleep…they had all gone, the fiddlers, fortune-tellers, pierrots, cheapjacks, waiters and sellers of peppermint and pineapple rock…Blackpool the resort was dead." His favourite moments appeared to be on the promenade, with his back to the town, facing out to sea and relishing the "great salty gusts" and the way in which the sea "sent sheets of spray over the glistening wet railings and seats." He didn't like his hotel, nor the American Bar in which he had a drink, but, compared with other towns he visited, Blackpool got off relatively lightly (unlike Gateshead, Wolverhampton, and the Potteries which all get a hammering).

It's probably just as well that Priestley didn't visit Blackpool in the height of the season, which is when other writers have struggled to find anything positive to say about it. In the most recent edition of *Crap Towns*, Blackpool comes in at 28th crappiest. One contributor records that he went to Blackpool once, and that "It was like walking through a Hieronymus Bosch painting. Hordes of topless folk hung out of pub windows, yelling, drooling, puking, pissed. Blackpool is all the proof I need that God doesn't exist. If He were looking, He would have burned the place!"

Paul Theroux travelled on to Blackpool from Wigan and was not impressed. Blackpool as a town was, he thought, "perfectly reflected in the swollen guts and unhealthy fat of its beer-guzzling visitors." It was "just swagger and sandwiches." The 'Golden Mile' was, in his view, "a hideous promenade." He wanted to leave

Blackpool as quickly as possible and was annoyed that "it was not possible to walk away" (it was of course; he could have reached the town's rural fringes in less than an hour). Instead, he caught a bus to Morecambe, which by the early-1980s was (unlike Blackpool) well past its sell-by date as a seaside resort, but which he liked for being "sedate and dull and unapologetic." Not necessarily a combination of qualities likely to get the crowds flocking back!

Bill Bryson also struggled to find positive things to say about Blackpool, although he did like it considerably better in daylight. "The promenade had some nice bits of cast-iron and elaborate huts with onion domes selling rock, nougat and other sticky things, which had escaped me in the darkness the night before." The beach, he thought was "vast and empty and very agreeable." Refreshing to find someone with a good word or two for Blackpool, even if the author had been underwhelmed by the illuminations the previous evening ("They are nothing if not splendid, and they are not splendid.").

Bryson returned in 2014 and was impressed with the revamped promenade, "two miles of broad, artfully sinuous thoroughly pleasing walkway; it isn't so much a promenade as a piece of sculpture you walk on." In his view, it's the nicest promenade in the world, "so long as you keep your gaze firmly out to sea and don't look over your shoulder at the town facing it." Oh dear, another damning verdict on its way? Yes, indeed. Whereas on his previous visit, in 1994, he'd thought that Blackpool was "cheerfully down-market, but good-natured and fun," in 2014 it was "depressed and half-derelict, its streets empty by day and intimidating by night." He reels off a set of depressing statistics: third highest percentage of job losses in the country (2004-13): the unhealthiest community in Britain (2013): the highest proportion of alcohol-related deaths in the country; and (according to the *Guardian*) the site of the 'worst hotel in Britain' – the New Kimberley. But, as Bryson points out, "the patrons of the New Kimberley weren't holidaymakers; they were the indigent and semi-homeless who stayed in a squalid dangerous fleapit because it was all they could afford." His tongue-in-cheek solution is to let Wetherspoons run the town. "They seem to know how to give working people a happy experience in decent surroundings at a reasonable price."

Mathew Engel, having reminded us of what former Conservative Minister and diarist Alan Clark thought of the town ("Isn't Blackpool appalling, loathsome… dirt, squalor, broken pavements with water lying in them… and on the Promenade vulgar, common 'primitives' "), adds his own voice to the chorus of disapproval. He found a town centre "so run-down the competition mainly comprises pound shops being undercut by 99p shops… it has ceased to be a venue for family summer holidays, but unlike the more southerly resorts has found no real replacements… the party conferences have migrated elsewhere, mainly inland; the Labour Party stopped going there when the guacamole tendency had seen off the mushy peas tendency."

He also notes that "the action now belongs mainly to stag and hen parties that have become Blackpool's most reliable source of business and aggravation." The Wikipedia entry on Blackpool makes the same point (so it must be true). But Blackpool has also become a magnet for another social category. According to an entry in *Crap Towns*, Blackpool has the greatest proportion of single male homeless divorcees in its population of any town or city in Britain. So "when you've lost your wife, lost your job and lost your house, there's always Blackpool!"

In *Pies and Prejudice*, Stuart Maconie returned to Blackpool, the location of many of his childhood holidays, for the first time in years. Once he'd emerged from the "deadening experience" of arriving at Blackpool North station ("it looks less like a railway station than a decontamination plant"), the sun came out, the North Pier came into view, and "my heart lifted and my step quickened; I was nine again." This change in mood inspired him to visit the famous Pleasure Beach, a mile or so to the south along the promenade, where he spent a happy hour or so, before emerging into the demimonde of the South Shore, which "even by Blackpool's own standards is supremely tacky." This observation was of particular interest to me, because Blackpool FC's Bloomfield Road ground is situated close to the South Shore. I looked forward to checking out his perception of it.

But those who have been brought up in Blackpool, as opposed to jaundiced travel writers, typically retain a great affection for the town and are quick to remind you of its positive qualities: the iconic Tower, the town's most famous landmark, visible from the hills around Kendal, where I live; the legendary Ballroom within the Tower with its sprung dance floor, spiritual home to the phenomenally-popular *Strictly Come Dancing* TV programme; the lovely ornate interior of the Grand Theatre, where I went to see Alun Owen's *Progress to the Park* with my Mum and Auntie Phil in the early 1960's; the continuing tradition of the donkey rides on the beach, where my wife Karen used to offer to help groom the donkeys in return for a free ride; and the survival of the tramway system, the only commercial example of the genre remaining in Britain.

My friend Phil Hartley remembers the time when most visitors arrived by train, and were met at the station by local lads (including his dad) with hand carts, who wheeled their luggage to their accommodation in the numerous guest houses, one of them run by his aunt, where he often stayed and helped out after his parents had moved away. Christine Seddon, vice-chair of Blackpool Supporters Trust (of which more later) has lived all her life in Blackpool and clearly loves the town (and the football club; so often these two affections are inextricably intertwined).

And whatever the travel writers think, the many thousands of visitors who still pour into the resort every year clearly think a lot of it. Okay, relatively few families now book a week's holiday in Blackpool's plethora of bed-and-breakfast establishments, but they still pile in for day visits, weekend breaks, stag and hen parties, and the long-surviving illuminations, in numbers that ensure that Blackpool remains Britain's most popular holiday resort. And you can't argue with that... can you?

When starting this book, I had only a superficial knowledge of both Blackpool and Wigan, based on occasional visits. I had vague childhood memories of Blackpool, although the relatives we visited lived in the infinitely superior environment of Lytham St. Annes, and we only rarely made sorties to its bigger brasher neighbour. In my previous existence as a local government guru, I had visited Wigan Borough Council offices on a few occasions, and had been impressed by its down-to-earth qualities – no poncey management-speak in Wigan, thank you very much! I resolved to explore both towns during the course of my regular match visits, keeping an open mind and disregarding the (often unfavourable) opinions of Messrs Orwell, Priestly, Theroux, Bryson, and Engel.

Blackpool FC was founded in 1887 and elected to Division Two in 1896, failed to get re-elected in 1899, but achieved a speedy return in 1900. They stayed in Division Two for the next 30 years, rarely challenging for promotion, and twice finishing in bottom place until 1930, when they achieved promotion. They survived in Division One for three seasons. Their glory years covered the period from 1937 – when they were again promoted to Division One – to 1967 when they were relegated. For 23 successive seasons (interrupted by World War Two), they were up there with the Arsenals, Evertons, and Manchester Uniteds of this world. Although they never won the league, they were runners-up to Manchester United in 1956, and between 1949 and 1958, only once finished outside the top ten. And, of course, there was the FA Cup, a much bigger deal in those days than it is now. Blackpool lost 4-2 to Manchester United in 1948, 2-0 to Newcastle United in 1951, but returned to Wembley in 1953, where they came from behind to defeat Bolton Wanderers four-three in the legendary 'Mathews final.' In the England team which lost 3-6 to Hungary at Wembley in 1953, there were four Blackpool players, which caused one observer to comment "It was like watching Blackpool playing Hungary."

Robin Daniels, in his official history of the club (published in 1972) draws parallels between Blackpool as a town and Blackpool FC. "Blackpool is now the world's most popular seaside resort, a town of show business, slot machines, holiday camps and donkey rides; a free-swinging town, wind-blown, even in the height of summer. It is not surprising to find that Blackpool's football is entertaining, open, breezy, fluctuating." That was certainly their reputation in the days of players with the individual skills of Stanley Mathews, Stan Mortenson, Jackie Mudie, and Ernie Taylor.

Following their relegation in 1967, Blackpool were always among the leaders in Division Two, and were promoted back into Division One in 1970, only to come straight back down again the following year. In seeking to retain their former status, there followed a succession of near misses (and never a finish outside the top ten), until 1978 when they went down rather than up, heralding a period in the wilderness of Divisions Three and Four (or One and Two, as they later became) which lasted for nearly 30 years. In 1983, the club suffered the indignity of having to apply for re-election to the Football League, having finished the season in 21st place.

It was in 1987, when Blackpool were struggling to survive (the board had tried and failed to sell Bloomfield Road as part of a rescue plan) that the Oystons first appeared on the scene. The owner of a large and successful estate agency, together with a varied range of other business interests, Owen Oyston acquired a substantial shareholding in 1987, and became a majority shareholder and hence outright owner a year later, reportedly purchasing the club for the princely sum of one penny, which would be a reflection of the state the club at the time.

But for the next 20 years, Blackpool continued their topsy-turvy trajectory. They went down to Division Four in 1990, but came back up again in 1992, finishing third in 1996, (when they would have reached the play-off final if they'd not contrived to lose 3-0 at home to Bradford City, having won 2-0 away in the first leg). They were down in the fourth tier again in 2000 but came straight back up in 2001. Finally, in 2007, they made it back to what was now the Championship, nearly 30 years after they'd last left it.

But in the meantime, there had been changes in the club's ownership hierarchy. In May 1996, Owen Oyston was jailed on a charge of rape, an offence he has always vehemently denied. In his absence, his wife Vicki became chairman (should it have been chairwoman or chairperson?) but resigned at the end of the 1998-99 season, having become increasingly unpopular amongst the fans and having suffered a good deal of verbal abuse from a group of them. Their son Karl Oyston took over, witnessed an immediate descent into Division Four, and has continued to operate as chairman ever since, although following Owen's release in 2000, the assumption has always been that his father has continued to be a major influence.

In the light of the present-day toxic relationship between the Oyston dynasty and the majority of the fans, it is interesting to note the attitude of the Blackpool fanzine *Another View from the Tower* during the club's period of instability at board level in the late-1990s. There was very little hostility displayed towards Owen (not surprising, perhaps, given that the club had only just missed out on promotion when he started his jail sentence), although there was a recognition of the gravity of the offence for which he'd been jailed. There was a good deal of criticism of Vicki's short period of office, with questions raised about her commitment to the club and her competence (indeed there was a pitch invasion in protest at her record as chairperson in the autumn of 1998). Karl's succession to the hot seat was seen in positive terms: "So far the heir to the Oyston millions has done well," (Summer 1999).

There had been changes to the ground, too. In 2000, plans were announced for a comprehensive redevelopment of the Bloomfield Road stadium. In 2003, when I saw Stockport County play there, the ground was in a state of transition. A gleaming new white seating area had been built at one end and along the west side of the playing area. The other end was derelict, and the east side of the ground was the site of a temporary stand open to the elements, which housed the away fans, and which came to be known as the 'Gene Kelly Stand' ('singing and dancing in the rain!'). It was not until 2010 that the project was completed.

The timing was fortuitous because it was in May 2010 that what must have seemed like a miracle to Blackpool's long-suffering fans occurred. After promotion from Division Four in 2001, the team experienced five uninspiring seasons in Division Three, finishing 19th in 2006, only three points clear of relegation. After 11 games the following season, Blackpool had recorded only one win, were firmly entrenched in the bottom four, and appeared much more likely to be relegated than to be promoted. But under the astute management of Simon Grayson, they turned the season round, finished third, and went on to beat Yeovil Town 2-0 in the play-off final at Wembley. Back in the Championship for the first time in nearly 20 years, Blackpool struggled to survive but just managed to do so, thanks to some crucial goals from Paul Dickov, finishing two points clear of relegation. 2008-09 saw some improvement, with the team finishing mid-table, but not before Simon Grayson had resigned to take over at Leeds. His replacement, Tony Parkes, was offered a permanent contract at the end of the season but turned it down (claiming an 'inadequate salary'). In came Ian Holloway, who had been 'between jobs,' having endured a miserable time in 2007-08, failing to save Leicester City from relegation to Division One.

Although no-one would have guessed it at the time, it was an inspired appointment. Ian Holloway had, at that time, experienced a chequered managerial career (and has since). Sometimes his idiosyncratic jokey managerial style had been highly effective, as at Queens Park Rangers in 2004-06. On other occasions (including Leicester) it hadn't. Either the chemistry worked, or it didn't. At Blackpool, it certainly did. It felt in some strange way that Holloway's destiny was Blackpool FC, and Blackpool's was Ian Holloway. Starting the season as relegation favourites, the team surprised everyone by reaching the playoffs on the last day of the season, finishing a single point ahead of Swansea City. They went on to beat third-placed Nottingham Forest (who had finished nine points ahead of them) 6-4 on aggregate (including a thrilling 4-3 victory in the second leg at the City Ground), before defeating Cardiff City 3-2 to make it to the Premier League, for the first time since 1971.

By any standards, it was an incredible achievement. In the year they were promoted, the capacity of Bloomfield Road, where the transformation work was still in progress, was a mere 9,500 (it rose to 16,000 the following season). Blackpool were at the time no longer seen as a 'big club'; that perception had faded in the 1970s when they began to slip down the divisions. The Oyston dynasty may have been in the multi-millionaire bracket, but they were not in the same league of opulence as the owners of Chelsea, Manchester City or Liverpool, nor had they shown much evidence of a readiness to pump resources into the club. But Holloway's signings were astute, in particular, the acquisition of D.J. Campbell, a loan signing from Leicester City towards the end of the season, who scored a hat-trick in the play-off semi-final win at Forest. And he brought out the best in Charlie Adam, who had been signed the previous season from Glasgow Celtic for £500,000, the money having been provided by new board member Valeri Belokon (see Chapter 7 for further details).

Blackpool's solitary season in the Premier League will be remembered fondly by all who witnessed it. They started off with a 4-0 win over Wigan at the DW Stadium, followed that with a 0-6 away defeat at Arsenal, and went on to defeat Liverpool twice,

Newcastle and Spurs. They persisted in playing attractive attacking football and ended up with 55 Premiership goals, the most achieved by a relegated side before or since. Charlie Adam was outstanding, and he, D.J. Campbell and Gary Taylor-Fetcher all scored freely and contributed 31 league goals between them. But relegated they were, on the last day of the season, when, in a manner which epitomised their season, they went down 2-4 at Old Trafford, having been 2-1 up in the first half. As a result, Wolves stayed up, and Blackpool went down.

Half-way through the season, Blackpool had been in a (misleadingly) comfortable mid-table position. When results began to deteriorate in the New Year, some thought that the Oystons ought to be making funds available to strengthen the squad, as a precaution against a continuation of this decline. But it didn't happen, and Blackpool paid the price. It was a complaint that would be heard many times again over the next few years.

The following season, with Holloway still in charge and the benefit of Premiership 'parachute money', Blackpool very nearly bounced straight back into the top division. They finished fourth and reached the play-off final, where a late goal by West Ham's Ricardo Vaz Te ended their hopes. Charlie Adam had been sold to Liverpool in the close season, but the evergreen Kevin Philips had done well as a replacement, netting 16 league goals. Blackpool had performed above expectations, and a degree of optimism remained.

Sadly, such optimism proved unfounded. Ian Holloway, complaining that he wasn't being given adequate resources to strengthen the squad, resigned in November to take over at Crystal Palace (with whom he succeeded in winning promotion). His replacement, Michael Appleton lasted a mere 66 days and 12 games, by which time Blackpool were perilously close to the relegation zone. He was succeeded by Paul Ince, under whose management results improved (helped by the prolific goal-scoring record of his son Tom). A mid-table finish was a disappointment, but a lot better than looked likely in late January.

With the benefit of hindsight, Holloway's departure proved to be the turning-point. It was downhill all the way after that. The following season began with what turned out to be a false dawn, with Blackpool taking 16 points from their first six matches. Without this cushion, they would certainly have been relegated. They amassed a derisory five wins and 30 points from their remaining 40 fixtures and escaped the drop by a mere two points. Paul Ince was dismissed in January. His replacement, Barry Ferguson (a midfielder currently on their books) lasted until the end of the season but was then also shown the door. 38 different players had been used during the course of the season, and in an unprecedented clear-out of the playing staff, only six of them were retained, including three goalkeepers. The club appeared to be in a state of meltdown. Not an encouraging start for new manager, former Charlton Athletic boss, Jose Riga.

David Perkins, now with Wigan Athletic, was recruited to Blackpool by Paul Ince in January 2014. Three days after he'd been signed, the manager was sacked. In a recent Wigan programme, Perkins describes the bizarre situation when the Blackpool players reported for training later that summer, "There were only six of us, and that went on for a few days. We had trialists coming in all the time. It was destined to go badly."

It was indeed! Jose Riga managed to cobble together a bunch of free transfers and loanees by the time the season started, but in the first game, away to Notts Forest, Blackpool were able to fill only four of the seven permitted substitute slots. Not surprisingly, *When Saturday Comes* and pretty much every other forecaster saw them as relegation favourites, an expectation that became a virtual certainty by Christmas. The club was in 24th position from mid-August onwards, and ended up winning only four games, all of them 1-0 at home. Riga was dismissed after five months in the job. His successor, Lee Clark, recently sacked by Birmingham City, resigned at the end of the season. Blackpool's final home game against Huddersfield Town was abandoned early in the second half, as the result of a pre-planned pitch invasion by hundreds of fans in protest at the way in which the Oyston family was running the club. The result was later declared a 0-0 draw by the Football League. In June, Karl Oyston lost his appeal against a decision by the FA that he had brought the game into disrepute by texting an abusive message to a Blackpool fan, whom he referred to as a "retard," and was banned from all football activities for six weeks.

It was indeed a bizarre (and unprecedented?) situation that a Championship club, which had three seasons ago been in the Premiership should find itself in a position where there were only six players on its books a few weeks before the start of the season. It was at this stage that the worst fears of some supporters about the attitude of the Oystons to the club were (in their eyes) confirmed. Would owners that really cared about the club conceivably have allowed this to happen? Did other investment priorities militate against the pre-season assembly of a group of players who might be expected to deliver at least an average season? Were the 38 players who managed to avoid relegation the previous season so devoid of talent that only six of them were worthy of retention? And if that was felt to be the reality, why had resources not been made available to the manager to recruit viable replacements? In 2012, following the Premier League season, the staggering sum of £11m had been paid out to a company owned by Owen Oyston, a transaction which was perfectly legal, but which raised plenty of eyebrows (see Chapter 7 for more).

David Goldblatt, in his excellent *The Game of our Lives*, identifies the Oystons as one of the few exceptions to the typical situation where owners are "primarily concerned with winning football games and not with making a profit."

"The Oyston family took the opportunity of a season in the Premier League to recoup their investment, rather than making a reasonable stab at staying up. The wage bill was frozen at Championship levels, Blackpool were duly relegated, and the Oystons scooped up around £40 million from a year of broadcast fees and four years of parachute payments. The club made an unheard-of £32 million profit." Such actions would inevitably impact upon the future of any football club.

As long-term supporter, Phil Hartley told me, "Some people are saying that Blackpool FC has lost its soul. That's not true; what's happened is that it's had its soul torn out of it." For him, and many others who decided to stop attending matches in the 2015-16 season, Blackpool will never regain its soul until the Oystons leave.

In July 2015, a month before the new season was due to commence. Blackpool Supporters Trust (BST) made a £16 million bid to buy the club from the Oystons. Their proposal involved a takeover of the playing staff, the stadium (including the loss-making hotel), and the training ground, with the remaining assets being retained by the Oystons. The Trust's spokespersons argued that the time was right for the Oystons to back out; the club was now a loss-making rather than a profit-making concern.

Three weeks later, a detailed response was received by the Trust from Owen Oyston. To the surprise of many (including, I suspect, the Trust) the bid was not summarily dismissed. The response asked a series of detailed questions, and although at times there were hints of incredulity in the wording ("are you really suggesting that we should...?"), on the face of it, the bid was being taken seriously by the owners. BST were asked for a response in September, which they duly submitted. The new season would start with just a glimmer of hope for the long-suffering fans that salvation might be around the corner.

A further wholesale clear-out of the playing staff had taken place at the end of the disastrous 2014-15 season. Of the 50 players who had turned out (many of them never experiencing a single victory), a mere seven were still with the club as the start of the next season approached. And it soon became clear that one of them, Nile Ranger, would not be featuring in the club's plans for the new season. This unquestionably talented player had proved a problem at his previous clubs – Newcastle United and Swindon Town – both of whom had terminated his contract for 'disciplinary reasons.'

His sporadic appearances for Blackpool in 2014-15 had been interspersed with lengthy unauthorised absences, so it was a surprise, to say the least, that he was retained at the end of the season, presumably as a result of a decision by Karl Oyston rather than the departing manager. His re-appearance late in July 2015, weeks after he was supposed to have reported for training, convinced the new manager Neil McDonald that his lack of commitment to the club should exclude him from being considered for selection. Yet he remained under contract.

Otherwise, the handful of survivors from the previous season – Henry Cameron, Tom Oliver, Tom Aldred, Jose Cubero, Bright Osayi-Samuel and Charles Dunne – were joined by 15 others. Amongst them was one relatively high-profile signing, Mark Cullen from Luton Town, where he had been their leading scorer in 2014-15 with 13 league goals. He was joined by another striker, Jack Redshaw from Morecambe, with 11 goals to his name. On the face of it, Blackpool would have an experienced and (reasonably) prolific strike force. Brad Potts, an industrious midfielder previously with Carlisle United, and Colin Doyle, an experienced keeper signed from Birmingham City, were amongst the other newcomers.

So at least Blackpool would be able to fill the substitute's bench on the opening day of the season. Indeed, they were in a position (unlike the previous season) to arrange the customary quota of pre-season friendlies, one of which (at home to Morecambe) had to be played in an empty stadium, because of fears of crowd trouble. Prospects for the new season looked somewhat more promising than for the previous campaign, but that wasn't saying much, and Blackpool were still seen as likely candidates for a second successive relegation. (At this rate they would be in the Conference by 2017!) The predictions in *When Saturday Comes* (an amalgamation of the views of contributors from the Supporters Associations of all the clubs in Division One) put Blackpool at 22nd in the table by the end of the season, with only Colchester and Crewe expected to do worse. The Blackpool contributor John Secker did not disagree, "We could be in any of three divisions come August 2016, and I would say League Two is looking the most likely at the moment," he wrote. It all depended, he felt, on the degree to which the board were prepared to back the manager in signing his targets, and then on how well he could get them to play as a team.

CHAPTER 3
AUGUST: HOPE SPRINGS ETERNAL

August is the month of hope. Anyone can win the league. Anyone can win promotion. A defeat in the first game of the season might generate some doubts, but this can be viewed as a temporary setback on the road to glory. It is only by early October, after ten or so games, that reality sinks in for the clubs occupying the lower reaches of the table; a rueful realisation that this is unlikely to be their year of triumph.

Blackpool's first fixture was away to Colchester United, who had narrowly escaped relegation to Division Two the previous season. They secured survival on the very last day, and also deprived Blackpool's traditional rivals, Preston North End, of automatic promotion. Five years ago, the Tangerines had started their one eventful season in the Premiership with an emphatic 4-0 victory at Wigan, whose first fixture – this time around – was away to Coventry City.

By 5 o'clock on August 8th, Blackpool could reasonably have been said to have made an encouraging start to the season, and Wigan a disappointing one. Blackpool managed a 2-2 draw at Colchester, which doesn't sound like a major achievement, but in the context of their recent history (and last season's fiasco of an opening game at Nottingham Forest, when they were three short of a full complement of substitutes), it could at least be seen as progress. The first half was good news, with Mark Cullen scoring twice; one a tap-in following a flowing move involving the lively youngster Bright Osayi-Samuel, and the second an impressive individual effort. In the second half, Colchester dominated play and equalised, but Blackpool held out and came away with a deserved point.

Wigan, on the other hand, succumbed to a 2-0 defeat at Coventry, whose loan signing from Newcastle – Adam Armstrong – scored with two impressive individual efforts. Wigan enjoyed plenty of possession, but rarely looked dangerous going forward, and appeared fragile defensively. Not a good start for a side widely tipped for promotion. But any team whose members had never played together before the pre-season friendlies (there was only a single surviving member of Wigan's 2014-15 squad playing at Coventry) perhaps needed a few league games together to develop some kind of coherence?

The mid-week League Cup games certainly did not inspire optimism. Blackpool lost ignominiously 3-0 away to Northampton Town of Division Two, conceding three goals in the space of nine minutes midway through the first half. Wigan went down to a 2-1 defeat at home to Bury, after leading 1-0 at half time. The scorer of the two Bury goals was Leon Clarke, who had failed to impress in a loan spell at Wigan the previous season (I saw him score the only goal he managed during his ten appearances, in a game in which Wigan were totally outclassed by a buoyant Bournemouth side).

But the League Cup is no longer a priority for many clubs, nor for their supporters (as the meagre 5,484 attendance at the Wigan-Bury game illustrated). There were plenty of upsets amongst the first round ties, as a result of which a few smaller clubs may go on to experience brief moments of glory in subsequent rounds. But I wouldn't expect the managers of either Blackpool or Wigan to lose much sleep over their teams' early exits. It's the league that really counts, and the imminent first home games of the season for both clubs would be of much greater concern. Fortunately for me (given my wish to see both first home fixtures), Blackpool were playing on Saturday, whilst Wigan had switched their game to Sunday (12.30 kick-off).

*

I travelled to Blackpool by train, on the line which arrives at Blackpool South station. This line (and station) is very much the poor relation of the Blackpool North route, from which it diverges at Kirkham and Wesham. But there were two reasons for choosing it. First, it involved a mere ten-minute walk from the station to

Bloomfield Road (from which Blackpool North is a mile-and-a-half distant). Secondly, it enabled me to experience a nostalgic journey through Lytham, Ansdell and Fairhaven, and St Annes-on-Sea, all places full of childhood memories, which I had not revisited for many years. The ghosts of Auntie Phyllis, Uncle Ambrose, Auntie Pam and Cousin Dan (amongst others) hovered above Fairhaven Lake, the Royal Lytham golf club, and the shopping arcades of St Annes high street.

I had anticipated that the train would pick up significant numbers of tangerine-shirt-clad Blackpool supporters as it stopped at the run of stations south of the terminus. But as I stepped off the train, it was clear that there were little more than a dozen. No bumper home gate for the first game of the season then! I followed the tangerine shirts across a large car park, at the far end of which stood the gleaming white façade of Bloomfield Road.

Outside the main entrance were to be found a large number of tangerine shirts, sported by a lot of angry men (and in a few cases, women). I had wondered whether there would be some kind of demonstration, given that very little had changed since the pitch invasion the previous May had caused the abandonment of the final home game of the season. The acrid smell of a (tangerine-coloured) smoke bomb filled the air, as did the incessant chants of "Oyston Out," and various more colourful variants on the same theme. I joined the world's slowest-moving ticket queue at 2.35 p.m. and watched the continuation of the demonstration, which I guessed would be repeated at every home game until some satisfactory outcome (like the sale of the club to the Supporters Trust) materialised. Welcome to Blackpool F.C.! Welcome to the new season!

At 2.55 I had still not reached the interior of the ticket office (what was going on here?), and the crowd outside the main reception began to disperse, though it was away from the ground rather than into it. At 3.05 p.m., I finally managed to purchase a ticket (the problem apparently was that at some turnstiles, season tickets were not being accepted by automated ticket readers), and five minutes later I was in my seat, a few rows below the Directors Box. It is always frustrating not to be in the ground before kick-off, particularly so on this occasion when it was the first assignment of the book. "Any score?" I asked the bloke next to me. "Nope." "Anything much happened?" "One good chance for Rochdale and two delays for injuries," was his response.

I looked around the stadium. This was my fourth visit. I'd seen Blackpool defeat Manchester City 1-0 in the 1970s, when the ground was still a traditional, unmodified stadium, which had a substantial terrace at one end, open to the elements (didn't they all!) and a splendid West Stand, which Simon Inglis described in his book, *The Football Grounds of Britain*, as "the quintessential British football grandstand, impossible to recreate in concrete and steel." Then in 1997 I was there to see Stockport County lose 2-1; a rare defeat in a season which saw them promoted to the second tier. Bloomfield Road was much as it had been in the 1960s if considerably more dilapidated. I returned in 2004 to see Stockport manage a 1-1 in the midst of an (ultimately successful) battle to avoid relegation. By this time, the metamorphosis of the stadium was well under way. Over half of the old stadium had been replaced by a new gleaming white structure. There was a temporary roofless seating area at one side, where the Stockport fans were located. The old open end was derelict and unusable.

Now, three sides of the new stadium (one of which incorporates a four-star hotel) had been completed. In the place of the open temporary structure of 2004, there was a much more permanent-looking covered stand, which was totally unoccupied, except for a few stewards. My neighbour told me that this too was "temporary," having been hurriedly erected to provide extra accommodation for Blackpool's arrival (also temporary) in the Premiership at the start of the 2010-11 season. Its safety certificate had expired in the summer, and the club were apparently in no hurry to renew it.

It was not difficult to understand this reluctance. What faced me was one of the most unusual crowd patterns I had ever seen at a football match. At one end of the stadium, in the section reserved for away fans were to be found around 1,500 (my estimate) vociferous Rochdale supporters, who totally filled the (relatively ungenerous) space allocated. Throughout the rest of the ground were haphazardly scattered the uncannily quiet home supporters. Where were the massed ranks of home fans you almost always see somewhere in the ground, if you're watching a Football League game? Nowhere to be seen, at Bloomfield Road! If ever there was justification for the familiar "You're supposed to be at home" chant from visiting fans it was here and now (the Rochdale supporters generously refrained from doing so). I surmised that the many gaps in the stands (and the lack of vocal support) must be due to a boycott of home games on the part of many disgruntled regular supporters (including those who had been demonstrating outside), a conclusion which was later confirmed.

It was not that there was any antagonism displayed by the Blackpool fans in the stadium. They made suitably supportive noises, in a low-key way, whenever the home side threatened the Rochdale goal, which it has to be said wasn't very often. Nor was it the case that Blackpool were awful; the first half was, in fact, relatively evenly balanced. Their two young midfielders Bright Osayi-Samuel and Henry Cameron were speedy and inventive. It was just that there was little penetration up front. Neither of the two strikers, Mark Cullen and Jack Redshaw, who had scored 26 goals between them in Division Two the previous season looked likely to add to their combined tally. Another new signing, Brad Potts, who had been impressive at Carlisle in 2014-15, struggled to make an impact. Rochdale looked better organised and (marginally) more dangerous, reflecting perhaps the fact that half of them had actually played together the previous season. The first half remained goalless, and Blackpool left the field to polite applause, Rochdale to a thunderous ovation.

Rochdale proved more dominant in the second half as Blackpool's young side ran out of steam, and it was no surprise when the visitors took the lead in the 58th minute through the impressive Donal McDermott, who broke through an (ineffective) offside trap and coolly side-footed the ball past the advancing keeper. Brad Potts should have equalised a few minutes later when presented with a free header, which he sent soaring over the bar. That was, in effect, Blackpool's last real chance, and Ian Henderson wrapped the game up shortly before the end, taking advantage of a defensive mix-up.

The match statistics confirmed my impression that although Blackpool had matched Rochdale for possession, the visitors had created many more chances (15 compared with 6). Some of the performance ratings allocated to the players in Sunday's *Football League Paper* were bewildering. Mark Cullen received a 7 when I thought his contribution had been minimal, whilst the unfortunate Jack Redshaw was awarded a 4, despite a couple of mazy (if ultimately unproductive) dribbles through the Rochdale defence. It made me wonder whether players take any notice of these ratings. Do they pick up the paper the next morning and howl with indignation at the perceived unfairness of a 4, or punch the air at the award of a 9?

I made my way back to Blackpool South Station, noting with amusement the sign that read "Trains to Preston and beyond" (so there is a world beyond Preston!). I also observed the poster depicting a smiling station manager named Chris, who was "here to help you," (except that he wasn't). In my young day, station managers used to be based at the stations for which they were responsible. At Blackpool South, there was nowhere for the incumbent to base himself, other than a small graffiti-covered plastic shelter for waiting passengers. He was no doubt available at the end of a phone, somewhere in Preston (or beyond). I wondered whether he had ever actually visited the station for which he was (nominally) responsible!

*

The next morning, I drove to Wigan for the 12.30 kick-off against Doncaster Rovers. In other circumstances, I would have travelled by train and enjoyed the walk from the town centre past the legendary Wigan Pier to the DW Stadium. But it was a Sunday morning, and the southbound service on the West Coast line started too late for me to reach the ground in time. The stadium is located in a singularly inaccessible part of Wigan but was helpfully signposted all the way from junction 27 of the M6.

Until 1999, Wigan played at Springfield Park, a traditional un-reconstituted ground which I visited in the mid-1980s when the club was in what was then Division 3. One end of the ground – the Shevington – comprised four or five steps of concrete terracing behind which was a grassy bank with hardly anyone on it. But that was then, and this is now. Soon after David Whelan purchased the club in 1995, he announced plans for a new state-of-the-art stadium which would become the home not just of Wigan Athletic, but also the town's rugby league club, in whose shadow Athletic at the time languished. It says a lot for David Whelan (and his millions) that ten years later, with the football club in the Premier League, there was almost an equivalence of status, although there is a sense amongst Latics fans that they still have to battle against the perception that Wigan is a 'rugby town.'

My only previous visit to the DW Stadium had been earlier in 2015 when I went to see the Latics (as they are widely known) take on Bournemouth, who were at the time amongst the top three in the Championship, and who went on to become champions. It was one of the best games of football I saw all season, but that had little to do with Wigan's contribution, and everything to do with Bournemouth's. Wigan were half-way through the brief and undistinguished managerial reign of Malky Mackay, who introduced four of his many new signings into the team. Wigan gave a dogged gritty performance but were totally outclassed by a Bournemouth side who gave the best display of team football I'd seen in years. They won 3-1, but it could have been 8 (as indeed it was in their away game at Birmingham City). Although I find it difficult to like new purpose-built grounds, I'd been impressed with the DW Stadium, which had a welcoming feel about it, and generated a lively atmosphere.

Certainly, the atmosphere outside and inside the stadium was in marked contrast to the tension surrounding Bloomfield Road the previous day. I was struck by the number of family groups approaching the stadium, not just father and son but mother and daughter too. There were lots of blue and white replica shirts to be seen, but hardly any with players' names on them, which was not surprising, as most of last season's squad had departed for pastures new. The only exception was Will Grigg, of whom much was expected after his 20 goals for MK Dons the previous season.

I was pleased to see that David Perkins was in Wigan's starting line-up. He had several productive seasons with Morecambe when they were in the Conference, where he was a favourite with the home supporters who relished his commitment, tenacity, and not inconsiderable skill. I'd followed his subsequent career with interest. He had a couple of seasons with Barnsley when they were in the Championship, where he was known as 'The Blond Boris,' on account of his perceived resemblance to the mayor of London. The previous season he'd been with Blackpool, where he'd been in the starting lineup for 45 of the league games; Mr Reliable, apparently, in a side in which 50 different players appeared over the course of the season.

The attendance looked disappointing (maybe the 12.30 kick-off wasn't such a good idea?). Last season's average home attendance was close to 13,000, but there didn't seem to be more than two-thirds of that number present today. There were acres of space in the area where I was sitting, high up in one end of the ground, opposite the end set aside for visiting fans (of which there were around 800). In Doncaster's first game of the season, at home to Bury, there had been a bizarre conclusion. In added time, a Bury player had sportingly kicked the ball into touch so that an injured Doncaster player could receive treatment. Doncaster's Harry Forrester then sent a speculative lob in the general direction of the Bury keeper, which sailed over him into the net (totally unintentionally, or so Forrester claimed!). There was an understandable outburst of anger from the Bury players, a hurried touchline consultation between the two managers, following which Bury's Leon Clarke was allowed to stroll through the Doncaster ranks unopposed, and put the ball into the net past an immobile keeper, who was no doubt not best pleased at forfeiting a clean sheet. Still, it was the right outcome, applauded by Bury manager David Flitcroft, who acknowledged that Paul Dickov, the Doncaster manager, didn't have to respond in the way that he did.

The game started slowly and continued that way. In the first half, Doncaster looked marginally more inventive than Wigan. New signing Andy Williams (21 goals for Swindon Town last season) missed a couple of reasonable chances and was understandably incensed to have a legitimate penalty appeal turned down when he was blatantly barged in the back. Some of Wigan's approach play was pretty, but generally too slow-paced to pose problems for Doncaster's well-organised defence. David Perkins was much in evidence, always in the thick of the midfield action, but Will Grigg, Wigan's new striker, was making little impression. It was clear that the game was not capturing the imagination of the crowd, but I was finding it fascinating. The advantage of sitting high up in a stand is that you can really appreciate the patterns of play, and the intentions behind the actions of the players, in a way which is much more difficult when you are closer to the action. If I'd been in Row A, I'd probably have been bored out of my mind!

Wigan proved a more potent attacking force in the second half but still could not break down the Doncaster defence. Youngster

Shaquile Coulthirst came on as a substitute and impressed with some positive running and tricky footwork, marred by a tendency to over-elaborate. You might have expected either Will Grigg or Andy Williams, who had scored 42 league goals between them the previous season, to revitalise the increasingly lacklustre proceedings with a goal, but neither looked like doing so. As a 0-0 draw became more and more likely, the natives became increasingly restless, or at least the younger ones did. Midway through the second half, most of them had lost interest and were either running around in the many vacant spaces which surrounded them, or were playing on iPhones, iPads, or games consoles, a phenomenon I recall only too well from previous visits to watch Morecambe with my two sons.

Nil-all was the way it finished. Eight days into the season, both Blackpool and Wigan had managed only a single point each, and both had been unceremoniously dumped from the League Cup. Things could only get better.

*

Sadly, three days later, things did not get better for Blackpool. They lost 2-1 at home to Burton Albion, an unfashionable small-town club who had been promoted from the Conference as recently as 2009, and whose first season this was in the lofty heights (for them) of Division One. As they had done against Rochdale, Blackpool started well and went into the lead half-way through the first half, when Jack Redshaw neatly tucked away a Harry Cameron cross. But in the second half, Burton's Abdenasser el-Khayati (who hails from Rotterdam) scored twice, to the delight of manager Jimmy Floyd-Hasselbank, and Blackpool ended up with nil points from their first two home games. The *Blackpool Gazette* reporter noted the lack of atmosphere inside the stadium, where there were a mere 6,197 hardy souls present.

Wigan, on the other hand, recorded their first win of the season a day later, 3-0 at home to a singularly unimpressive Scunthorpe United side. It all looked relatively straightforward from the video footage. As early as the third minute, Will Grigg had his shirt grabbed by a defender in full view of the referee as he burst into the penalty area, and scored decisively from the spot. A few minutes later, Michael Jacobs lofted a dangerous ball into the box, which fell kindly to Donervon Daniels, who slotted the ball home from an acute angle. In the second half, a good through ball from the same player gave Craig Davies a clear run on goal, which he took advantage of with a confident finish past the out-rushing keeper. But Wigan will face much more challenging opponents than Scunthorpe.

*

The next Saturday, Blackpool were away to the division's best-supported club, Sheffield United, who were widely tipped for promotion, and who had won their two previous games after an unexpected 4-0 thrashing at the hands of Gillingham on the first day of the season. Realistically, it did not look like a promising source of points for the visitors, but they were still level at half-time, and early in the second half, David Ferguson hit the post with a curling free-kick. Then, predictably, manager Neil McDonald's 'defend in depth and hope for a goal on the break' strategy came to nought, when first Billy Sharp and then Mark McNulty scored to give Sheffield the points. The propensity of the young Blackpool side to fade in the second half was again apparent. If there were a league table based on half-time scores, Blackpool (played four, won two, drawn two) would be near the top. Unfortunately, there isn't and they aren't. Meanwhile, Wigan were finding a visit to Gillingham as unrewarding as Sheffield United had, going down 2-0 to two Bradley Dack goals. It was another unconvincing away performance, a source of some concern for one of the promotion favourites.

*

On the last Saturday of August, I returned to Bloomfield Road for Blackpool's make-or-break game (the first of many, I suspect) against the current joint Division One leaders Walsall. I travelled again along the Blackpool South line, past the Pleasure Beach, which was buzzing with activity (it was Bank Holiday weekend) to the terminus, where there was still no sign of smiling Chris, the station manager. This time, a mere four or five tangerine shirts exited the train, a worrying two-thirds reduction from the Rochdale game. Had the Lytham St Annes supporters' fraternity lost interest already? No problems about waiting in a queue this time; I'd been loaned a season ticket by a long-term supporter who was currently boycotting home games until the ownership problem was resolved (he may be in for a long wait!). As I'd expected, there was another angry demonstration outside the main reception. A number of banners were displayed. "You said 'Judge us in May'…we have done, now f*** off," read one.

Once inside the stadium, I was, at 2.45, the only customer at the refreshment bar. Having located my seat, I looked across to the away fans enclosure, which had been extended into the temporary stand (safety certificate or no safety certificate) and where there were, even more Walsall fans present than Rochdale had brought with them (1,803 as it turned out). They were making a lot of noise, unlike the widely-scattered Blackpool contingent. Gone are the days when Blackpool had one of the highest decibel ratings in the Football League (yes, a few years ago, someone actually took readings at every ground!).

Neil McDonald was relatively upbeat in the programme notes. "We're continuing to show signs of improvement… we've been excellent in patches and highlighted plenty of potential… it's now about bringing it all together for the full 90 minutes." But then he had to be, hadn't he. What manager is going to write: "We're clearly not up to it. The lads just can't hack it at this level. Relegation stares us in the face." Another run of defeats and he may be reduced to something approaching this level of honesty!

Blackpool started brightly, with David Ferguson testing the Walsall keeper in the first minute. Brad Potts was bursting with energy in midfield (sadly, he couldn't sustain the momentum). For the first 25 minutes, the teams were evenly-matched. Henry Cameron went close for Blackpool, Romaine Sawyers likewise for Walsall. There was little to indicate the 22-place disparity between their respective league positions. Then Sawyers found himself with space in the Blackpool penalty area and jabbed the ball past the advancing Kyle Letheren. Blackpool, once they had recovered from this reverse, came back into the game, and could count themselves unfortunate to be one down at half-time. Certainly, league-leaders Walsall hadn't outclassed their hosts.

But in the second half, they certainly did! Early on Blackpool had come close to equalising, when Jack Redshaw directed a header invitingly into the box, to a location where a team-mate should have been waiting, but no-one was. Then, after 57 minutes, it all began to go wrong for the home side. Walsall's Rico Henry wove his way into the box, sent over a sharp low cross, and amidst scenes of panic, the unfortunate Tom Aldred turned the ball into his own net. Then Sam Manton rose to direct a powerful header past Letheren, at which point a goodly number of the Blackpool faithful decided they'd had enough and left the stadium. They missed the best goal of the game, a superlative long-range curler from the impressive Romaine Sawyers, before Tom Bradshaw hit the post and was then foiled by an excellent save from Letheren. It finished 4-0, but it could easily have been six or seven.

Although there was some booing at the end, I was pleased to note some sympathetic applause as Blackpool's dejected young side trooped wearily off the field. You couldn't fault them for lack of effort, but in the second half, the vast gulf in class was only too apparent. Walsall had been excellent.

Sitting next to me in the Stanley Mathews Stand were a couple in their fifties, regular supporters who had not felt inclined to join the boycott (I noticed that most of the fans around me were in this age category, or older, with a few father-and-son duos also scattered around). Their unhappiness with the current state of the club (on and off the field) was apparent, but they felt, reasonably enough, that the right thing to do was to continue to turn up and support a team which was clearly in great need of support. I asked them about Nile Ranger (see Chapter 2). "A formidable talent," they told me, "who most of the time just couldn't be arsed," (this is a paraphrase of their comments). It sounds like it was good judgement on the part of Neil McDonald to dispense with his services, although Blackpool could have done with some 'formidable talent' or at least 'flashes of inspiration' today.

I made my way back to Blackpool South station through the South Shore area of town. This is certainly not the 'golden mile'; more like 'the mile of tat and tack,' a depressing melange of cut-price stores ('Almost everything under a pound'), down-market cafes displaying pathetic attempts at humour ("Don't walk past bored; come inside and get fed up!"), and uninviting-looking pubs outside which were gathered groups of sturdy middle-aged men with shaven heads. (I uneasily entered one such establishment so that I could check the final scores.) The only redeeming feature was the view of the imposing Blackpool Tower to the north.

Meanwhile Wigan Athletic had scraped an unimpressive 1-0 home win against a Crewe Alexandra side yet to record a league victory. The headed goal by Michael Jacobs early in the game was hotly disputed by Crewe, who claimed that George Ray had been fouled in the build-up to the goal. One way and another, Wigan have so far failed to live up to the expectations of *When Saturday Comes* (amongst others).

CHAPTER 4

SEPTEMBER: ERRATIC LATICS AND CLUELESS POOL

Early September brought encouragement to both Blackpool and Wigan. After the Walsall game, I couldn't see where Blackpool's next points (or any point for that matter) were coming from. Even Neil McDonald, who had done his best to remain positive throughout a dismal August was struggling to maintain an upbeat attitude. Well he surely felt a whole lot better at 4.55 p.m. on Saturday September 5th, having watched his side record their first league win since January (that was 24 games ago!) and their first away league win since April 2014 (at Wigan, as it happens, a win which effectively kept Blackpool in the Championship for another season). Glanford Park, Scunthorpe, was the place and 1-0 the score. It wasn't pretty, nor was it deserved, but who cared; certainly not the 237 ecstatic Blackpool supporters who'd made the long trip, no doubt more in hope than expectation. Appropriately, the crucial goal was a scruffy close-range effort from the much-maligned Brad Potts, in a goalmouth scramble following a Tom Oliver corner, late in the first half. Scunthorpe managed 23 shots (10 on target) to Blackpool's 5 (2), but couldn't find a way past Colin Doyle who had an inspired afternoon, and was rewarded with inclusion in *The Football League Paper's* Division One team of the day. "England's number one," chanted the Blackpool fans (wrongly, as it happens; Doyle is Irish).

I was pleased for Neil McDonald, who strikes me as an honest, decent bloke, doing his best in difficult circumstances. He'd made some changes from the previous settled (if singularly ineffective) line-up. Redshaw and Osayi-Samuel had both been relegated to the substitutes bench (despite the former's allocated score of 7 in the Walsall game; he must have been indignant). Costa Rican international Jose Cubero was given his first start of the season as was John Herron, who had recently recovered from injury. New signing David Norris, an experienced midfielder from Yeovil made his Blackpool debut halfway through the second half. Blackpool played in a 4-1-4-1 formation, which doesn't sound particularly exciting (and wasn't). But it did the trick and helped to lift the blanket of despair which had settled over Bloomfield Road, at least for the next week.

*

Meanwhile, Wigan were involved in a topsy-turvy game at Chesterfield which might just prove a turning point in a so-far lacklustre season. Eighty minutes into the game, they were losing 2-0, and heading for a third consecutive 2-0 away defeat. After an uneventful first half, Chesterfield had apparently taken control, courtesy of a stunning long-range strike from Dan Gardner, and a bizarre own-goal from Leon Barnett, who headed neatly into his own net with no-one near him (definitely a contender for the 'gaffe of the season' award). But then, in the 81st minute, Barnett redeemed himself by blasting home a volley from outside the area. Soon afterwards Craig Davies scored from the spot having been (unnecessarily) fouled by Sam Hird, and finally, well into stoppage time, the ball ran kindly for Jordy Hiwula, a 20-year-old loanee from Huddersfield, whose goal sent the travelling fans (over a thousand of them, although many had departed early, before the late comeback) into a state of delirium. As with Blackpool's win at Scunthorpe, it probably wasn't deserved. But it may prove the boost in confidence that Wigan clearly needed.

*

The next Saturday, both clubs were away again. Could they repeat their successes of the previous weekend? Blackpool's task was particularly daunting; they were in Kent, facing league leaders Gillingham. Wigan looked to have a more promising opportunity in Burslem, against an inconsistent mid-table Port Vale side.

By all accounts, Blackpool performed creditably and looked likely to come away with a draw until ten minutes from the end, when the ball fell kindly, via a deflected pass, to the prolific Bradley Dack, who scored his 5th league goal of the season. Blackpool had started brightly, with a rejuvenated Brad Potts frequently surging forward from midfield. But Gillingham had gone ahead early in the game; a simple tap-in for defender Doug Loft resulting from a misdirected punch from keeper Colin Doyle following a corner. Shortly after half-time, Blackpool levelled when Brad Potts' cross cannoned off Gillingham's Ryan Jackson into the net. A spectacular long-range effort from Potts was then cleared off the line, and Blackpool looked like they'd done enough to earn a point, before the late Bradley Dack decider. Despite the disappointment, Blackpool could take some comfort from the quality of their performance. "This is not the worst side we've played this season," said Gillingham's manager Justin Edinburgh graciously. Neil McDonald was pleased that his team had given the league leaders a good run for their money (which they certainly hadn't when Walsall visited Bloomfield Road a couple of weeks before).

At one stage in the second half of Wigan's game at Port Vale, it looked like a repeat of the comeback at Chesterfield the previous Saturday might be on the cards. Vale went ahead through Anthony Grant midway through the first half and added a second (Louis Dodds) with 25 minutes to go. Wigan's performance had been distinctly uninspired, and the home side looked to be coasting to an unproblematic win. But then Chris McCann slotted home a low cross from Craig Davies, and with seven minutes remaining, Leon Barnett headed a Michael Jacobs corner into the net (later registered as an own-goal; unjustly in my view). It was proving an eventful couple of away visits for Barnett; two goals at the right end – not bad for a centre back – and one into his own net. His high profile exploits continued, although not in a way he would have wished when he was sent off in the 89th minute for bringing down Enoch Andoh who had a clear run on goal. Shortly afterwards, Vale's Uche Ikpeazu scrambled the ball home to deny Wigan a hard-earned (albeit undeserved) point.

After the euphoria of the win at Chesterfield, this result (and performance) felt like a real setback for the Latics. In each of their four away games, they had conceded two or three goals. Until they started replicating their impressive home results on their travels, predictions of a playoff slot were looking premature. The jury is still out on the newly-assembled squad, and indeed the manager.

*

On the train from Kendal to Wigan the following Saturday, to see the match against Fleetwood Town, I was meditating (as one does) on the appeal of football, from a spectator's perspective. It occurred to me that every football game is like a play (in two acts, with an interval). All the familiar ingredients of plays can be seen from time to time: tragedy, comedy, farce, pathos, villainy, heroism and unexpected twists at the end (like Wigan's three goals in the last ten minutes at Chesterfield). The difference with a football match is that you don't know, as you take your seat, how it's going to end, or indeed how the plot is going to develop! In a theatre production, you know that Hamlet and Macbeth are going to get killed (unless you've never seen or read the play before, which is possible but unlikely). One of the great appeals of watching football is that you just don't know what's going to happen.

I'd arranged to meet Martin Tarbuck before the game at the Wigan Central pub, close to Wigan North-Western station, which can be recommended for its imaginative range of micro-brewery real ales. Martin is the co-editor of *Mudhutter*, one of the best of a decreasing number of fanzines. The decline of the fanzine is a source of great regret to me (and to Martin). In the 1990s and early 2000s, almost every Football League club had one, and some had two or three. There was an annual publication called *Survival of the Fattest* which contained retrospective reviews of the season by fanzine editors of all the league clubs (excluding the much-despised MK Dons). They had titles like *The Pie-Muncher* (Preston North End), *Grorty Dick* (West Bromwich Albion), and (my favourite) *One F in Fulham*. The fanzines provided a welcome antidote to the blandness of the 'official programme,' which invariably put a positive slant on the club's fortunes, even when it was palpably obvious from more objective sources that the manager was useless, the team was hopeless (or both), and that relegation was a near certainty (in this connection, it would be interesting to get hold of some examples of Blackpool – or indeed Wigan – programmes towards the end of their dismal 2014-15 campaigns). At most clubs, social media, in one form or another, has replaced the fanzine, but social media is typically too piecemeal, shallow, and unanalytical to provide a viable substitute. As far as I'm concerned, long may *Mudhutter* and the remaining examples of the genre survive and indeed flourish.

Martin is also the author of a truly remarkable book entitled *The Life of Pies* which details his journeys across the length and breadth of Britain in search of the perfect pie (an appropriate venture for someone born and brought up in Wigan!). You wouldn't think this topic could sustain one's interest, but it does, partly because the book also includes some very funny descriptions of the places he visited. Martin helpfully provided me with a well-informed fanzine editor's perspective on what went wrong last season, and its legacy (see Chapter 7).

At first glance, Fleetwood Town (today's visitors) and Wigan Athletic exemplify as great a contrast between clubs that you could possibly imagine; Wigan, a big club fallen on hard times, and Fleetwood, a little club, punching well above its weight. Eight years ago, Wigan were in the Premiership, whilst Fleetwood were playing the likes of Kendal Town in level three of the non-league pyramid, before crowds (on a good day) of around 200. But look further back (and indeed more recently) in time, and you'll discover more common ground than you might expect. Wigan were only admitted to the Football League in 1978, before which fixtures between the two clubs were a regular occurrence in the Lancashire Combination and (later) the Northern Premier League. And just as Wigan's fortunes improved after multi-millionaire Dave Whelan took over the club in 1995, so did Fleetwood's when

Andy Pilley (not quite as well off as Dave Whelan, but still very rich by most standards) became its owner in 2004. So, both clubs emerged into the Football League from the world of non-league football, albeit 35 years apart, and both have prospered following their acquisition by rich local businessmen. Equally, both are vulnerable to loss of interest (or bankruptcy) on the part of their owners. Wigan fans, in particular, must be wondering what the impact would be if Dave Whelan were to pull out. There are worrying recent precedents. Who now remembers Rushden and Diamonds, who disintegrated in 2008, following the withdrawal of the multi-millionaire owner of Doc Martins footwear? (Level Five of the non-league pyramid is where they are at present.) And Newport County look destined for a rapid return to the Conference, now that Chairman Les Scadding's EuroMillions have run out.

The Wigan/Fleetwood programme made reference to the 'Cod Army,' which is apparently what Fleetwood fans call themselves. A bit of a time-warp in evidence here, I reckon! It's a long time (over 30 years?) since any cod was unloaded in the (now defunct) Fleetwood docks. Still, one of the endearing qualities of football clubs' nicknames and songs is the way in which they conjure up a long-departed industrial heritage. They still chant "Sing when we're fishing," at Grimsby Town's Blundell Park, even though fishing in Grimsby is a thing of the past. Stockport County are still known as the 'Hatters' (when was a hat last manufactured in Stockport?). And Braintree Town, I discovered on a recent visit, are still known as the 'Iron,' even though the small iron-smelting plant there closed before World War Two.

So how did my 'football as drama, but you don't know the ending' metaphor stand up to scrutiny at today's match? In my (admittedly self-interested) view, pretty well. Wigan dominated the first half with some fluent and creative approach play, which brought its just reward shortly before half-time when 19-year-old Jordan Flores found space in the box to hook home a cross from Michael Jacobs.

Flores sounds like he might be an import from Spain or Portugal, but is, in fact, a local lad, who has supported Wigan throughout his childhood and youth. This was his first league goal. He looked understandably delighted, as well he might. Fleetwood had hardly created a scoring opportunity and had played as if their collective mind was on other things. A minute after the interval, the impressive Reece James made rapid progress down the left, before his cross found Michael Jacobs, who scored with an emphatic first-time drive, to put Wigan two-up.

It felt like it was game over, and I envisaged a subsequent lack of dramatic action (well you do get some plays like that, albeit not particularly good or memorable ones). Certainly, there was little evidence that Fleetwood could turn around a two-goal deficit. But Wigan's second goal inspired a degree of urgency in their play, and they began for the first time in the game to create chances. After 60 minutes, a free-kick from the left found its way, via a deflection, to the impressively-named Tyler Hornby-Forbes, lurking by the far post, who scored with ease. Fleetwood then piled on the pressure, and the game unexpectedly became a real contest. Wigan were limited to breakaways, from two of which substitute Samni Odelusi should have increased their lead, but didn't, first slicing a good opportunity so wide that it really did hit the corner flag, and then failing to beat the Fleetwood keeper when put clean through. Fleetwood continued to threaten, but Wigan held out for a deserved win (at least on the evidence of the first hour). It was their third home win of the season, enabling them to equal the total of last season's home wins as early as September 19th. The drama of the game lay in the way in which, with Wigan seemingly coasting to a routine home win, Fleetwood unexpectedly shook off their lethargy and made a game of it.

The atmosphere at the game was very different to the muted climate of the Doncaster game. The crowd was much more animated and vocally supportive, although to be fair, their team's performance was giving them much more to be enthusiastic about.

CHAPTER 4

Walking away from the ground towards the railway station in the evening sunshine, I began to feel an affinity with the club and its supporters. Observing the many family groups (including young daughters as well as sons, many sporting replica blue and white shirts) and listening to their animated chatter in a broad mid-Lancashire accent, I formed a strong impression of a local (family-friendly) club for local people.

*

At Bloomfield Road, there were no doubt celebrations underway in the local pubs, following Blackpool's first home point of the season, a one-all draw against Barnsley. By all accounts, the first half was dire, particularly from Blackpool's perspective. An untidy goal from Hourihane had given Barnsley a seventh-minute lead, in a half which the visitors dominated. Neil McDonald made two changes at half-time, bringing on Redshaw and Thomas for Cameron and Cubero respectively, but admitted at half-time, "I could have taken anybody off to be fair because they were all rubbish." They must have been because McDonald is usually much more restrained in his criticism. As it happened, the changes paid off. Ten minutes after half-time a pass from the rejuvenated Brad Potts gave Redshaw a clear run on goal, and he scored with a crisp low shot into the corner of the net, eliciting recollections of many similar finishes for Morecambe (maybe he will yet prove to be a worthwhile signing). Blackpool then gave a much-improved second half display and had chances to win the game. McDonald, having recovered from his half-time despair, thought that, "the lads showed a lot of character," before expressing a guarded degree of optimism for the future. "It's nice to hear people say we might have turned a corner." We shall see. Four points from the last three games (in which only three goals have been conceded) is an improvement. Unfortunately, Crewe's win at Shrewsbury meant that Blackpool returned to the bottom of the table, and still haven't won at home since the end of January. Maybe, just maybe, the next home game against an inconsistent Chesterfield side will see the finish of that unenviable run.

*

Within a week, Blackpool's hope had turned to despair, particularly for the couple of hundred Blackpool fans who made the trip to Shrewsbury, but also for the long-suffering manager Neil McDonald. After an away win at Scunthorpe and a good performance at high-flying Gillingham, Shrewsbury Town (away) looked like a match that might yield some reward, given that their home record read played 4, lost 4, goals for 2, goals against 6 (which is even worse than Blackpool's!). But after a goalless first half (dominated by the home side), Blackpool capitulated meekly, conceding two goals in quick succession to Jean-Louis Akpa-Akpro (now there's a name to relish; resurrected football fans of the sixties would be incredulous when faced with the names on the team-sheets 50 years later!).

Neil McDonald is clearly a 'glass half full' sort of person, who has always sought to find positive features in his team's performances, without entering the realms of fantasy (he'd been upbeat, in his laidback kind of manner, about Blackpool's second half display against Barnsley the previous week). But he could find no positives in this performance. "We're definitely at rock bottom," he admitted. "It was the worst performance since I came to the club. We came up against a team that hadn't picked up a point at home, and we were outplayed in the second half. We forgot how to move, tackle and pass, and got what we deserved." It's beginning to look like the best that Blackpool can hope for this season is still to be in there with a chance of avoiding relegation in April. The worst case scenario is that by then their future will have been sealed.

The manager's mood will not have been helped by further developments in the bizarre Nile Ranger saga. This talented, unstable, and inconsistent character had turned up for training at Blackpool the previous week and had posted photos of himself on

FaceBook, in the club's kit, at the training ground. As he is still under contract to the club, they apparently have to offer him the opportunity to train, if he turns up, which (after a long absence) he had now done. Neil McDonald made it clear in a pre-season interview that, due to his palpable lack of commitment to the club, he would not be featuring in the manager's plans. So why, one wonders, is he still under contract? Given his long-term absences, surely it would be possible for the club to cancel it? Since his appointment, McDonald has been loyal to the club chairman Karl Oyston (probably a wise move given the rate of turnover of previous Blackpool managers), on one occasion going out of his way to emphasise his chairman's commitment to the club. For the first time, there was a hint of criticism in his statement of annoyance at Ranger's continued involvement with the club. There was clearly a sub-text of 'this guy needs to go; but it's not up to me, is it.'

*

Whilst Blackpool were evoking despair at Shrewsbury, I was at Boundary Park, watching the 'Battle of the Latics.' It was Wigan's first visit there since 2003, the year they won promotion to the Championship (amassing an impressive 100 points in the process). I'd not been to Boundary Park since the early 1960s, when Oldham were emerging from the depths of what was then Division Four, inspired by the skills of Bobby Johnstone, coming to the end of his illustrious career (he had scored in successive Cup finals for Manchester City in the mid-1950s). Oldham eventually made it to the Premiership for three seasons (1991-94) under the stewardship of Joe Royle, since when they have been a declining force. The ground didn't appear to have changed much over the 50 years since my last visit, apart from a gleaming new – but as yet unoccupied – North Stand, the first phase of which was due to be opened in late October.

I was hoping that at an unfashionable Division One club, it would still be possible to stand up somewhere, but it was not to be, The

Rochdale end from which I'd watched Bobby Johnstone weave his magic was now all-seated, as was everywhere else, including the Chadderton end opposite, in which were gathered over a thousand Wigan fans. The new stand apart, the ground had a neglected appearance, epitomised by the primitive nature of the gents' toilets at the top of the Rochdale end.

After an early shock, when Richard O'Donnell managed to palm a powerful header from Oldham's recent loan signing Michael Higdon onto the post and out, Wigan quickly recovered their composure, and began to dominate the game, gradually assuming (almost) total control. They passed the ball around well with David Perkins again dominant in midfield, hardly ever wasting a ball. The build-up was patient, indeed at times laborious, with too many passes back to the keeper, and rarely resulted in goal opportunities, but it was more than the home side could deal with. Oldham, who had dispensed with their manager two weeks previously, after a 5-1 thrashing at home at the hands of Peterborough United, were clueless, showing little idea of what to do with the ball on the rare occasions they moved into the Wigan half. Ten minutes before half-time, Wigan got the reward that their possession and superior organisation merited, when Max Power hit a superb drive on the volley from well outside the penalty area into the top corner of the net. Just before the interval, they nearly doubled their lead when Oldham's keeper just managed to keep out a close-range header from Chris McCann.

Wigan's domination continued in the second half, and they looked set for a routine if unexciting away win until the 70th minute when it all went wrong. Jordan Flores was clearly fouled as he gained possession in the Oldham half, but unwisely retaliated with a swinging arm, and inevitably received a red card. Glory to infamy for the youngster within a week! The game then changed totally in character. Oldham began to demonstrate a modicum of self-belief and equalised shortly after the sending-off when, after good work from the tank-like Michael Higdon, the ball fell kindly for substitute Dominic Poleon, who scored emphatically from close range. Oldham pushed men forward and the last 20 minutes must have seemed like an eternity for the Wigan players and fans. But they held out and came away with a deserved point. Wigan were now functioning better as a team than in the earlier games I'd seen but were struggling to transform their possession and territorial dominance into goal opportunities. Jordy Hiwula had made little impact up front in this game or the Fleetwood match the previous Saturday. Will Grigg (20 goals with MK Dons last season), who was on the subs bench today, was maybe due for a recall.

One comes away from some grounds with a warm feeling, reflecting the good-humoured, albeit partisan behaviour of both home and away fans. Boundary Park was not one of those grounds! There was something unpleasant about the atmosphere in the Rochdale Stand: incessant mindless chants of "Blue Army," and a number of solitary individuals sustaining a barrage of alcohol-fuelled invective, mainly at the referee (who seemed to me to be reasonably competent) or at Wigan players who (in their eyes) were too robust in their tackles. The spectators were predominantly white (strange in a town with such a large Asian population), with tattoos, shaven heads, obesity and foul language all much in evidence. I decided to choose Bury or Rochdale, rather than Oldham, for a later Lancashire trip to see a Blackpool away game.

*

A few days later I was in Scotland at the excellent Wigtown Book Festival and didn't find out the results of the Tuesday evening fixtures until I bought a paper on Wednesday morning. There's always a degree of nervous anticipation involved in opening the sports section and checking the results. Had Blackpool managed to register their first home win since January? Indeed they had, and more than that they had won by more than one goal! (The first time since March 2014.) And they had outplayed Chesterfield. Watching the video recording the next day, it was clear that the first early goal was somewhat fortuitous; a mishit shot from Jack Redshaw conveniently found its way to Mark Cullen, who could hardly fail to score. But the second was class, a flowing move on the left, which ended with Brad Potts finishing with an emphatic left-foot drive. Whatever Neil McDonald had said and done in the 72 hours between the end of the limp performance at Shrewsbury and the visit of Chesterfield had inspired a transformation.

Meanwhile, Wigan were leaving it late to earn a point at home to Millwall. They led through a Michael Jacobs goal (similar to the one scored by Blackpool's Brad Potts the very same evening). But in the second half, Millwall scored twice in quick succession, and it was not until injury time that the home side managed to equalise through a close-range shot from Will Grigg. The anticipated move into a play-off spot would have to wait until Saturday when Wigan were up against second-in-the-table Walsall at the DW Stadium.

CHAPTER 5

OCTOBER: A MONTH OF MELLOW FRUITFULNESS

I had been sorry to miss out on Blackpool's first home win since January 2015 but was able to make it to Bloomfield Road the following Saturday for the game against Swindon Town. It was September 2013 when Blackpool last recorded consecutive league wins. Could they confound the doubters and end yet another unenviable record of failure? Swindon Town had reached the play-off final last season, where they were beaten comprehensively by Preston North End, and although they had started this season well, they had failed to win any of their previous four games.

For a change, I travelled to Blackpool North, which, unlike Blackpool South is a real station with ticket barriers, a Costa Coffee outlet, and an in-situ station manager. I made my way past the Town Hall to the North Pier and then proceeded along the Promenade. It was a warm autumnal day, and the place was packed. At 2 o'clock on a sunny Saturday in early October, the town was not living up to its 'stag and hen night' reputation. There were a few groups of stags or hens in evidence, in some cases looking somewhat the worse for wear, but the sea-front population was dominated by families with young kids (no doubt the rest of the stags and hens were sleeping off the excesses of the previous night or were still making their way to Blackpool). All the familiar attractions of the resort were in evidence: the donkey rides, the sticks of rock (with letters all the way through), the amusement arcades, the fish and chip shops and restaurants, and the Tower looming above the promenade, its summit dramatically wreathed in mist. I'd forgotten how little beach space is accessible when the tide is in. In Blackpool's heyday, on hot summer days, there must have been a huge degree of overcrowding (and frustration) at high tide, with hordes of children sat on the prom, buckets and spades in hand, waiting for the waters to recede.

What was new to me were the tacky spherical Cinderella coaches, drawn by pairs of horses, which mingled with the road traffic adjacent to the prom. But who am I to be judgmental?! The little girls who occupied these coaches all looked happy enough. Indeed, a sense of joie de vivre was apparent, albeit with a disconcerting element of shrillness. You wouldn't recognise the picture painted in *Crap Towns*. But doubtless, by ten o'clock in the evening, there would be a totally different ambience to the place.

As soon as you move inland from the Central Pier, you're back amongst the cheap cafes, the many variants of Poundland, the money lenders, and the uninviting pubs. One sweetshop close to Bloomfield Road was advertising 'Swindon Town rock' for sale, an imaginative piece of entrepreneurship I thought, although there didn't appear to be any takers.

The demonstration outside the main entrance to the ground was smaller in numbers and quieter than had been the case on my two previous visits. Surely the first home win for ten months hadn't caused significant numbers of protesters to change their minds? Inside the stadium, too, the atmosphere was different. Blackpool emerged to an enthusiastic welcome, and although the game started quietly, with Swindon passing the ball around prettily, but to no great effect, every Blackpool attack was accompanied by higher decibel roar of support than had been apparent in the Rochdale and Walsall games. Jack Redshaw went close with a powerful long-range drive after ten minutes. Swindon continued to dominate play, but neither they nor the home side were creating much. Then, a few minutes before half-time, Blackpool won a corner on the left. Henry Cameron took it, Clark Robertson flicked it on at the near post, and Mark Cullen forced the ball past Swindon's keeper. It was not one of those satisfying goals which hits the back of the net – a Swindon defender hooked it clear before it got that far – but the ball had clearly crossed the line, and the referee had no hesitation in awarding a goal (nor were there any protests from the Swindon players).

The goal sparked the game into life. Blackpool grew in confidence, and just before half-time a stunning 30-yard free kick from Brad Potts was acrobatically saved by Lawrence Vigouroux. The home side left the field at half-time to a deserved ovation, in which I enthusiastically joined.

It was becoming increasingly difficult to maintain the neutrality which I'd thought at the start of the season would be an important position to take in writing this book. Here was a team which had suffered an abysmal couple of seasons (they only stayed in the Championship in 2013-14 as a result of taking 16 points from their first six games) suddenly beginning to win games again and displaying long-absent qualities of commitment and self-belief in doing so. I realised that I wanted them to win this game, and I wanted them to stay up. Similarly, at Oldham the previous week, I'd celebrated (undemonstratively rather than enthusiastically, given that I was surrounded by some belligerent home fans) when Wigan managed to hold on for a deserved point. I wanted Wigan to win promotion. Readers will just have to live with the implications of this change of approach!

As the second half progressed, Blackpool displayed an attacking flair almost totally absent in the Rochdale and Walsall games, helped no doubt by the fact that Swindon were now pushing men forward in their quest for an equaliser. Bright Osayi-Samuel came on for an injured David Norris, and immediately made an impact with a series of surging runs down the left. Sadly, his finishing was not of the same high standard as his approach play, and he pulled two good one-on-one chances wide. Then Brad Potts hit the post with another thunderous drive which was deflected along the goal line but somehow failed to cross it. Vigouroux continued to live up to his name in the Swindon goal.

This was all heart-warming stuff which delighted the home supporters, who could hardly believe what they were seeing. If Blackpool had been able to increase their lead, which their attacking flair merited, we could all have relaxed. But they hadn't, and in the final 20 minutes, Swindon increasingly threatened to level the game. It was the time for a heroic rear-guard action, which Blackpool duly delivered. Bodies were thrown in all directions to block shots, cut out corners, or in one way or another prevent Swindon from breaking through. Tom Aldred, in particular, caught the eye on numerous occasions when performing all these last-ditch functions (he later deservedly won the man of the match award). There was a tense moment when Swindon's James Brophy went down in the penalty area, but referee David Webb (what was he doing officiating a Division One game?) awarded a free-kick to Blackpool and booked Brophy (who then received an earful from an aggrieved (but relieved) Aldred). After a long five minutes of added time, the final whistle was blown, and the ground resounded to a mighty roar of mingled celebration and relief. The Blackpool players hugged one another in scattered groups. You could see the delight on their faces. The whole scene epitomised the way in which football can engender profound emotional reactions.

The next day, I returned the season ticket to Phil, its rightful owner, and told him he would have been proud of the team he has supported since boyhood. But his dilemma remains. If Blackpool continue to improve and climb up the table, the likelihood is that the weight of protest against the Oystons will diminish, as it did when Blackpool made it to the Premiership in 2012. But for those like Phil who have increasingly (and understandably) come to resent the way in which the Oystons have run the club, the only acceptable outcome is that the Oystons sell up, ideally to the Supporters Trust, but failing that to someone who would put the interests of the club first. That outcome is more likely to result if Blackpool's fall continues, perhaps as far as the Conference. It's not a problem for me, but I can well see that it is for him, and many other long-term supporters.

*

Meanwhile, Wigan were involved in yet another draw – their third in succession – at home to second-in-the-table Walsall, who had so ruthlessly demolished Blackpool a couple of weeks previously. After a tepid first half, both teams had good chances to win the game, with Wigan's Will Grigg missing two close-range opportunities in quick succession. Wigan then made things difficult for themselves when captain Craig Morgan was sent off in the 70th minute for a professional foul on Walsall's Kieron Morris. That's the third sending-off in five matches, all coming at critical times in the game, and in the first two cases (at Port Vale and Oldham) costing the club points, as the home side scored soon afterwards on both occasions. But today, Wigan managed to hold out against an impressive Walsall side, and manager Gary Caldwell was relatively upbeat about his team's performance ("I'm sure if we finish with eleven, we'll start winning games").

*

Both Wigan and Blackpool were involved in midweek games, at Crewe and Port Vale respectively, in the Johnstone's Paint Trophy round two. I really can't take this competition seriously, a view echoed by both managers, who gave starts to various players who had not yet appeared in league games, and by the fans, who turned up in derisory numbers (well below 2,000 at each game). Even the final is remembered, one suspects, more for the day out at Wembley rather than any real sense of achievement on the part of the winners, who would happily have settled for promotion, if offered the choice. As it happened, both teams won, Blackpool extending their winning streak to three, with goals from Clark Robertson (his first ever) and the previously-unused Jarrett Rivers, whilst Jordy Hiwula scored twice for Wigan, whose third goal was apparently a spectacular long-range effort from one Yanic Wildschut (where has he sprung from?).

*

The following Saturday, Blackpool had a free day; their opponents Bradford City having successfully applied for a postponement, on account of having three players involved in Euro 2016 fixtures being played over the weekend (three current internationals at Bradford City? Hard to believe!). Wigan and Bury (their scheduled opponents) had no such problems. At Gigg Lane, Wigan once again demonstrated their ability to stage late recoveries. One-nil down after six minutes, and two-nil down after 60, it looked like there was no way back despite Wigan's usual domination of possession (an impressive 72%) and superior creation of scoring opportunities (18 to 6). Then Bury's Chris Hussey was sent off with ten minutes remaining after which the customary comeback soon materialised. Bury's Nathan Cameron obligingly headed into his own net, under pressure from substitute Grant Holt, whose first Wigan appearance this was since sustaining a long-term injury in the 2013-14 season. In the final minute of normal time, captain Craig Morgan found space on the edge of the area and drilled a low shot into the corner of the net, to the delight of the large contingent of travelling supporters. There was time for Michael Jacobs to hit a post and Chris McCann to bring out a great save from Bury's keeper, before Wigan had to settle for the draw.

So that's five games unbeaten for the Latics. However, the last four have all been draws, so the team is still hovering in mid-table. And why do they so often leave things so late in away matches? In the last four games, seven of the eight goals scored have come in the last 15 minutes of the game. Their loyal and numerous visiting fans will no doubt have been delighted by the series of late comebacks, but much less happy with the content of the previous 75 minutes, in the games at Chesterfield, Port Vale, and Bury.

*

The following Saturday I was back at the DW Stadium, where the visitors were Colchester United. Not, on the face of it, a fixture to set the pulses racing. It's a measure of how far Wigan have fallen that on the equivalent Saturday three years ago they were at home to West Ham. Both Wigan and Colchester were currently becalmed in mid-table. The visitors, a side typical of the majority of Division One's participants (average home attendance last season 3,886; no wealthy owner) had managed a run of four straight wins in September but had suffered three consecutive defeats since then. They had the leakiest defence in Division One (22 goals conceded in 12 games) but had compensated by also being amongst the leading scorers (with 19). So at least a goalless draw didn't look on the cards today. Wigan started with loan signing Yanic Wildschut (from Middlesbrough) on the left and 40-year-old Jussi Jaaskelainen preferred in goal to Richard O'Donnell.

Any fears of a goalless draw were dispelled within five minutes. Wildschut, showing an impressive combination of speed and strength, muscled his way to the goal-line. His low cross was palmed away by the Colchester keeper straight into the path of Donervon Daniels, who scored with ease. Six minutes later, another ball from the left found Max Power on the edge of the penalty area and his shot took a wicked deflection and sailed into the top corner of the net, leaving Jamie Jones stranded. An element of good fortune about that one, but this wasn't the case with the next goal in the 50th minute, when Daniels scored his second, with a crisp shot after good work on the right by Jacobs. Colchester, who had contributed little in the way of counter attacks, looked dead and buried, an impression that was confirmed in the 33rd minute when David Perkins surged into the penalty area and laid the ball back for Will Grigg to calmly slot the ball home. There could have been more, but four-nil it remained at the interval. Not that the Wigan supporters were complaining. When had they last seen their team score four in the first half? Lost in the mists of antiquity!

The scoreline was a fair reflection of Wigan's dominance. They had played fluent attacking football throughout the first half. In the previous games I'd seen, they had enjoyed a lot of possession involving patient passing movements in midfield, but had typically lacked the ability to turn those qualities into goal-scoring opportunities. Today there was much more urgency about their play. Yanic Wildschut was a constant danger on the left and gave Wigan greater width and more attacking options, which they put to good use. There wasn't a weak link in the team.

But the game wasn't providing a particularly good illustration of my 'football as drama' metaphor. That's the problem when a side goes three or four goals up in the first half. Except in very exceptional circumstances, the result is no longer in doubt. That was certainly the case today. Colchester had shown no evidence that they could overturn a four-goal deficit and the second half was an anti-climax, devoid of drama. Wigan did create further chances, but only took one of them, just before the end, when Will Grigg exquisitely chipped the ball over the hapless Jamie Jones. So five-nil it ended, the first time Wigan had scored five in a league game for 11 years. And I was there to see it!

*

Meanwhile, Blackpool were battling their way to a commendable goalless draw at Coventry, who were unbeaten at home and still in a playoff position. This was the third league game in a row that Blackpool had kept a clean sheet; "From rock bottom to rock solid," as the *Blackpool Gazette* put it. Although Coventry dominated possession and created more goal-scoring opportunities, Blackpool gave a good account of themselves, and could have won it in the second-half when Mark Cullen created the best opening of the entire game but then contrived to miss it. But a point was probably more than the visitors expected and continued the sense of momentum generated by the successive home wins. There followed a few days of uncertainty, in the aftermath of Sam Allardyce's appointment as the manager of Sunderland. Neil McDonald had been Allardyce's assistant at West Ham United for several years prior to his appointment at Blackpool in the summer, and there was expectation in the media that McDonald could be enticed to the North-East to work alongside his former boss again. But he soon made it clear that he was staying put, showing a nice touch of humour in doing so – "It's amazing isn't it; a Blackpool manager who actually wants to stay!" This was excellent news for the Seasiders, as McDonald had managed to turn a disparate group of individuals into a coherent and committed team, in a matter of two months, and in far from easy circumstances. His departure would have been a big blow.

*

The following Tuesday, Wigan were away at Peterborough, who were positioned just below them in the table. Within 15 minutes, the Latics were two goals ahead, repeating what they'd achieved against Colchester a few days previously. First Yanic Wildschut embarked on a run from the half-way line, surged into the box and side-footed the ball past the Peterborough keeper; a hugely-impressive individual effort. Then Reece James, on the edge of the penalty area, hit a low shot which according to the *Wigan Observer* "Hit Will Grigg on its way into the net." That's a misrepresentation; it's clear from the video footage that Grigg delivered a neat back-heeled flick, which deliberately and conclusively changed the ball's trajectory. In the second half, Peterborough dominated the game and pulled a goal back. Ten minutes from the end they equalised, and no doubt had aspirations to go on and win the game. But within a minute, Max Power received the ball on the edge of the box (via a deflection from a defender), and strode forward to finish confidently. Wigan held on to record their second away league win of the season, and as a result moved for the first time into a play-off position. They are clearly on a roll – seven games undefeated in the league – with the recent introduction of Wildschut having made a major contribution to a more attacking style of play.

*

Blackpool were entertaining Millwall (who came down with them last season) and showed further evidence of their new-found resilience. The visitors took the lead late in the first half and appeared to be coping comfortably with Blackpool's second half pressure, until ten minutes from the end, when Jack Redshaw was unfairly upended as he prepared to shoot. Under the 'last man' rule, the culprit was sent off, before Redshaw scored from the spot in emphatic style. So Blackpool's unbeaten run in the league extended to four games, a totally unexpected turnaround after the 'rock bottom' display at Shrewsbury late in September.

But, as so often with Blackpool, news off the pitch was vying for attention with events on it. The club president and board member Valeri Belokon, who holds a 20% stake in the club and is currently suing the Oystons over alleged financial irregularities in their business relationship, announced that he had made progress in assembling a group of local businessmen who would be prepared to make a takeover bid for the club. So it may be that there will soon be a second bid on the table, in addition to the one from the Supporters Trust, about which nothing has been heard in the past few weeks. Belokon is seen in a much more favourable light by the fans than his co-directors; it is widely believed that it was he, rather than the Oystons who provided the resources to bring Charlie Adam to the club, a signing that was a major influence in Blackpool reaching the Premiership in 2010. Such a consortium would, I guess, probably prove an acceptable alternative to the BST bid as far as the fans are concerned. There is no love lost between Belokon and the Oystons.

Oh, and Nile Ranger is pleading (again) for an opportunity to show what he can do for Blackpool. He has seen the error of his ways, foresworn a life of crime, and is certain that he deserves one more chance. How certain, *Sky Sports* asked him? "100 million percent," was the answer. Well, you can't get much more certain than that. Maybe, given his undoubted talent, it would be worth giving him one last chance.

What a month it was turning out to be for both of my chosen clubs. Both continued their unbeaten runs on the penultimate Saturday of the month. Wigan returned from Bradford with a creditable point, at a ground where the home support is formidable. There were over 19,000 present (a figure which reflected, inter alia, some very attractive season ticket deals). Wigan went ahead early in the second half when a pass from substitute Donald Love found Michael Jacobs free on the edge of the box, from whence he scored with a well-placed curling shot. He then proceeded to do a silly dance, as his team-mates descended on him. Personally, I've no time for silly dances, nor any of the increasing range of similarly fatuous celebratory rituals. Whatever happened to spontaneity? Whenever anyone scored a goal for Parrswood Athletic or St. Theresa's FC (Chester), two teams I turned out for in my playing days, we were all so delighted we just coalesced in a big mutual hug. I would make silly celebratory dances, or any other such contrivances, a red card offence, and if the whole team chose to indulge in them, then they take the consequences! The fourth official could be the arbiter of whether the offence was silly enough to merit a sending-off; it would give him or her something to distract them in a job with long periods of inactivity.

Where was I? Oh yes, shortly after the Jacobs goal, Bradford equalised, through a James Hanson header. It was a good game full of flowing football (*The Football League Paper* gave it four stars (they rarely give five) which either side could have won late on. Both managers seemed happy with a draw (a rare occurrence, in my experience), and as a result, Wigan remained in a playoff position (fifth) thanks to unexpected defeats for Bury and Sheffield United.

*

Meanwhile, at Bloomfield Road, Blackpool were facing bottom-of-the-league Crewe Alexandra, whom they deservedly beat two-nil. After a lacklustre first half, in which Crewe dominated possession but carved out few chances, Blackpool developed some momentum and went ahead when debutant on-loan signing Hayden White scored from the edge of the area with a shot which took a wicked (as they say) deflection. Jack Redshaw wrapped up the game late on when he scored from a clear penalty after Dave Norris had been upended in the box.

What is happening to Blackpool? They've already won as many games as they did in the whole of the previous season, and we're still only in October. They are unbeaten in the last five league games, in which they have conceded just one goal (they haven't scored many, but with a defensive record like that, they haven't needed to). After today's game, they found themselves clear of the relegation zone for the first time since the opening day of the season, and they have a game in hand over the four clubs above them. A lot of credit must go to Neil McDonald who has somehow managed to generate a level of commitment, cohesion, and self-belief in a team which was short on all three qualities a month ago. His achievement was rewarded (although I'm not sure 'rewarded' is the right word) by an extended interview on the Channel Five *Football League Show* (which has yet… how can one put it… to find a convincing format). He comes over as a modest, likeable guy, whose thoughtful comments are mercifully free of the hype and bullshit which are delivered by many of his fellow managers. As long as he stays, the prospect of Division Two is likely to continue to fade into the background.

*

On the last day of October, I travelled to Gigg Lane to watch Bury play the resurgent Blackpool. I used to watch Bury occasionally in the 1960s when I lived in South Manchester. They were in what was then Division Two. I always enjoyed the tranquil surroundings of Gigg Lane – the ground is flanked on three sides by trees, which are visible above the roofs of the stands. So if you sit in the main stand, as I did today, the rest of the ground has a (misleadingly) rural feel to it.

As I fumbled for change near a cash turnstile, I was approached by a middle-aged man who offered me a free ticket; his dad couldn't make it today, and didn't want to see the ticket wasted. I gratefully accepted. In my *Conference Season* visit to Lincoln, a couple of seasons ago, the same thing happened. Maybe I have an air of vulnerability or need which makes me a target for such generosity? But I'm certainly not complaining.

Inside the stadium, it was clear that a large contingent of Blackpool fans had made their way across Lancashire to see if their team could continue its six-match unbeaten run. It turned out that there were over 1,700 of them, packed into the visitors' enclosure. They were making a lot of noise too, maybe trying to re-establish their position in the decibel rating league! Strange that they have been so quiet at recent home matches. The decibel level soon dropped, however, when two minutes after kick-off, a well-flighted in-swinging corner on the right taken by Chris Hussey found a Bury team-mate at the far post, whose header then hit various people before going in off a Blackpool defender. It dropped even further seven minutes later when the same sequence of events was repeated except this time Bury forward, Danny Rose, poked the ball home from close range, in the ensuing confusion.

The mood then turned ugly in the Blackpool-populated enclosure. Goaded by the taunts of the Bury fans in the adjacent stand who had positioned themselves as close as possible to the Blackpool contingent, a number of the latter rushed to the barrier separating the two areas and had to be restrained by police. The earlier carnival mood was rapidly turning sour. However, things improved shortly afterwards when Mark Cullen took advantage of the debutante Bury keeper inexplicably losing possession on the edge of the penalty area, to score with ease. But they then got worse again when the ubiquitous Ian Hussey took a free-kick from close to the right-side corner flag, from whence he had set up the first two goals. This time, he curled the ball directly into the net, past an ill-prepared Colin Doyle, who really should have saved it. Could it get any worse for Blackpool? Indeed it could. In the 34th minute came the best goal of the game (so far) a 30-yard thunderbolt from Bury's Tom Soares. At this stage, significant numbers of Blackpool fans strode angrily out of the stadium, arguably a premature reaction given the rate at which goals were being scored, particularly when just before half-time Clark Robertson reduced the deficit with a powerful header from a Jack Redshaw corner.

Although Bury were two goals to the good, Blackpool had carved out just as many chances. It could easily have been four-all (or indeed five-all). At four-one, it felt like 'game over,' but the second Blackpool goal just before the interval had introduced an element of uncertainty as to the final outcome. Both defences had looked extremely vulnerable, and Bury looked to have acquired a prime example of a 'dodgy keeper.' From the start of the second half Blackpool dominated possession, and produced some fluent attacking play of the kind almost totally absent in their early season games. They generated few scoring chances but always looked more likely to score than Bury, who were defending in depth and relying on the occasional breakaway. Then in the 85th minute, substitute Martin Paterson was pulled down in the area, and Jack Redshaw scored emphatically (again) from the spot. In the ten minutes (including added time) which remained, Blackpool continued to dominate, but couldn't produce the decisive finish that would have earned them a famous (and arguably deserved) 4-4 draw.

Despite the four goals conceded (so much for the 'rock solid' metaphor) which demonstrated a worrying vulnerability to set-pieces, there were several positives about Blackpool's performance: three goals scored away from home for the first time since the spring of 2013; a strength of character demonstrated by a preparedness to fight back from an apparently hopeless position of four-one down; and further evidence of the effectiveness of the Cullen/Redshaw strike-force. The Blackpool fans who had stayed the course gave the team a deserved ovation at the final whistle. Their team remained just clear of the relegation zone, one point ahead of Fleetwood Town.

Late the previous day it had been revealed, to no-one's surprise, that the Blackpool Supporters Trust bid for the club had been rejected by the Oystons (one wonders why it had taken them so long to decide). Owen Oyston's response included the following statement, "I believe that if you were left to run the club, you would go to the wall, because you do not have any money or the experience necessary to support the club in its present moment of need," (so who is responsible for this 'moment of need', one might ask?). Importantly for the Oystons, the offer involved no cash, and was seen as "an invitation for me to give you all the assets and cash, without you producing a penny of new money." So the remaining hope for a change of ownership rests with Valeri Belokon's efforts to assemble a group of sympathetic local businessmen. But even if he does, the chances of the Oystons conceding ownership to someone who is pursuing legal action against them look decidedly slim.

What I hadn't realised until I checked the internet the next day, was that the rejection of the BST bid was common knowledge amongst Blackpool fans as they made their way to Bury and that a lot of the noise emanating from the away fans enclosure was an expression of anger and frustration at the news. Secondly, the adjacent Bury fans were waving pro-Oyston banners, an action calculated to incense the visiting supporters, which indeed it did; and thirdly that trouble in the wake of the news had been expected – hence the large police presence. Owen and Sam Oyston, who were present, had been advised not to sit in the Bury Directors Box but were located elsewhere in the ground, where they were less likely to be recognised. I guess this kind of scene is likely to recur at away grounds within easy reach of Blackpool throughout the season unless the current impasse is resolved.

*

Elsewhere, Wigan were making hard work of defeating declining Swindon Town at the DW Stadium. This was Swindon's owner Les Power's last game as manager (well, team selector at least) and he reportedly felt 'sick as a parrot' when his side went down to a 0-1 defeat after conceding a scrappy 95th-minute goal, scored by substitute Francisco Junior (his first for the club). The win leaves Wigan well-positioned in fifth place. But it was clearly a game to miss; I was glad I'd gone to Bury.

*

Three days later, following Blackpool's 0-1 defeat at Bradford (for details see next Chapter) and Coventry City's 4-3 victory over Barnsley, all the clubs in Division One had played 16 matches and were one-third of the way through the league season. It felt like a good time for some reflections on progress. As far as Blackpool and Wigan were concerned, their records and positions were more or less what had been predicted. Blackpool were in 20th position with 16 points from 16 games, one place above the relegation zone. Wigan were fifth in the table, in a play-off place, with 27 points from 16 games. Blackpool had lost four more games (8) than they had won (4), whilst Wigan had won four more games (7) than they had lost (3). All nicely symmetrical if, like me, you have autistic tendencies. Blackpool were in the midst of a group of eight teams propping up the table, with a mere four points separating bottom-placed Crewe (13 points) from Shrewsbury Town (17). In the upper reaches of the table there were four clubs on 32 or 31 points, headed by Walsall, and followed closely by Wigan and Bury, both on 27.

But these predicted outcomes have been reached in diverse ways. After five games, Blackpool had managed a single point, were bottom of the table, playing badly, and looking certainties for relegation. After nine games things were not much better; still bottom, five points on the board, and a 'rock bottom' performance at Shrewsbury in the last of these games. Then came a revival, not just in terms of results, but in also in the quality of their performances. Blackpool embarked on an unbeaten run of five league games, in the course of which only a single goal was conceded. Although goals scored were still in short supply, the team was also developing a degree of attacking flair, which had been absent in the earlier games. The higher-profile new signings –

Jack Redshaw, Mark Cullen, Brad Potts, and Emmerson Boyce – were making an increasing impact and Colin Doyle was excelling in goal. The whole team was developing a coherence that had previously been lacking, and also an enhanced team spirit, including a commendable resilience when under pressure. Much of the credit must go to Neil McDonald, whose post-match comments had always involved a refreshing blend of praise, encouragement, and realism. Then came a couple of setbacks; narrow and arguably undeserved defeats at Bury and Bradford. But even in these games, the team had demonstrated positive qualities largely absent in the earlier games. There was no way Blackpool were going to make the playoffs, but there was a reasonable chance that they could avoid the widely-predicted further drop into Division Two.

Wigan started the season more slowly than many expected. Their away form, in particular, was unimpressive; three defeats and only one win in their first four visits. After eight games they were becalmed in mid-table, strong at home, but defensively vulnerable away from the DW Stadium. Doubts began to be expressed as to whether Gary Caldwell was up to it as a manager. But eight games later such doubts had receded. Wigan began to look like a real team, as opposed to a disparate collection of individuals assembled in the close season (which had been the reality). Several of the new signings began to turn in impressive displays: David Perkins, Donervon Daniels, and Max Power in midfield, Michael Jacobs up front, and Reece James as an attack-minded defender. Yanic Wildschut added width and penetration when signed on loan from Middlesborough. Wigan embarked on a still extant unbeaten run and by late October had climbed into a playoff position, which is what the pundits had predicted.

At this stage in the season, no obvious contenders for promotion had emerged. In all honesty, there appear to be a sizeable contingent of mediocre teams in Division One this year. Walsall have proved the most consistent of the front-runners and certainly looked impressive when trouncing Blackpool at Bloomfield Road.

CHAPTER 5

Wigan had shown what they were capable of in their 5-0 demolition of Colchester. Otherwise, there was little I had seen live or on video that suggested that Wigan didn't have as good a chance as anyone of promotion to the Championship, or that Blackpool were not eminently capable of reaching the safety of mid-table. We shall see.

CHAPTER 6

NOVEMBER: THE SEASIDERS SLUMP AND THE LATICS STUMBLE

On a foggy Tuesday evening, early in November, Blackpool crossed the Pennines to play the re-arranged fixture against Bradford City. A repetition of the seven-goal bonanza at Bury was unlikely; Bradford are not prolific scorers, but they don't concede many either. If Blackpool managed to win, it would send them soaring up the table to 17th, well clear of the relegation places.

Unfortunately, neither outcome materialised. By all accounts, Blackpool gave a gritty performance, matching the hosts for possession and chances created, but lost to a solitary goal, a header from James Hanson just before half-time. Neil McDonald was disappointed, but not unduly perturbed; it had been one of Blackpool's better away performances, and with more decisive finishing, they could easily have come away with a draw.

*

The following Saturday, it was the first round of the FA Cup. Wigan were at Bury (again) and Blackpool at Barnet. The diminished status of this venerable competition was well-illustrated by the fact that each club fielded what was close to a reserve team line-up. Both clubs paid the price. Wigan were hammered 4-0, and Blackpool went down meekly 2-0. So much for the magic of the Cup! (The memories of Wigan's euphoric success at Wembley in 2013 have clearly faded).

Wigan's cause was not helped by a costly error by (reserve) keeper Richard O'Donnell, who gifted Bury their first goal, after an evenly-contested first 20 minutes. Blackpool also suffered from an attack of 'dodgy keeping.' Regular keeper Colin Doyle was injured half-way through the first half, and his replacement Kyle Letheren was at fault for both of the Barnet goals, which followed in quick succession shortly afterwards (*The Football League Paper* awarded him a performance rating of three). Both managers made predictable 'this was totally unacceptable' comments. Gary Caldwell claimed that this was the lowest he'd felt since taking over as manager. "Everything that could go wrong did go wrong." Well, maybe you should have fielded a stronger side, mate! He did have the grace to apologise to the large contingent of Wigan fans who had made the short trip.

Neil McDonald at least gave a justification of sorts for fielding a weakened team. "I don't regret the changes. We've got a very thin squad, and we needed to protect the team." Apparently, there had been 'plenty of individuals knocking on his door, saying they should be in the team,' but none of them, he felt, had taken their chance. So it's presumably a return to the bench (or possibly not even that) for Messrs Higham, Dunne, Rivers, Cubero, and Thomas. One suspects neither manager will really have been that bothered about their early exit. They can now, in the time-honoured parlance, 'concentrate on the league.'

But the possibility of a day out at Wembley remained for both clubs in the shape of the Johnstone's Paint Trophy (please stifle your yawns). The Tuesday after the cup defeats, Wigan and Blackpool met at the DW Stadium, striving to gain a place in the semi-final of this (rightly) underrated competition. 'Striving' turned out be a misrepresentation of Blackpool's efforts. Wigan cantered into the semi-final with an emphatic 4-0 win. It would be more accurate to report that Wigan Reserves beat Blackpool Reserves 4-0.

As was the case the previous Saturday, the bulk of the first-team regulars of both clubs were conspicuous by their absence. Wigan's scorers were Joey Hiwula (long absent from the first team) with two, Sean Murray (where did he spring from?), and Yanic Wildschut after coming on as a substitute. Blackpool managed three shots (one on target), and must have made the 480 fans who made the trip wonder why they'd bothered. Neil McDonald remained unapologetic about his team selection for cup matches, claiming that he always "picked teams to win games." But Neil, you've just fielded a close approximation to the team that failed (miserably) to win at Barnet! Had you forgotten?

*

The following Saturday, I'd planned to go to Rochdale to watch Wigan attempt to continue their unbeaten run in the league (currently stretching to nine games). But the weather forecast was predicting up to two inches of rain in the vicinity of Rochdale, so I decided against it. A missed opportunity, as it turned out, because Wigan gave a thoroughly professional performance, controlling the game throughout, and ending up with a convincing 2-0 win against one of the early season pace-setters. Once Jason Pearce, making a rare appearance, had headed home a well-directed free kick from Michael Jacobs in the 60th minute, the outcome was never in doubt (although the video suggested that there was more than a hint of offside about it).

The second goal, early in the second half, was set up by the impressive Yanic Wildschut (what a difference he has made) who stormed past a hapless Rochdale defender to set up a chance for Michael Jacobs, whose powerful shot went in off the bar. David Perkins, who is every week demonstrating his terrier-like qualities in midfield, could have added a third, with a powerful drive which brought out the best in the Rochdale keeper. *The Football League Paper*, in an untypical example of original prose, characterised Perkins as, "a fizzing pinball of trips, tugs, and tackles that prevented Rochdale building any kind of rhythm." This doesn't quite do justice, however, to the creative qualities which are an equally significant element of his contribution.

The win meant that Wigan remained in fifth position, but were now only four points behind the leaders (Gillingham). The bookies now make them joint favourites to come top of the division (with Coventry City and Walsall). And it was their first clean sheet of the season away from home. There is a real sense of a developing momentum.

Blackpool, on the other hand, have followed an unbeaten run of six games (in all competitions) with a sequence of five consecutive defeats, in the last four of which they have not scored a single goal, but have conceded ten. Their 0-2 defeat at home to improving Doncaster Rovers deposited them back in the relegation zone and made recent dreams of mid-table security appear premature.

Having conceded an early goal to Andy Williams – a neatly curled strike following a poor clearance from Chares Dunne – Blackpool never looked like making a match of it (they managed only a single shot on target). They fell further behind just before the interval to a messy short-range goal from Taylor-Sinclair and ended up fortunate not to have conceded more. Neil McDonald felt that it was the team's worst home display of the season: "We were outplayed and didn't perform half as well as we could," he claimed. "We're in a fragile state, I suppose. The fans had every right to boo."

As so often the case, there was an accompanying off-field story to compete for attention. A Blackpool fan who had made defamatory comments about the Oystons on social media was ordered by a judge to pay £40,000 in damages to the club's owners; yet another example of the toxic relationship which has developed between the Oystons and the club's fan base.

*

It was a bitterly cold late November day as I boarded a crowded Transpennine train at Oxenholme Station. I was on my way to watch Wigan Athletic play Shrewsbury Town and to see whether they could extend their unbeaten run of league games to 11. On the face of it, there seemed every likelihood of them doing so. Shrewsbury were languishing near the bottom of the table, one point ahead of Blackpool. They'd started the season by losing five home league games on the trot (a sequence halted by the fortuitous visit of Blackpool in mid-September). Since then, they'd won all their home games, but had lost the knack of picking up points in away matches.

I was becoming familiar with the 20-minute walk from Wigan Station to the DW Stadium: under the railway bridge, past Poundsavers, past the currently non-operational Wigan Pier leisure and tourism complex (the brown tourist signs scattered around Wigan need to go; anyone following them would be sorely disappointed!), over the canal bridge, and then a right turn onto the canal towpath, which takes you close to the stadium. The journey is a grim reminder of the coming of the post-industrial age; what would once have been a thriving industrial area is now a blend of deserted premises and derelict land, interspersed with small factories, retail outlets or car showrooms. Orwell would have hardly recognised the scene, 80 years after his visit.

There was a sizeable contingent of Shrewsbury fans in the North Stand, making a lot of noise. Hope springs eternal, particularly after a few pints of lager. The first 30 minutes were relatively uneventful. Wigan, as usual, had most of the possession but were unable to turn it into clear-cut chances. They were forced to make an early substitution when Michael Jacobs was injured following a heavy Shrewsbury tackle (one of many). This was a blow, as Jacobs has been influential recently both as a goalscorer and provider. His replacement, Will Grigg, had proved much less consistent in his recent appearances.

There was a developing sense that this could be a frustrating afternoon for the home side. But ten minutes before half time, the deadlock was broken. A lovely through ball from Daniels found Yanic Wildschut on the left, who left defenders trailing in his wake before crossing for Alan Revell (making his home debut) to score with a well-placed header. Cue a sequence of synchronised crawling motions towards the fans in the East Stand. Book the lot of them, I say!

Then Wildschut who was looking increasingly dangerous again stormed past a series of defenders on the left and provided a cross, which resulted in opportunities for Grigg and then Tim Chow, neither of whom could take advantage. Wildschut's ability to get to the by-line on a regular basis and put over dangerous crosses is a rare and welcome quality at this level. Wigan are going to miss him when his loan spell expires in January.

In the first half, Shrewsbury had proved well-organised in defence but had offered little in attack. They started the second half throwing more men forward, but still found it difficult to create clear-cut chances; yet another team (like Doncaster, Swindon, and Colchester) capable of fluent approach work, but lacking incisiveness. Wigan, now given more room, always looked more likely to score. Daniels should have done better with a free header, and on a couple of occasions low crosses scudded across the six-yard box narrowly evading incoming forwards. A second goal would have killed the game. But in its absence, there remained a level of uncertainty which at least maintained spectator interest, especially when a Shrewsbury free-kick crashed inches wide into the advertising hoardings behind the goal, with Jaaskelainen apparently unsighted. Nonetheless, Wigan survived to make it 11 undefeated games in the league. In a not particularly distinguished game, any result other than a Wigan win would have been an injustice.

In 'Captain Morgan's' column in the excellent Wigan programme, Craig Morgan argued that Shrewsbury posed a threat and that that's the case for every team in the division. "We haven't had an easy game yet," he claimed. Not even Colchester? No, that wasn't a case of them being poor it was that "We were very very good on the day." I'm not sure I agree with his perception of how tough Division One is proving. In my view, it contains a lot of mediocre teams. I've witnessed high-quality performances from Wigan, Walsall and (at a pinch and disregarding their defensive frailties) Bury. The remainder have been nothing to write home about, which is good news for Wigan's promotion prospects, and, at the other end of the table, Blackpool's hopes of survival.

*

Blackpool were at Southend and went down 1-0 to a late header from a defender. If Wigan are on a roll, Blackpool are currently rolling backwards. That's now six defeats in succession, including four in the league. Since scoring three at Bury, they have failed to find the net in five consecutive matches. The revival, which peaked with the 2-0 win over Crewe in mid-October has petered out. Neil McDonald did his best (as ever) to find some positives, "We had some great chances to score," he said, "but we aren't getting enough goals at the moment." To be frank, Neil, you're not getting any. The (unofficial) club social media sites have begun to despair of the team's lack of quality, as well as continuing to express unqualified hostility to the Oystons. One contributor berated the 4,000 or so fans who still turn up regularly at home matches, arguing that if the current boycott by around 2,000 season ticket holders were to spread more widely, the pressure on the Oystons to withdraw from the club (or at least rethink their attitude to it) would intensify. It made me feel uneasy that I was continuing to attend home matches. But then I do have a book to write.

*

The following Tuesday, Wigan, having disposed of Shrewsbury, had a more testing fixture at home to Burton Albion, who were positioned fifth in the league, one point behind Wigan, but with a game in hand. Burton were proving the surprise package of Division One. Promoted from the Conference in 2009, they narrowly missed out on further advancement in 2012-13 and 2013-14, reaching the playoffs in both seasons. Last season they had been doing well under the management of Gary Rowett when he left in November to take over at Birmingham City. He was replaced by Jimmy Floyd-Hasselbaink, whose first managerial appointment it was. Under Hasselbaink, Burton lost only three games over the remainder of the season and finished as Division Two champions; not bad for a club whose average home attendance was a mere 2,713.

To the surprise of many, Burton have been amongst the leaders from the start of the season. At the end of September, they were top of the division, and although their results have been more erratic since, they have never been out of the top six. Their success has been built on a strong defence, the meanest in the division, with only 14 goals conceded in 17 league matches (it would have been ten had it not been for an uncharacteristic 4-0 defeat at lowly Fleetwood Town). On the other hand, they don't score many either; only Blackpool, Crewe, and Doncaster have managed fewer than Burton's paltry 16. So a high-scoring game tonight was not to be expected.

The reason that the game was particularly important for Wigan was that, although they have prevailed against the likes of Crewe, Scunthorpe, Colchester and Swindon, their record against sides in the leadership group has been uninspiring, to say the least; defeats at Gillingham and Coventry, and draws against Walsall, Bury and Bradford City. A win against Burton would greatly aid the credibility of their promotion aspirations.

There were no more than a couple of hundred Burton fans dotted around the North Stand, a predictably small contingent for a small-time club, on a wet Tuesday evening in November, with a 160-mile round trip involved. But it's surprising how much noise 200 fans can make. Not that they, nor the Wigan fans, had much to shout about in the first half. For once, Wigan's measured approach play, involving squares or triangles of short-range inter-passing wasn't working. Usually, it can be relied upon to progress well into their opponent's half, even when it doesn't penetrate any further, but not tonight.

Burton were proving adept at stifling at an early stage such attempts at a leisurely build-up. A potent mixture of tight marking, and hustling and harrying opponents as soon as they received the ball, meant that Wigan's quota of misplaced passes was far higher than usual. There were more balls played back to the keeper (which always, beyond a certain point, irritates the crowd, and understandably so) and, totally uncharacteristic of Wigan this season, several futile long balls out of defence aimed at solitary forwards, always well-policed. Even the irrepressible Yanic Wildschut was subdued, out on the left. He rarely received the ball, and when he did, he found progress difficult in the face of close attention by multiple defenders. I don't recall a single Wigan shot – on or off target – throughout the first half. Not that Burton did much better, although their few attacks usually looked more threatening than those of the home side.

Overcoming my disappointment at not winning a jar of Uncle Joe's Mint Balls in the half-time raffle, I settled back into my seat to see what impact (if any) Gary Caldwell's pep-talk during the interval had made. For a while, there was an improvement in Wigan's play. More defenders and midfielders were taking the ball forward into Burton's half. The home side won a series of corners, none of which came to anything. But it felt for a while that Wigan were getting the upper hand and the tempo of the play had certainly increased, drawing vocal support from the fans which had previously been lacking.

But a goal wouldn't come, and in the end, it was the tendency for Wigan midfielders to stride forward with the ball, rather than passing it around, which proved their undoing. Max Power, in the process of an up-field run, was dispossessed. Immediately a bevy of black-and-gold-shirted Burtonians surged forward. The ball reached Timmy Teale on the left, and his immaculate cross found Abdenessar El Khayati in acres of space in front of goal, who had no problem beating Jaaskelainen. El Khayati who is from Holland (but doesn't sound as if he is) had contributed very little up to that point, a shortcoming which I'm sure his team-mates were now prepared to overlook.

Wigan never really looked like equalising, although late on, a shot from Reece James hit the outside of the post. But Burton had few problems in playing out time (including the seven added minutes). Although not particularly attractive to watch (nor I suspect do they strive to be), Burton proved to be a well-organised well-drilled side with an effective game plan. And despite their emphasis on defensive solidity, the match statistics show that they managed seven shots (two on target) to Wigan's paltry three (none on target). Jimmy Floyd-Hasselbaink is clearly proving an extremely able manager, so much so that he may not be with Burton for much longer. Queens Park Rangers are reportedly closing in on him!

Finding my way out of Wigan in the dark in torrential rain proved a nightmare. My futile attempts to reach the M6 (northbound) resulted in a series of visits to places I've never been to before (nor would ever wish to revisit). I passed through the deserted, windswept streets of Orrell, Billinge, Wigan (again), Platt Bridge, Hindley, and Westhoughton, before reaching the M61, which eventually joins the M6 south of Preston. A glance at a map of Lancashire will show you what a bizarre circuitous journey this was. But at least it gave me the chance to tune into Radio Lancashire and hear about the latest misfortunes of Blackpool. They had been at Port Vale, where they had lost (again) to two late second half goals. This outcome made it seven defeats on the trot (five in the league) and no goals scored in any of the last six games. As a result, they found themselves next to the bottom of the table, with the same number of points as Crewe, but with a marginally better goal difference. Had it been a repeat of the earlier 'rock bottom' performance at Shrewsbury? It would appear not. Blackpool had created and missed numerous opportunities, 13 shots in all (6 on target) to Port Vale's 11 (5 on target). According to the reporter, they should have had the game sewn up long before conceding the late goals. "It's as if they're afraid to score," he commented; an interesting concept which to me lacks credibility. But if Blackpool fail to get anything from the local derby at home to Fleetwood Town five days hence, then the perception of a major crisis on the field will become much heightened. Added to this, there is a pre-match demonstration planned outside Blackpool Tower by the Tangerine Knights, followed by a protest march the short distance to Bloomfield Road. There is a growing sense, given the run of appalling results and the Oystons' rejection of BST's takeover bid, that the stand-off between owners and supporters is becoming increasingly bitter and indeed potentially explosive.

*

The weather on Saturday turned out to be horrendous; gale force winds and bouts of squally horizontal rain. Not a day to be on Blackpool's seafront and not a day for an outdoor protest. The rain-sodden Tangerine Knights and their supporters eventually made their way to the main entrance of Bloomfield Road to join the Blackpool Supporters Trust and other aggrieved groups of fans, for the customary pre-match demonstration. 'We want our club back' proclaimed one banner; 'Where's our money gone?' asked a second; 'RIP Blackpool, killed by the Oyston Family' another. The profound affection and commitment which football clubs inspire amongst local people is well-captured by the vehemence of these (and other) sentiments, as is the readiness to stand in the pouring rain and gale-force winds expressing them.

Inside the ground, there was a lively pre-match atmosphere, as you would expect for a local derby. It was the first ever league fixture between Blackpool and Fleetwood, seven miles apart on the Fylde coast. The Cod Army occupied the whole of the area reserved for visitors in the North Stand, with an equally large contingent in the (so-called) temporary stand adjacent to it. Fleetwood had recently appointed a new manager, Steven Presley, who had already made his mark, masterminding consecutive home wins against Swindon (5-1) and Millwall (2-1). They must have been confident of making it three wins in a row, against a team which had lost their last seven games. And if they managed to do so, what a symbolic achievement that would be. As the BST leaflet, which was distributed to fans before the game pointed out, in 2010 Blackpool were in the Premier League and Fleetwood had just been promoted to the Conference. What a difference five years had made. "One club is steadily on the rise, one in rapid decline," the leaflet argued. "One owner plans to succeed, the other fails to plan. One stadium is buzzing, the other is two-thirds empty. Is Conference football coming to Bloomfield Road?"

The early stages of the game were not encouraging for Blackpool. Fleetwood looked dangerous every time they went forward. Hayden White headed a Joe Davis shot off the line. Other efforts went close. But then, in the 17th minute, Blackpool scored a goal, the first (by my calculations) for 650 minutes! It would have been good if it had been a thunderous volley from the edge of the area, but predictably it was a messy effort, as so many of Blackpool's goals this season have been. Brad Potts found space on the right and sent over a dangerous low cross, which, with two Blackpool players waiting to convert it, Fleetwood's Nathan Pond saved them the trouble of doing so, by diverting the ball into his own net. Without there being a goal-scorer to congratulate (Pond clearly did not qualify) all ten Blackpool outfield players converged in a mass mutual embrace to celebrate the fact that a goal – any kind of goal – had been scored!

This reverse took the wind out of Fleetwood's sails (an appropriate cliché, given the town's nautical history) and the rest of the first half was more even. Given the appalling weather conditions, the quality of football (especially from Fleetwood) was pretty good, and there was a sense of excitement, befitting a local derby, as the Blackpool fans found their collective voice in the wake of the unexpected goal. On the stroke of half-time, Blackpool could and should have increased their lead. A misjudgement by Nathan Pond (who wasn't having the best of games) left Jack Redshaw clear with only the keeper to beat. He screwed the ball high into the North Stand.

That miss looked like it would prove costly, as the second half progressed. Neil McDonald had withdrawn Bright Osayi-Samuel at half-time; a pity, in my view, because the youngster had been prominent in the relatively few attacks that Blackpool had managed. His replacement, debutant Elliot Lee was proving ineffectual. Blackpool also switched to a 4-3-3 formation to match (and presumably seek to nullify) Fleetwood's effective use of this pattern in the first half. But the visitors dominated from the start, and created chance after chance, including an effort from David Henin which cannoned off the frame of the goal. Blackpool were reduced to aimless up-field punts and rarely got anywhere near the Fleetwood goal.

It was a rear-guard action reminiscent of the last 20 minutes of the Swindon game, except that this one lasted for the entire half. Blackpool's on-loan keeper Dean Lyness rose to the occasion, keeping out everything Fleetwood threw at him, although the well-organised Blackpool defence limited most of Fleetwood's goal attempts to long-range efforts. To the frustration of the visiting fans (at least 2,000 in number) and to the delight (and surprise) of the home supporters, Blackpool managed to hold out right through to the sixth minute of added time, for a long-awaited, (but totally undeserved) home win.

Steven Presley, the Fleetwood manager certainly felt hard done by. "There's no doubt we deserved more from the game than we got," he said afterwards. The statistics certainly support his view. Fleetwood had 16 shots, 9 of them on target. Blackpool had a paltry four, none of which troubled the keeper. So we'd all witnessed a rare occurrence, a team winning a game in which they hadn't managed a single shot on target. Remember that if you're ever involved in a pub quiz in Blackpool!

Neil McDonald, unsurprisingly, had a different view. "Without a shadow of a doubt we deserved it," he claimed. The basis of his claim appeared to be that his side had undeservedly lost games recently (for example the recent 2-0 reverse at Port Vale in a game which Blackpool dominated). "We just haven't had the luck; we've been on the wrong side of a fine line." It's a not unfamiliar managerial argument and one for which evidence can always be adduced ('remember that last minute penalty we were denied by that clueless referee!'). For me, the only possible justification for claiming that it was a 'deserved' victory was Blackpool's sterling defensive performance throughout the game, particularly from the back four and the goalkeeper. Whatever problems exist at Blackpool (and there are many) lack of team spirit is not one of them. In each of the games I've seen recently (Swindon and Fleetwood at home and Bury away) the commitment and fighting spirit of the team has been there for all to see, which reflects well on the manager's motivational skills.

*

Meanwhile, Wigan were at Southend, seeking to make amends for the disappointment of their first home defeat of the season the previous Tuesday. Gary Caldwell had made several changes, resting Jacobs, Perkins, and Chow, who were all on the substitutes bench, and Morgan and Wildschut, who weren't. There were recalls for Leon Barnett, Jason Pearce, Francesco Junior, Doug Cowie and Will Grigg. In an evenly-contested game, Leon Barnett, a central defender, came closest to scoring with three powerful efforts, one of which came back off the bar. But neither side could break the deadlock, and both managers felt that it was a fair result (so it probably was).

Wigan remain in fifth place, albeit four points behind second-placed Gillingham, whilst Blackpool have moved up to 22nd, two points away from (temporary) safety.

CHAPTER 7

BLACKPOOL AND WIGAN: WHAT WENT WRONG AND WHAT'S BEING DONE ABOUT IT

When I started watching Blackpool and Wigan in August, I had researched the outlines of what had gone wrong the previous season (and in the case of Blackpool, since well before that), which I have summarised in Chapters One and Two. However, I knew it would be beneficial to include perceptions and insights from those with a detailed knowledge of the clubs concerned. Armed with a series of questions, I arranged interviews with Christine Seddon and William Watt in Blackpool, and Martin Tarbuck and (some time later) Jonathan Jackson in Wigan. Given Blackpool's recent turbulent history, there is more to write about them than there is about Wigan, whose disastrous 2014-15 season is beginning to look like a one-off interruption in a period of success dating back to the 2002-03 season.

Three days after Blackpool's fortuitous 1-0 victory over Fleetwood Town, I returned to the town to interview Christine Seddon, vice-chair of Blackpool Supporters Trust. Christine was taken to her first match at Bloomfield Road when she was five-years-old, by a family with a long tradition of support, and vivid memories of the post-war greats including Stanley Mathews, Stanley Mortensen, Jackie Mudie and Jimmy Armfield. She has been a committed fan since her teenage years, including the entire 29-year ownership span of the Oyston dynasty.

I had arrived early to give myself the opportunity to explore some unfamiliar areas of Blackpool. It was a wild and windy day, and there were very few people around, as I made my way from Blackpool North station towards the sea front and the North Pier. But I was taken aback to be hailed by one of the few who were – a bloke in his twenties with a large menacing-looking bull terrier on a lead. "Where are you going?" he shouted from the other side of the street I was walking down. "Mind your own business," felt like too high-risk a response, so I settled for the admittedly lame reply "just wandering around," and hurried onwards.

My plan to brave the elements and make my way to the end of the Pier was thwarted by the fact that access to the Pier was barred by a locked gate. It wasn't clear whether this restriction was due to the weather, or whether the Pier was closed for the winter (or perhaps closed on weekdays?). Disappointed, I turned back inland to explore the area of cheap hotels (one of them offering bed-and-breakfast "from £10 per night") and shabby rooming houses. Blackpool boasts a large number of houses in multiple occupation; you can recognise them by the multiple doorbells (many of which probably don't work) and the tangled disparate curtains. By the 1970s such accommodation appeared to be dying out; the widespread availability of council housing was then a better bet for anyone in housing need. But given the subsequent decimation of the council house stock, and the resulting acute shortage of 'social housing' options, it was clearly making a comeback. Such areas are profoundly depressing; a walk around the streets to the east of the Metropole Hotel is a real eye-opener.

I spotted a sign for Bethany's Equestrian Tack Shop; an unlikely establishment, I thought, in this part of Blackpool. It was closed and empty; not a bridle or harness in sight ('there's just no demand for it nowadays, you know'). Not far away was a shop selling seaside rock (and other such delicacies) including what were labelled 'adult rock': confections shaped to resemble male and female genitalia. I passed on quickly; if there is anything which so vividly epitomises the tawdry, tacky side of this town, I have yet to come across it!

I returned to the sea-front and passed a terrace of classier hotels, which looked like they were trying to outdo the 'different-coloured house, sitting by the sea' of the Childrens' TV series *Balamory* (which is in reality Tobermory, on the Isle of Mull). There was a pink one, a yellow one, a purple one, and a green one. But somehow it seemed to work much better at Tobermory.

It was time to meet Christine. This is what she told me.

When Owen Oyston purchased the club in 1987, there was an initial surge of goodwill towards him on the part of the fans; he had, after all, rescued Blackpool FC from possible extinction. But it soon became clear that the Oystons were not investing in the club in the way that fellow millionaire Lancastrians Jack Walker and David Whelan did at Blackburn and Wigan respectively. When the Oystons took over, Blackpool had spent most of their years of league football in the first or second tier. Throughout the first 20 years of their ownership, the club alternated between the third and fourth levels. For a club like Blackpool, with its previous high-profile history, this was a huge disappointment. Although many of the fans remained broadly supportive (the fanzine *A View from the Tower* between 1996 and 1999 contained little of the anti-Oyston feeling so apparent today), others (including those currently leading the Supporters Trust) ultimately came to believe that the Oystons were not doing enough to support the club.

To be fair, the Oystons did begin to invest in the modernisation of the Bloomfield Road stadium in the early-2000s, although the project was not completed until 2010 when the South Stand (the Jimmy Armfield Stand) was opened, funded at least partly by Valeri Belokon (see below). It incorporated a new luxury hotel.

At the time that the revival began, with Blackpool's promotion to the Championship in 2007, the board had recently been joined by someone who was to play a major part in the club's progress – the Latvian-born businessman Valeri Belokon. Initially, there was a good relationship between Belokon and Owen Oyston. It was Belokon who made resources available for some of Blackpool's key signings, notably Charlie Adam who played a central role in helping the club win promotion to the Premiership in 2010 (and nearly keeping them there the following season). In the triumphal post-promotion parade through Blackpool in 2010, Belokon and the Oystons played prominent roles. It felt like a minor miracle had been achieved; Blackpool back in the top tier after an absence of nearly 40 years.

But then the relationship deteriorated. There is a widespread view amongst Blackpool fans that if a couple of new signings had been brought in, in January 2011, when (after a good first half of the season) Blackpool were beginning to struggle, it could have kept them in the Premiership for (at least) another season. But Belokon was by then experiencing problems with his businesses, and was not in a position to respond to manager Ian Holloway's requests, and the Oystons were reluctant to pay out large transfer fees at this stage. In May 2011, Blackpool returned to the Championship, a single point behind Wolves, who survived.

The next season Blackpool continued to prosper under Ian Holloway's quirky but inspirational management style, and nearly made it back to the Premiership, losing narrowly to QPR in the play-off final. But mid-way through that season, Belokon's assets were frozen, and he has subsequently played little part at boardroom level.

In the run-up to the following season, 2012-13, there was little in the way of expenditure on new players, and in November 2012, Ian Holloway resigned. It was widely assumed that this was because resources were not being made available to him to sign the players he wanted. If this were the case then, in Belokon's absence, it would have been the Oystons who were refusing to respond. Holloway's resignation heralded the start of Blackpool's downward spiral and an intensification of the tensions between the Oystons and a growing number of the club's fans.

In the wake of Holloway's departure, a small group of fans decided to set up an independent supporters group called SISA (Seasiders Independent Supporters Association). This group had by then become convinced that under the present ownership, Blackpool's prospects looked bleak. They were dismayed at Holloway's departure and angered at the fact that earlier that year, the unprecedented sum of £11 million had been paid out to a company owned by Owen Oyston, a payment that is perfectly legal under company law. Twelve months later the SISA members voted to form a legally-appointed trust, whose first meeting was held in July 2014.

In the meantime, the fortunes of the club on the pitch had deteriorated. Paul Ince's spell as manager had started well, but then lost impetus, and after a bad run of results, he was dismissed in January 2014. Blackpool only survived in the Championship because of their impressive start to the season – 16 points from the first six games. There was a glimmer of hope in the close season, when former Charlton manager Jose Riga (who had an impressive track record) was brought in, a move which, coupled with an attractive two-year season ticket deal, led to a surge in sales, many of them to Supporters Trust members.

Then came the unprecedented pre-season fiasco in which, in July, only six players had been registered with the club. By the start of the season, the arrival of a motley crew of trialists and on-loan players had swelled the squad to 15, which left three vacancies on the substitutes' bench for the opening fixture at Nottingham Forest. Blackpool had become everyone's hot tip for relegation. But having purchased their season tickets, the members of the newly-formed Trust were prepared to suspend disbelief, at least for a while.

Disbelief was not long in returning! With the benefit of hindsight, Riga did a reasonable job with his ever-changing crew of loanees and rejects from other clubs. He also had the reputation of being prepared to stand up to the Oystons, which gave him a degree of credibility with many of the club's supporters, especially BST members. His dismissal in October 2014, after a mere five months as manager, and his replacement by someone who had himself been summarily dismissed from his previous job with Birmingham City was the last straw.

For the BST members, all their worst perceptions about the Oystons' lack of commitment to Blackpool FC were confirmed.

From then on, there was no realistic prospect of reconciliation. Previously BST members had (just about) clung on to the (remote) possibility that the Oystons might re-evaluate matters, and experience a change of attitude towards the club, both in relation to the fans, and in terms of financial investment. That was no longer seen as realistic. The priority was now to somehow persuade or influence the Oystons to relinquish ownership, in favour of the Trust itself, or a different group of financial backers.

This brought BST's main priority into line with that of the Tangerine Knights, who are a protest group with the sole and specific remit of unseating the Oystons (BST's mission has always been more wide-ranging). Although both groups are committed to operating within the law, it's probably fair to say that the Tangerine Knights are more prepared to push at the boundaries to achieve their goals. For those whose memories go back to the 1960s, they are in a similar relationship to BST as the Committee of 100 were to the Campaign for Nuclear Disarmament. The two groups do work together at times, and see themselves as 'on the same side, but operating in different ways.'

In the demonstration on the pitch which resulted in the postponement of Blackpool's final home game of the 2014-15 season (see Chapter 2), BST were certainly not involved, and the Tangerine Knights are adamant that they did not organise the pitch invasion.

BST's membership is currently approaching 2,000 and growing. They make a point of behaving responsibly and democratically, even when under great provocation. If change does come about, it will come about through their efforts, organisation and commitment. It was they who worked up and submitted a well-argued takeover bid for the club in the summer of 2015 (see Chapter 2). The way in which their bid was eventually rejected (a response posted late one Friday evening on the club website) was dealt with in an appropriately restrained and logical manner. This is the hallmark of BST's way of working.

There are two other supporter-based organisations in existence. There is still an official supporters group – the Blackpool Supporters Association (or BSA), which has, however, now detached itself from the club and its owners following the Textgate scandal (see Chapter 2). It operates on a low-key basis, its main function being to organise coach travel to away fixtures. Following this detachment, the club set up a replacement, initially known as a Fans Parliament, which comprised 12 individuals who were interviewed and selected by the club (significantly, Jimmy Armfield, former player Trevor Sinclair, and local MP Gordon Marsden declined to be involved). It is now known as the Fans Progress Group, but given the recent resignation of its chairperson, it has downsized to five. It continues to lack credibility within the fan base.

In the long unhappy history of the relationship between the Oystons and a large section of Blackpool's supporters, the fans have not been blameless. Vicki Oyston (Owen's then wife) was subjected to a good deal of verbal abuse from a group of fans, during her brief spell as chairperson, after Owen was jailed in 1996. Karl has experienced similar problems, and the road outside the Oyston family home in Waddington has been subjected to occasional demonstrations (organised by the Tangerine Knights). But these activities have involved only small numbers of Blackpool fans and do not justify a number of Karl's responses (including legal actions).

One of BST's continuing objections to the way the Oystons run the club is their propensity to make loans and payments to their other companies (of which there are many), using income generated by the football club. This practice is legal and Owen Oyston (in a *Blackpool Gazette* article in October 2014) explained that payments have been made to repay existing loans (including those from other Oyston companies to the football club), and to finance ground redevelopment.

Following the rejection of the BST bid, the one remaining hope of a change of ownership lies in the recent announcement by Valeri Belokon, now free of financial problems and with his assets unfrozen, that he is striving to assemble a consortium of local businessmen prepared to make a takeover bid for the club. There is, of course, the problem of the legal action he is currently taking against the Oystons. But if the view of BST (and others) that the club is currently making a loss is correct, and the Belokon bid were (unlike BST) to involve 'real money,' then maybe, just maybe, the Oystons might be tempted. Christine was confident that the Trust could work with Belokon (he has previously been much more supporter-friendly than the Oystons), and would push hard for BST representation on the board, in the event of a successful takeover.

Following the dismissal in October 2014 of Jose Riga, a sizeable proportion of BST members (and indeed non-affiliated supporters) decided to stop using their season tickets in protest. Many fans have chosen to take part in an ethical boycott of club facilities, including purchasing the alternative shirt endorsed by BST rather than the official club shirt, only attending away matches when a pay-on-the-gate facility is available, and not buying food or drink or a match-day programme if they do attend home games. The BST's estimate is that at least half of current season-ticket holders are choosing not to attend home games, which means that you have to subtract up to 2,000 from the published attendances at Bloomfield Road to figure out the real crowd figures (in my visits this season, I'd certainly felt on each occasion that there were significantly fewer people present than were later reported; now I know why!). Attendance at away games is seen as okay because that doesn't result in a source of income to the club.

But for Christine, Phil Hartley, and many other BST members there is a real dilemma here. Is there any enjoyment to be gained from attending games (home or away) if you're not sure you want your team to win? Their concern is that if Blackpool's results on the field start to improve (as they did throughout October) the likely outcome is that fans who are undecided about attending start returning to Bloomfield Road. In turn, if the club's financial position marginally improves, the Oystons claim credit for the upward turn (e.g. 'we knew we would pull through the crisis'), and the possibility of their stepping down recedes. On the other hand, if the November slump in form were to continue and Blackpool fell to the bottom of the table, with relegation looking increasingly probable, then (so the argument goes) the Oystons would be more likely to opt out, or at least feel under increasing pressure to do so.

One of the saddest outcomes of the bitter resentment between the Oystons and a sizeable proportion (probably a majority) of the club's supporters is that Christine and her colleagues are faced with this dilemma. She feels that the long-term future of the club (which she sees as unsustainable under the Oystons) is more important than winning games, and so is almost relieved when the club she has supported for over 40 years experiences defeat rather than victory. But BST members, nor indeed football fans anywhere, should not have to face this awful choice. Football clubs are not like other businesses; they are community assets in which many thousands of local people have invested time and energy, and experienced joy (and suffering) because the clubs symbolise their deep-rooted sense of belonging to a particular place. At the very least, one can make the case that there should be a legal requirement that football clubs are run as discrete entities so that they could not be used to support other business interests of the owner(s), an outcome as desirable for Manchester United as it is for Blackpool.

A couple of weeks later I interviewed William Watt, who has been reporting on Blackpool FC for the *Blackpool Gazette* since 2010, Many of his views about the club's recent history were similar to those of Christine Seddon, but his 'insider' status (until the *Gazette* was ostracised by the club in the summer of 2015) meant that he had a further range of insights to offer.

In his view, the Oystons had never been popular, despite their rescue operation in 1987. The club had underperformed for 20 years under their ownership. In the mid-2000s, there were few expectations of any change amongst the supporters. Then in 2007 Valeri Belokon joined the board, and was seen as a 'breath of fresh air.' He got on really well with Karl, put money into completing the ground improvements, and provided resources to pay for Charlie Adam, Neil Eardley, and others who were crucial in getting the club into the Premiership.

The other key element in Blackpool's promotion was the appointment of Ian Holloway in the summer of 2009. Initially, he was telephoned by Karl Oyston and told he wasn't going to be interviewed (the chairman had an aversion to dealing with agents, including Ian Holloway's). A short time later, Holloway rang back and offered a meeting (saying he'd negotiate without involving his agent), a proposal to which the chairman agreed. At the ensuing meeting (at the Tickled Trout, near Preston), they talked for 3-4 hours not just about what Holloway could offer Blackpool, but also about a wide range of other topics. The two men got on well, and Holloway was duly appointed. Less than 12 months later Blackpool won the Championship play-off final and were in the Premier League for the first time since the late 1970-71 season, an outcome few would have predicted. On the open top bus in the victory parade were both Karl Oyston and Valeri Belokon, waving to the cheering crowds. By this time, any reservations the fans had previously had about the Oystons were (temporarily) forgotten in the euphoria of the occasion.

Most of the players who went on to win promotion had been there when Holloway arrived. His contribution was in motivating them. In this, he was helped by the board's commitment to paying out a £5 million bonus to the players (in proportion to appearances) if promotion was achieved. The players weren't on particularly high salaries and some (e.g. Keith Southern) still had mortgages to pay off, so this was indeed motivational. There was a poster in the dressing room informing the players of the commitment needed, and Holloway regularly reminded them of it.

Then came the one season in the Premiership. At the end of 2010, Blackpool had 29 points and looked well-placed to at least survive. When things began to go off the boil in the New Year, there was a strong case for strengthening the squad; so why didn't this happen? The money was there, as was the financial incentive for the chairman (in terms of the income that would be generated by another season in the Premiership). The main priority was a replacement for the regular keeper (Michael Gilks) who was injured at a crucial time. But no significant new signings were made (although the board did go out of its way to hang on to Charlie Adam when Liverpool and other clubs were pushing hard to sign him), and Blackpool went down, one point behind Wolves, having delighted everyone with the quality of their attacking football throughout the season.

The next season, money was made available to strengthen the squad, with Kevin Phillips and Barry Ferguson proving particularly effective signings. Blackpool nearly made it back to the Premiership, losing narrowly to West Ham in the play-off final. There remained a feeling of Blackpool being amongst the top clubs.

But from then on, it all went wrong. Blackpool started the 2012/13 season well, with Tom Ince proving a star turn (Neil Warnock thought they were the best team in the Championship, at this stage). However, Ian Holloway appeared to have lost heart when Blackpool failed to win promotion the previous season and was disappointed when his wish to re-sign D.J.Campbell (and others) was not supported. He resigned in November and went on to become the Crystal Palace manager. Blackpool appointed Michael Appleton, slid down the table, and then replaced him with Paul Ince, who pulled them back to a mid-table position.

The following 2013/14 season was worse. After a flying start (16 points from 6 games) there was a slump in form which led to Paul

Ince being sacked in January 2014. He was replaced by Barry Ferguson (as 'caretaker' player/manager), who just managed to keep Blackpool up (they finished two points above the relegation zone), with the help of a number of short-term loan signings. This was the season when protests from the fans began to develop momentum. SISA had been formed the previous season, following Holloway's departure, and staged a demonstration at the home game against Burnley (18th April 2014), throwing over 200 tennis balls onto the pitch, whilst the game was in progress. This led to a statement from Karl Oyston to the effect that he would have no dealings with SISA, a position he maintained after SISA became a Trust (BST) later that year.

In the summer of 2014, with the final season of parachute payments ahead, there were two crucial changes of personnel. Following the departure of Barry Ferguson, Jose Riga was appointed as manager (a popular choice among the fans, given his achievements at Charlton the previous season). The problem was that from the start, Riga and Karl Oyston didn't get on. The second key factor was the departure of Matt Williams, the club secretary and Karl Oyston's right-hand man and trouble-shooter. Williams had played a major part in running the club. Karl tended to make the big decisions, but Williams put them into practice. Williams was a tough negotiator and adept at implementing what the chairman wanted. When he left, Karl Oyston lost a key ally and facilitator; roles that Williams' successor proved less effective at filling.

The third critical factor was the fact that that there was a big clear-out of personnel at the end of the 2013-14 season. Many of the Premier League squad were now out of contract, and Ferguson's on-loan or short-term contract acquisitions also departed. Several key players declined the deals which the club offered them, including Gary Taylor-Fletcher. Hence the meagre playing staff of six, four weeks before the new season commenced. Had Karl Oyston and Jose Riga been able to work together, or had Williams still been around, this shortfall could have been dealt with sooner.

As it was, Riga was left to hastily assemble enough new signings (including several on loan) to start the season.

In William Watt's view, the Oyston/Riga partnership never stood a chance. Their personalities and priorities clashed from the start. The chairman used his column in the *Gazette* to criticise Riga who, in turn, made his dissatisfactions clear in his briefings to the press. When he was sacked in November 2014, and Lee Clark was appointed, Karl Oyston made one final attempt to stave off the threat of relegation, sanctioning the signing of a number of high profile players (Eagles, O'Dea, O'Hara, O'Keefe) on short-term contracts, but it didn't work out and Blackpool's fate was sealed well before the end of the season.

William sensed that during this disastrous season, Karl Oyston lost some motivation. His invaluable right-hand man (Matt Williams) had moved elsewhere, the fans were on his back, and on the pitch, the club was in freefall. He felt that Karl was still committed to the club and wanted Blackpool FC to do well, but had become increasingly vulnerable and isolated. In the spring of 2015, the *Gazette* decided to stop publishing Karl's weekly column, in which he was typically outspoken, writing things which really riled the fans. The 'Textgate' incident was the last straw, which precipitated the end of the column. Karl's response was to restrict the *Gazette's* access to normal press facilities (no longer a 'favoured media partner'!), although the 'official' explanation was that this was because the *Gazette* had ceased to buy advertising space at the ground. The new manager, Neil McDonald, was instructed not to speak to them, and William Watt was barred from attending the press conference which announced McDonald's appointment.

Moving to the present date and on the basis of recent performances, William felt that Blackpool would probably avoid relegation. They are certainly not attractive to watch, relying on a strong well-organised defence, but there is a high level of commitment from the players (partly due to the fact that for some of them – Redshaw,

Cullen, Aldred, Potts – the move to Blackpool involved a step up from Division Two, and better money; they want to prove themselves at this level). Neil McDonald has, he thinks, done a reasonably good job, in the (difficult) circumstances. He has managed to assemble a reasonably competent squad in a relatively short space of time in the close-season, whilst having to cope with the fact that Blackpool's reputation now meant that many players did not want to come there. He is not the problem. But is 18th in Division One an acceptable outcome? Possibly it is to McDonald, given last season's debacle, and the parlous state of the club when he was brought in. But for the fans, who remember the promotion to the Premier League, and the glorious failure in the year they were there, 18th in Division One is not acceptable. They have a longer time perspective than McDonald.

In William's view, there was a real missed opportunity at the end of last season. Karl Oyston could have said 'Okay, it's been a disaster, I take responsibility for that, now let's work together to get the club back on its feet again.' In particular, he could have made overtures to BST, inviting them to fill a couple of places on the proposed 'Fans Parliament' so that a regular channel for their views could be established. It was clear in the aftermath of the May demonstration that BST had played no part in the pitch invasion, and had become the responsible arm of the protest movement with by far the highest level of support. But Oyston has a stubborn streak and was not going to retract his earlier statement that he would have nothing to do with them. So the opportunity was missed, and the tension between the Oystons and the majority of the fans was exacerbated by the 'Textgate' incident and the chairman's determination to proceed with legal action against a range of fans and other critics (including Joey Barton!). Recently he has taken action against a fan who was seen on TV holding up a doctored copy of the *Gazette*, in which the headline 'We are not thieves' had the word 'not' erased. In William's view, for any kind of positive change to take place, he has to stop doing this kind of thing.

He doesn't agree with the argument that the Oystons' primary motive has always been to make as much money as possible from the club and that they are not really concerned about success on the field. If this were true, why didn't they try to sell the club during the first 20 years of their ownership, when it certainly wasn't making money? And why would they have invested in major ground improvements well before the revival which occurred in the late 2000s? Even in the recent years of decline, Karl Oyston has stepped in to try to stop the rot (see the examples noted above when Ferguson and Clark were managers). But these arguments have to be set against the issues raised by BST including the large sums paid out of the club, and the lack of investment in players at crucial times in the club's recent history.

Four future scenarios can be identified. First, that a prospective owner comes along who is prepared to do a deal which the Oystons find acceptable. This is probably the most desirable option (discounting a takeover by BST, which has already been rejected, although BST are looking to negotiate with others to make another bid). William thinks that the fans would return in significant numbers if this happened. But it won't be a Belokon-led initiative, at least not whilst the legal action he is taking, which alleges 'unfair prejudice' in the way the club has been run financially (and a claim that he is owed £25 million), is in progress.

The second scenario is that the relationship between the Oystons and the protesting fans (particularly with BST) changes, following a genuine change of heart on the part of the board. However, this outcome doesn't look at all likely at present, given Karl Oyston's stubborn streak, and the potential loss of face if he did change tack (and maybe it's too late anyway; the big opportunity was in the summer).

The third (and most likely) scenario is that Karl Oyston gambles on a turnaround in the club's fortunes on the field; survival this season, a strengthened squad and a push for promotion next season, resulting in a gradual increase in attendances stimulated by the improvement in form (and possibly including at least some BST members, whose principled boycott stance would be under pressure, if Blackpool looked to be on an upward surge). The nightmare scenario is that the upward surge doesn't happen, Blackpool find themselves in the Conference in a couple of seasons, and the Oystons lose interest and sell Bloomfield Road for housing. William regards this outcome as unlikely. The Oystons already own a great deal of land with planning permission for housing, and Bloomfield Road is not the most attractive of locations.

As a postscript, William told me that he has often, over the years, done talks in schools about Blackpool FC. Before Holloway arrived, when he asked the kids how many of them supported Blackpool, only three or four hands went up. Then in the glory years (2009-2012) it would be most of the class. Now it's back to two or three. He finds this very sad: a lost generation of fans!

*

The 2014-15 season had been equally disastrous for Wigan Athletic, although their eventual relegation, unlike Blackpool's was unexpected. The future had looked so promising in August, given how close the Latics had come to regaining their Premier League status just three months previously, under Uwe Rosler. It soon became apparent, to both Jonathan Jackson (the club's chief executive) and Martin Tarbuck (editor of the influential fanzine *Mudhutter*) that several of the players who had played in the Cup-winning side of 2013 were underperforming; they were not happy about playing for a team in the bottom half of the Championship and were beginning to look elsewhere. Results proved disappointing, and Rosler was sacked in November. The *Mudhutter* editorial team, who admired his patient inter-passing style of play, thought he should have been given more time to turn things round. But Dave Whelan had lost patience, and his choice of new manager was Malky Mackay.

The *Mudhutter* team opposed his appointment from the start, on the basis of the discriminatory content of Mackay's text exchanges, which had recently been made public. Many other fans were critical of the appointment, although they might well have become reconciled to it had he managed to reverse the club's downward trend. With the benefit of hindsight, Jonathan Jackson acknowledges that the appointment was a mistake. Results got worse rather than better, his long-ball direct route of football proved unpopular (and was not in the more creative Wigan tradition which had prevailed under Martinez, and which had also been favoured by Rosler). In addition, the club, which was justly proud of its reputation as a family- and fan-friendly outfit, had been unwittingly dragged into media-accentuated controversy once Dave Whelan added fuel to the fire with his public statement of support for his beleaguered manager.

From Christmas 2014 onwards, it began to look increasingly likely that Wigan would be relegated. Unlike Blackpool, the club began to prepare, at this stage in the season, for this eventuality. Jonathan knew that in the event of relegation, the club would have great difficulty meeting the current wage bill, which still covered the salaries of the players inherited from the Premier League days. It was fortunate, given this dilemma, that many of them were only too happy to move to clubs in better positions. McManaman, Maloney, Epinoza and Watson were all allowed to move elsewhere. Had they been reluctant to do so Wigan would have started the following season with a much higher wage bill than it did.

The club also began to plan for the increasing probability of life in Division One by rethinking its recruitment policy. The aim was to change the age profile, by seeking out good, ambitious younger players from outside the top two tiers. The player-recruitment team of five full-time staff, supported by a part-time scouting team of eight, led by Matt Jackson, a former Wigan player, began to identify targets such as 22-year-old Max Power, then with Tranmere Rovers, and 24-year-old Will Grigg (a prolific goal-scorer with MK Dons). This level of foresight would pay dividends in the close season.

Then came David Whelan's resignation as chairman during his period of suspension. Taking his place was his 23-year-old grandson David Sharpe. At the same time, the board was reconstituted, with three directors who were former business associates of Whelan's voluntarily stepping down (although they still attend home games). The new slim-line board comprises the new chairman, his brother Matt (who plays a less active role than David), and Jonathan Jackson. A board of this size is well-placed to make speedy decisions, one of the first of which was to dispense with the services of Malky Mackay.

In looking for a new manager, there was a feeling that it would be advantageous to appoint someone who was familiar with the club and its ethos. A range of football criteria was identified (identity, philosophy, work ethic, style, and continuity) and after various options had been considered, former club captain Gary Caldwell (who was still registered as a player) was appointed ('he ticked all the boxes'). He was seen by some as a high-risk appointment due to his lack of any previous managerial experience, but the Board, recognising that by then relegation was almost inevitable, felt that the choice signalled the direction they wanted to go in.

The club was well-positioned to recruit the players it had identified as having the potential to take the club back to the Championship, now enhanced with new ideas from Caldwell. The recruitment budget benefitted significantly from Wigan's third tranche of parachute payments (£10 million). The newcomers comprised a blend of youth (Jacobs, Grigg, James, Daniels, and Power) and experience (Morgan, Perkins, and (later) Jaaskelainen), with an emphasis on the former. Understandably, Caldwell had a preference to build a team around new signings rather than former team-mates where there could have been difficulties on both sides in adjusting to the new relationship. There was a residue of players from previous campaigns (including McCann, Pearce, Barnett and

Cowie). At the end of the season, however, other established players on high salaries such as Scott Carson, Emmerson Boyce, James McClean and James Perch were not re-engaged.

Much time and effort then went into seeking to blend the new squad of players into a cohesive unit, both socially (shared dormitories were the order of the day on the pre-season tour) and on the pitch, where the new manager's approach was much more in line with that of Martinez and Rosler than that of Mackay. So far, the new direction in which the club embarked early in 2015 appears to be paying off. Wigan are currently in fifth place, on a ten-match unbeaten run in the league. But this success has not happened by chance. It has resulted from a readiness to admit mistakes and to take determined and strategic action to deal with the problems which ensued. What a contrast with the situation at Blackpool, where little appears to have been learned from last season's fiasco, and any kind of long-term vision for the club is conspicuous by its absence.

CHAPTER 8
DECEMBER: DOWNPOURS AND LOCAL DERBIES

The first Saturday of the month was FA Cup second round day. Neither Blackpool nor Wigan had survived the first round, so both would have had a rare Saturday off, were it not for the fact that Wigan had brought forward their Johnstone's Paint Trophy Northern Section semi-final tie against Barnsley, due to be played the following Tuesday. Probably a wise move in terms of attracting a larger crowd. There would be a sizeable contingent from Barnsley, and the fact that all adult tickets were priced at a fiver would also help.

Was I intending to go? I was not. My views about this competition have already been made clear. And if I had begun to waver, the fact that on the Saturday, Kendal and the rest of Cumbria were hit by a storm of biblical proportions would have dissuaded me from venturing out. By late afternoon, the River Kent had burst its banks and large tracts of the town were underwater. If I'd travelled to Wigan by train, I wouldn't have got back until Monday!

Sometime after five o'clock, Wigan's dream of Wembley glory was over for another year. In what the *Wigan Observer* described as "a lacklustre performance," the Latics twice went behind to the visitors (who were currently propping up the Division One table) and twice equalised, each time through Will Grigg. A 2-2 scoreline meant that the tie had to be decided on penalties. Craig Davies and David Perkins both contrived to miss theirs (against one of their former clubs), as a result of which Barnsley won the shoot-out 4-2. A Northern Section final against either Fleetwood or Morecambe awaited them (it turned out to be Fleetwood). Gary Caldwell had claimed to be taking the game extremely seriously, fielding his "strongest side so far in this competition," but it was still a long way short of his strongest side per se. No McCann, Morgan, Daniels or Wildschut in the starting line-up, which included two relative unknowns in Andy Kellett and Jack Hendry. So no crocodile tears please, Gary!

*

The following Saturday, Wigan were at home to Blackpool. This was a big test of where my sympathies really lay! Did I want Blackpool, who sorely needed the points to win? But then so did Wigan, if they were to remain in a playoff position, after gaining a mere point from their two previous league games. I vacillated in the hours before kick-off. Maybe a draw? But that felt like a cop-out.

A few days earlier, Wigan had won a Football Supporters Federation award for the 'Best Away Day' in the Football League (including the Premier League). The shortlist for the award was drawn up on the basis of an 'away fans survey' (covering the second half of last season and the first half of this), which canvassed views on such things as access, view, safety and security, pricing, and catering facilities, on all of which Wigan scored consistently highly. So that's at least one trophy for the display cupboard this season.

I'm not in a position to judge whether Wigan really is better in this respect than other contenders such as Rotherham, Brighton, or Derby, but I can see why it's on a shortlist. Plenty of room for everybody in the away end (which must have a capacity of close to 5,000), no inflated admission prices for visitors and ample food and drink facilities. Also, there are the more subjective qualities that the DW Stadium (and indeed Wigan itself) possess: a friendly, unthreatening, family-oriented ambience (in contrast to Boundary Park and Bloomfield Road, to name but two).

It was another very wet day as I caught the train for Wigan at Oxenholme (Lake District) station. The game had not (as yet) been postponed, but the way the rain was sheeting down suggested that a mid-game abandonment was by no means unlikely. I'd arranged to meet Martin Tarbuck for a 'how do you think the season's gone so far?' discussion, at a hostelry in Springfield, near the site of Wigan's former ground. The Bird I'th Hand (known locally as the Henhole) is a friendly traditional pub in the middle of an unspoilt area of terraced housing, which reminded me of Edgeley in Stockport. It was full of Wigan fans, eagerly anticipating a win against a side with only one away victory to its credit so far.

Martin told me that he would have been prepared to settle for a mid-table position at this stage in the season, after the traumas of 2014-15, so a playoff position was a bonus. He was supportive of the way that Wigan had ditched the long-ball tactics which had operated during Malky Mackay's time as manager and had re-introduced the more patient inter-passing style of play favoured by Martinez and Rosler. But we agreed that this approach had on occasions become sterile and boring, with sequences of passes too often going sideways and backwards, rather than forward. The 5-0 win against Colchester had shown it at its best; the most recent home game against Burton had shown it at its least effective, with Burton's hustling and harrying tactics preventing it from developing any kind of momentum.

Although Martin thought Gary Caldwell had done well as manager, given his lack of previous experience, he was critical of the way he had chopped and changed the team around in recent weeks (some, but by no means all, of these changes had been necessitated by injuries). The rhythm that had been established during the unbeaten run of 11 league games had gone (hopefully temporarily). The last four games of 2015 would be crucial in establishing which direction Wigan were going in.

We agreed that David Perkins had proved an inspired signing; Mr Perpetual Motion in midfield, where he rarely misplaces a pass. Yanic Wildschut, on loan from Middlesbrough, had made a big difference, opening up attacking options on the left which had previously been less apparent, apart from the occasional upfield surge from the capable Reece James. Michael Jacobs had impressed both as goal-scorer and goal-provider, although Martin had noticed that he had become more subdued since a clattering tackle from a Shrewsbury defender had resulted in him limping off the pitch three weeks previously. Craig Morgan and Donervon Daniels had proved solid at the back (with occasional lapses) and in Daniels' case, a real threat going forward (and indeed as a marksman). Others had proved more inconsistent. Will Grigg had not lived up to the reputation as a prolific goal-scorer with which he arrived from MK Dons, and had been in and out of the team. And the jury was still out on Max Power, Alex Revell, Tim Chow, and Craig Davies.

We discussed the way in which Wigan were still perceived as a 'big club' whose rightful place was (at the very least) in the Championship. That's the way many supporters still see things. And managers of this season's opponents have typically (particularly after a defeat) drawn attention to the disparity in the resources available to their own clubs and Wigan. Rochdale's manager Keith Hill recently commented, "Financially, Wigan are the Manchester United of League One. The resources they've got, the players they can afford – we cannot contend with that." (I think he meant to say 'compete'.) The *Football League Paper* referred to Wigan as being "still fat on parachute money."

Martin challenged this perception. He felt that Wigan were only a 'big club' by virtue of their recent history. With parachute payments finishing next season, David Sharpe is unlikely to be in a position to bankroll the club the way his granddad did, and with attendances having settled down at around 8,000, the reality is that they may have found their appropriate level, with the eight years in the Premiership a wonderful but unsustainable episode in the club's history. Even if they did get back into the Championship, their circumstances would be similar to those of Rotherham or Huddersfield, rather than Derby or Nottingham Forest. He, for one, is quite relaxed about this, but doubts whether the majority of the fan base are.

We made our way through the rain to the DW Stadium, to discover that the game was still on. As I took my seat in the East Stand, I was surprised to see how few away fans there were in the North Stand. There were 400 at most, less than the number who had travelled from Shrewsbury on an equally wet Saturday in November. Strange, because Fleetwood apart, Wigan was the nearest Division One location to Blackpool. There had been well over 1,000 of their fans at Bury, a month or so ago, so why had so few travelled today? Okay, it was two weeks before Christmas, but for what was, in effect, a local derby you'd have expected a more substantial turn-out, wouldn't you?

Blackpool have happy memories of their match at Wigan in their one Premier League season. On its opening day, they travelled there and thrashed the hosts 4-0. And today, five years later, the visitors were more than a match for the home side in the early exchanges. Although Wigan had more of the possession, it was one of those days when they didn't seem to know what to do with it. Blackpool looked more dangerous in their counter-attacks and came close on a couple of occasions. The pitch was sodden but perfectly playable; it wasn't one of those farcical situations where the ball regularly stuttered to a halt in a puddle.

Ten minutes before half-time, I felt the need for a warming cup of Bovril. Neither side at the time looked like scoring, so I left my seat and made my way to the refreshment bar. As I was being served, there was a burst of noise which I guessed reflected a near miss from the home side. As I returned, however, I noticed the TV screen near the bar indicating a score-line of Wigan 0 Blackpool 1. What? The first person I saw on re-entering the stadium confirmed that this was indeed the case.

I was distraught! The first goal scored by a Blackpool player since the game at Bury six weeks ago and I'd missed it! It turned out that defender Tom Aldred was the scorer – a rare goal for him – with a decisive near-post header from a Ferguson corner. The video recording which I watched the next day indicated that the goal bore all the hallmarks of a carefully-rehearsed training ground move. Blackpool continued to look the more enterprising side. At half-time, the match statistics on the TV screen revealed that they'd managed three shots (all on target) to Wigan's one.

From this point onwards, I was clear what outcome I wanted: a rare Blackpool away win. Their lead was thoroughly deserved. The home supporters had become increasingly restive, and there had been some sporadic booing as the players left the field at half-time. But could the visitors hold out? On the evidence of recent performances where they'd taken a first-half lead, one would expect a 'backs-to-the-wall' rear-guard action for the remaining 45 minutes. And that is precisely what transpired. Neil McDonald has managed to weld Blackpool's defence into a well-organised unit, which had little trouble dealing with Wigan's waves of attack. There were missed opportunities; Daniels with a free header and Power with the kind of chance he had buried at Oldham. Lyness was again impressive in the Blackpool goal, handling the ball cleanly and making a couple of crucial saves. For all their possession, the home side lacked penetration. Few of their many shots were on target.

Wildschut was having a particularly frustrating afternoon; the wet conditions didn't suit his familiar surging runs, which today invariably led down cul-de-sacs. Neither Davies nor Grigg were finding space when it mattered. The crowd's frustrations increased. The Blackpool fans alternated between chants of "We want Oyston out" and "Up the league we go". As the game neared its end, Blackpool introduced Emmanuel Boyce, formerly with Wigan, as a substitute. He received a heart-warming reception from the home supporters, who clearly remembered him with great affection.

At the final whistle, the joy on the part of the Blackpool players was again transparent. The six defenders on the pitch, close to where I was sitting, converged in a mutual celebratory embrace. Whatever the problems off the pitch, you can't fault the commitment of the players. The squad is thin on creative talent, but in all the games I've seen recently have pushed themselves to the limits to protect one-goal leads, or, at Bury, to fight back from a seemingly hopeless position (4-1 down after half an hour). They and the manager deserve a better climate in which to operate than the bitter divisions between the boardroom and the fans that sadly prevail at the club.

Wigan, for the moment, seem to have lost the plot. After a run of eleven games undefeated in the league, they have managed one point from the last three games, scoring no goals in the process. Given the characterization of Wigan as a 'big club' and the (possibly unrealistic) expectations that they will at least make the playoffs, Gary Caldwell must be feeling a little uneasy at present. There has been a high casualty rate amongst Division One managers this season. If Wigan's barren run continues into the New Year, he may well be amongst them.

On the Wigan North Western station platform, there were three middle-aged ladies wearing tangerine scarves and looking understandably delighted (they were heavily outnumbered by the police contingent, obviously expecting trouble, but not finding any). I congratulated them on their team's gritty performance and asked why they thought there were so few Blackpool fans present. "It's Christmas isn't it," said one. "And there were no coaches running," added another. I was not wholly convinced. For a local derby, involving a 40-minute car or train journey, you'd surely have expected more than three or four hundred, whatever the time of year, state of the weather, or availability of coaches!

*

Blackpool's last fixture before Christmas was a home game against Peterborough United, the in-form team of Division One. Under Graham Westley, who was appointed in October when the team was struggling in the lower-middle reaches of the league, Peterborough have soared up the table, scoring freely. They came to Blackpool on the back of a seven-match unbeaten run, which would have been seven straight wins if Shrewsbury had not scraped a draw at London Road the previous Saturday. This was a real test for the Seasiders. If Peterborough could be defeated, Blackpool really would be back in business. And it would be the first time since September 2013 that they had managed three league wins in a row.

Once again, the weather was appalling. Torrential rain had been falling all day, and, as at Wigan the previous Saturday, I wondered whether the game would be called off, or, if started, not completed. The train I caught at Preston, bound for Blackpool South, didn't get any further than Kirkham and Wesham, in central Fylde. The previous train on its way back from Blackpool South was running so late (and it was a single track line) that it was deemed a waste of time to continue. The disembarking passengers had the option of joining a Blackpool North-bound train 20 minutes later, which most of us did. I just made it to Bloomfield Road in time for the kick-off.

The familiar pre-match anti-Oyston demonstration was more sparsely attended than previously, but then it was very wet, and Christmas was a mere six days away. Inside the ground, about 300 Peterborough fans had braved the elements (and undergone a journey of over 200 miles) to cheer their team on. On days (and at times of the year) like this, the commitment of such fans is remarkable (remarkably impressive to me; remarkably stupid to Karen!). Half a minute into the game, they must have wondered why they had bothered. A Blackpool attack saw Mark Cullen head a clearance into the path of recent loan signing Elliot Lee, who with a clear sight of goal was blatantly impeded by a Peterborough defender. A clear penalty in my view (and more importantly the referee's). However, Ben Alnwick, the visitors' keeper strongly disagreed and spent a lot of time making his views clear. He then went through a series of goal-line antics designed to disconcert the penalty-taker, Mark Cullen. It looked like he'd succeeded when Cullen's kick hit the angle of post and bar and was clawed out by the keeper. But justice was done when the ball fell kindly for Cullen, and he poked the ball home from a couple of yards out. Another typically messy Blackpool goal. But 1-0 it was, with two minutes on the clock.

On the evidence of previous games when Blackpool had taken a first half lead (Swindon, Fleetwood, Wigan), I feared that this would be the signal for a rearguard action, with the team defending in depth for the remainder of the game. Hopefully not; there were another 88 minutes to go, for heaven's sake! Peterborough then began to dominate play, spraying the ball around (literally so, given the state of the weather and the pitch) with a fluency that the home side couldn't match. But for all their dominance, the visitors were creating very few clear-cut chances, and when they did, Dean Lyness dealt with them confidently.

Blackpool's long-ball approach looked more appropriate to the worsening conditions than Peterborough's pretty football, and after half-an-hour, the home side scored again. After Mark Cullen had caused confusion in the Peterborough defence, the ball found its way to Brad Potts on the right, and he scored confidently from a narrow-angle. A few minutes later it could have been three when Cullen had only the keeper to beat, but shot straight at him. Still, the Blackpool fans, who had been untypically vocally supportive, were happy to settle for an unexpected (but deserved) two-nil interval lead.

The second half progressed in a predictable fashion. Peterborough dominated possession, persisting with their intricate passing game, frequently involving sideways or backwards movement. Blackpool sat back and let them do so, breaking the monotony with the occasional breakaway. As the half progressed, I became aware of the significance of the term 'shape,' which is used by many managers (including Neil McDonald); 'we kept our shape well today' or 'unfortunately we lost our shape.' Watching the sequence of abortive Peterborough attacks, it became apparent that

Blackpool's 'shape' was indeed proving an effective barrier to progress. The visitors just couldn't find a way through, and most of their goal-scoring opportunities were restricted to long-range efforts which went high or wide (or both).

The two Blackpool strikers Cullen and Lee, having run themselves into the ground, were replaced on the hour by Martin Paterson and Andy Little. Lee is an on-loan signing (one of many this season) from West Ham United, and for all his hard work today has so far failed to impress. He lacks the spark of creativity – the ability to do something unexpected that can unsettle a defence – which Blackpool sorely need up front. Only Jack Redshaw, absent (injured?) today and Brad Potts have (sporadically) shown this capacity.

Towards the end, Blackpool managed a flurry of unproductive corners, whilst at the other end Lyness, who is proving a most worthwhile temporary acquisition, made a couple of important saves. Peterborough persevered with their patient build-up right to the final whistle, but it was still getting them nowhere, and this was the first time they had failed to score since mid-October. Blackpool came off to a standing ovation from the regulars in the Stanley Mathews stand. Tom Aldred won the man-of-the-match award, but in all honesty, it could have been any of the back four, all of whom had again performed heroically.

I arrived soaking wet at Blackpool South station in time to meet a disconsolate group of people coming away from it. The 5.20 to Preston had been cancelled, and the 6.20 was doubtful. Where was Chris, the smiling station manager when we needed him? A frantic dash, by bus and foot to Blackpool North enabled me to catch an alternative train and escape from this waterlogged resort.

*

Meanwhile, at Barnsley, Wigan's slump in form was reversed with a 2-0 win against their struggling opponents. Andy Kellett, making his first league start for the Latics, justified his manager's confidence in him by curling the ball neatly past the Barnsley keeper after 18 minutes, having been put clear by a shrewd pass from Michael Jacobs. Wigan were then content to sit back and soak up pressure for a long period before Yanic Wildschut, who had only just come on as a substitute, made the points safe shortly before the end, taking advantage of a mix-up in the home defence to tap the ball into an unguarded net.

It sounds like a routine win against mediocre opposition. Barnsley, for all their second half territorial dominance, didn't manage a single shot on target. They remain in deep trouble. *The Football League Paper* was singularly unimpressed, giving the game a single star rating (the only Division One game of the day to achieve this accolade). But Gary Caldwell was happy enough ("I think you could see that the players were hungry,") and will no doubt sleep a little easier, at least until the next game.

The post-match reaction of Lee Johnson, the Barnsley manager certainly captured one's attention. Having told us that "players have got to be strong not to let their mindsets drop," (now there's an interesting concept – a dropped mindset), he went on to add, "I just want to see people being bold and brave, and if you're going to fail, fail being bold, because football-wise you're going to have more longevity if you're consistent." Perhaps you could you run that past us again Lee? It brings back memories of the obtuse utterances of Colin Murphy, the one-time Lincoln City and Stockport County manager. Programmes which contain them are now collectors' items.

*

Both Blackpool and Wigan's Boxing Day fixtures (at home to Oldham Athletic and Sheffield United respectively) were called off, on another Saturday of torrential downpours, which resulted in widespread flooding in the Ribble Valley and West Yorkshire. A pity, particularly for Blackpool, who would have had a good chance of making it four wins in a row, against fellow strugglers

Oldham. Earlier in the week, Neil McDonald had suggested that a play-off place was not out of the question for the Tangerines, in the light of the recent run of form. A tad over-optimistic, I felt.

*

Two days later, Wigan were at Fleetwood and Blackpool at Barnsley. Wigan achieved a thoroughly deserved win at the Highbury Stadium, although they left it late. Midway through the first half, Andy Kellett cut in from the right, and his long-range (though relatively tame) shot squirmed through the grasp of the home keeper. That's two goals in consecutive games for the youngster. Early in the second half, both Craig Morgan and Max Power saw shots come back off the woodwork. In a rare attack, Fleetwood's David Ball was fouled in the area by Craig Morgan, and Antoni Sarcevic dispatched the penalty decisively. But Wigan took this reversal in their stride, and went ahead in the 83rd minute, when substitute Jordy Hiwula scored from close range after Fleetwood defenders had failed to clear a shot from Will Grigg. In injury time, Michael Jacobs wrapped up the three points, when put clear by Donervon Daniels, neatly slipping the ball past the out-rushing keeper. So Wigan finished 2015 in fifth place, with 40 points from 23 games, having overcome their late November/early December wobble.

Blackpool's run of wins came to an untimely end at Barnsley. The writing was on the wall when the home side's Sam Winnall scored with a close-range header in the third minute. When Blackpool's opponents have scored first this season, they have almost always gone on to win (only Millwall failing to do so, at Bloomfield Road in October). Although Mark Cullen equalised with a superb strike from the edge of the area (possibly the best goal Blackpool have scored all season), Barnsley regained the lead a couple of minutes later (Winnall again) and added a third shortly afterwards. Bright Osayi-Samuel then contrived to head over the bar from two yards out (scoring goals is clearly not this otherwise talented young man's forte), before Andy Little found himself in space in front of goal in the 90th minute to make it three-two.

Any chance of an undeserved draw in injury time soon disappeared when Templeman immediately restored Barnsley's two-goal advantage. Despite the rare feat of scoring two goals away from home, it had been a disappointing performance from Blackpool. The defence, which had been so resolute in the previous three games, looked vulnerable throughout. So Blackpool finished 2015 in 18th place, with 25 points from 23 games, and with a lot of work still to do. I think we can forget the playoffs, Neil.

CHAPTER 9

JANUARY: HALF THE SEASON REMAINS - EVERYTHING TO PLAY FOR

The New Year. Half the league fixtures completed; half to go. Time for a new start. Forget what's happened so far, a team can transform themselves in the months of the season that remain.

Such transformations can happen. On Boxing Day 2012, Mansfield Town lost 2-1 at home to little Alfreton Town in the Conference, and finished the year in twelfth place. Of their remaining twenty-five games, Mansfield won 21, lost 4, and ended up champions. Closer to home, Blackpool were comfortably placed in the middle reaches of the Premier League at the start of 2012. Five months later they were relegated.

Hence, the first fixtures of 2016 had a symbolic significance for both Blackpool and Wigan: an early indication of an upward trajectory or a downward spiral. Blackpool had a tough task away to Burton Albion, second in the table, with only one home defeat so far. Wigan were at mid-table Scunthorpe, whose form throughout the season had been consistently inconsistent.

Wigan emerged with a creditable one-all draw, which extended their unbeaten away sequence in the league to nine. Scunthorpe had taken the lead in the 20th minute, when a low cross from Scott Laird was volleyed into the net by Luke Williams, with the Wigan defence in disarray. But 15 minutes later, Michael Jacobs neatly controlled a long pass from midfield and beat the Scunthorpe keeper with a low shot into the far corner; an impressive strike which elicited a eulogistic post-match response from his manager. Jacobs has developed an impressive habit of scoring good goals at crucial times in away matches (Bradford, Rochdale, Fleetwood). He has become Wigan's most prolific striker. In an evenly-contested game, either side could have won it, with Wigan having the better chances. Yanic Wildschut, in his last game before returning to

Middlesbrough, gave another impressive display; he will be sorely missed. Both managers agreed a draw was a fair result. As a result, Wigan remain in fifth place, nine points adrift of an automatic promotion place.

Towards the end of a first half in which Blackpool effectively contained high-flying Burton, they must have felt they had a real chance of victory when Burton's Robbie Weir was sent off after a second yellow-card offence. But the home side continued to dominate the game, raining shot after shot (26 in total) on the Blackpool goal. When Mark Duffy (ex-Morecambe) scored with an impressive individual effort, it was no more than they deserved. It was only in the last 15 minutes that Blackpool began to create chances, but with no success. The contingent of travelling fans voiced their displeasure, and manager Neil McDonald could (for once) find little in the way of positive features to take away ("In the second half we never got going, and we didn't stop them from playing."). Blackpool ended the day back in the relegation zone. The illusory security of a lower-middle position in the table had proved short-lived. The reality is (and probably always has been) that Blackpool's challenge is to avoid relegation. The next few weeks will be crucial.

*

Wigan's next fixture was at home to Gillingham, on the following Thursday, brought forward from Saturday to fill a slot in the Sky Sports programme of live matches. Ticket prices had been reduced, presumably to tempt more folk out of the comfort of armchairs or pubs into the chilly DW Stadium. My senior citizen ticket cost a mere tenner; exceptionally good value I thought (depending on the quality of the game, of course). It was a crucial game for Wigan, a big test against a side second in the table, who had beaten Wigan convincingly at home in August. Wigan had not yet recorded a victory against any of the four front-runners (Burton, Walsall, Gillingham, and Coventry). A victory tonight would add credibility to their prospects of promotion.

Before the game, there was a minute of applause to pay respects to a former Wigan player, Steve Gohouri, an Ivory Coast international whose body had recently been found in Germany, a week after having been reported missing by his family. Gohouri had been in the Wigan Premiership squad in the 2010-12 period and was clearly remembered with affection by those around me in the West Stand. His death was a poignant reminder of the stresses, as well as the glory of top-class professional football (he was still registered with TSV Steinbach when his untimely death occurred).

Both sides strung some good moves together in the early stages. Gillingham's Bradley Dack looked dangerous every time he had the ball, not least when his brilliant long-range free-kick came back off the post, fortunately for Wigan at too great a height for Rory Donnelly to net the rebound. Soon afterwards, the visitors did take the lead, when Bradley Dack (yes, him again) sent a perfectly-weighted through pass out to Dominic Samuel on the right, who cut in unopposed to beat Jaaskelainen at the near post, eliciting a burst of cheering from the sparse contingent of Gillingham fans at the other end (well it was a Thursday night, and Gillingham is over 200 miles away).

Wigan came back strongly and should have equalised when first Jason Pearce missed a good headed opportunity, and then Andy Kellett, who had looked lively on the right, somehow managed to head over the bar, from two yards out, with no-one near him ("It takes a rare talent to miss a chance like that," muttered the bloke next to me). Chances were being created at both ends, and Wigan were unlucky to be one down on the balance of play. But I had the misfortune to be surrounded by a right bunch of moaners, who complained at every misplaced Wigan pass (well you're always going to get some at this level) and at every ball played back from a midfielder to a defender, which seems to me to be usually a better option than an optimistic punt upfield to a marked striker.

Wigan came out strongly in the second half, but it was not long before they went further behind. A high floated cross from the right found Rory Donnelly in space (Donervon Daniels, who was supposed to marking him, hadn't seen him bearing in from the left) and his powerful header evaded Jaaskelainen. The moaning around me increased in intensity. Wigan looked dead and buried. Gary Caldwell understandably decided that changes were needed. Off came Reece James (who had had a good game) and Andy Kellett (who'd had his moments) to be replaced by Chris McCann and Jordy Hiwula.

What followed was 35 minutes which made you realise why you come out on cold winter nights to a windswept stadium, in the hope of seeing something special. What transpired was indeed memorable. A new urgency began to permeate Wigan's play. Chris McCann made surging runs down the left. Jordy Hiwula, playing deeper than usual, found more space than he normally does and passed the ball around well. With 25 minutes of normal time remaining, a high cross from the left from Hiwula was met by Michael Jacobs, leaping higher above his marker than you would expect from someone of his (average) height. He headed the ball into the path of Will Grigg, who couldn't miss.

Three minutes later, a pass from the left found Max Power with space to try a long-range shot. It wasn't one of his best, but it squirmed through the grasp of Gillingham's previously impressive Stuart Nelson into the net. Two-all. But the visitors weren't giving up on the chance of what had seemed until then a routine away victory, and when Bradley Dack was put clean through, it looked inevitable that they'd retake the lead. Uncharacteristically, he over-ran the ball, and the chance was gone. Back came Wigan. Daniels went close. Craig Davies was brought on for Jacobs as added time (six minutes of it) got under way.

The home side forced a succession of corners. Then in the last minute of added time, Max Power swung over a final corner from the right, and there was Craig Morgan in space to score with an emphatic header. The comeback was complete. Delirium ensued in the West Stand (including the erstwhile moaners), and indeed throughout the entire stadium, with the exception of the North Stand, from which the disconsolate Gillingham fans were quietly departing.

I'd never seen Gary Caldwell so animated. Normally he just stands there passively, making the occasional incomprehensible hand gesture. Indeed, he and his counterpart Justin Edinburgh had been like a pair of statues all evening. At the final whistle, he was leaping around like a lottery winner, in utterly spontaneous mode (who needs silly dances at times like these!).

This is what the game (at its best) is all about, Brian. Football as drama. Football as a play with a totally unexpected twist at the end. Football full of heroes who never give up and can (sometimes) transform defeat into victory in the space of 30 minutes. Football as a spectacle which sends thousands of local residents on their way home with smiles on their faces and memories to share with their mothers, fathers, children, and grandchildren. Football as an outburst of collective euphoria, equalled only (in my experience) by rock concerts by the likes of Neil Young or Bob Dylan. Football as a phenomenon which expresses and strengthens a sense of community identity, epitomising Wigan people's pride in their town.

And that wasn't the end of the good news. The very next day it was announced that Yanic Wildschut, who had earlier in the week returned to Middlesbrough, after a hugely impressive loan spell with the Latics, would be back at Wigan shortly, the clubs having agreed a £1 million fee.

*

After the exhilaration of the Wigan Gillingham epic, it was difficult to get too excited about Blackpool's home fixture against Port Vale two days later. But it was an important game for the Tangerines (aren't they all!). After their run of three successive victories in

December, they could ill afford another losing streak. A win, however, would take them clear of the relegation places (it was FA Cup third round day, and there were only four Division One fixtures). The auguries were not promising. Craig Robertson was out injured, as was leading scorer Mark Cullen. His fellow striker of recent weeks Elliot Lee had returned to West Ham (who had been prepared to extend his loan spell) because he was missing his mum and dad, a justification which understandably caused a degree of disbelief and derision amongst the Blackpool management team. Dean Lyness had returned to Burton, after a short period on loan in which his prowess had contributed significantly to the run of wins. Fortunately, Colin Doyle was fit again to take over in goal.

Two new signings had been secured earlier in the week, both from fellow strugglers Oldham Athletic; Danny Philliskirk, a striker with a reasonable strike record over the previous few seasons, and Mark Yeates, a left-sided midfielder. Both were in the starting line-up, but after a single training session with their new team-mates, it was unreasonable to expect too much of them. Andy Little, whose loan from Preston had been extended until the end of January, was Philliskirk's strike partner. There is a real problem for clubs like Blackpool, who rely heavily on loan signings, when the loanees depart; it undermines continuity and disrupts a (temporarily) settled line-up.

Port Vale were comfortably ensconced in mid-table, unlikely to make the playoffs, but well clear of the relegation places. Their away record was as unimpressive as Blackpool's (eight points from 12 games) but at home they had suffered only a single defeat. On the face of it, they had little to play for, but with a sizeable following in the away fans section (at least 800 and in good voice) they would, no doubt, want to make their journey worthwhile.

The outcome of the game was decided, as is so often the case, by two key moments. In the fifth minute, Andy Little found himself clear, rounded the keeper, and then contrived to shoot wide from six yards, when everyone's proverbial granny would have scored. The remainder of the first half was relatively even, albeit uninspiring. There were alternating spells of pressure from first Port Vale and then Blackpool, but few clear-cut chances. There was a good deal of space in midfield, of which both sides took advantage, but little inspiration up front to capitalise on it. Andy Little limped off after half an hour, to be replaced by Jack Redshaw (good to see him back), so at least there was now a Blackpool striker on the field who had scored a few goals.

The second crucial moment came four minutes into the second half. Blackpool had a convincing penalty claim for a handball turned down (the video evidence indicated that it was indeed justified). Their players were understandably aggrieved but made the costly mistake of allowing their anger to affect their concentration. Port Vale immediately counter-attacked, Byron Moore's cross found Ajay Leitch-Smith, whose header was brilliantly saved by Colin Doyle, but the ball came out to the striker, now in a prone position, and rebounded off him into the net. Another messy goal to add to all those previously seen at Bloomfield Road this season.

Blackpool struggled to create chances until the final ten minutes when they bombarded the Port Vale goal. Bright Osayi-Samuel, who had been brought on as a substitute early in the second half, went close on a couple of occasions and was a potent attacking threat (maybe he should be in the starting line-up more often). Philliskirk had a close-range effort saved in the final minute of added time. But Port Vale held out, and Blackpool's run of defeats increased to three.

The mood around me in the main stand was one of resignation. There was a widespread expectation that Blackpool would be relegated, although their present position (25 points from 25 games) provides ample opportunity for escaping this outcome. The average age of the supporters surrounding me was much higher than those at Wigan. I sensed that these were fans who had supported their team for the past 30 to 50 years, and weren't going to stop now, whatever doubts they might have about the Oystons. The members of the Supporters Trust (and the other protest groups) had a younger age profile, judging from the turnout in the pre-match protests, and clearly felt more inclined to take radical action to (in their terms) 'save the club.'

The downbeat atmosphere at Bloomfield Road was in marked contrast to that at the DW Stadium two days before. But how could it be otherwise, given the continuing behind-the-scenes tensions between the Oystons and a large section of the fanbase? The previous week had seen two Blackpool supporters found guilty of public order offences, which had occurred when they tried to storm the directors' box during the protest which halted the game against Huddersfield Town the previous May. But during the trial, a police officer who had been present on the scene gave evidence that Karl Oyston had "beckoned and enticed" those charged. The Football Association has been made aware of the chairman's behaviour, and may (but probably won't) take further action.

Even the good news that Tom Aldred, the Blackpool defender, had been awarded the PFA Fans Division One 'Player of the Month' for December was soured by accounts of an incident at the end of the previous week's game at Burton Albion, when one of the many disgruntled visiting fans shouted at the team "You're not fit to wear the shirt." Aldred understandably (but unwisely) confronted the fan in question and had to be dragged away by his team-mates. Another unsavoury episode in a season sadly full of them.

The comments on the web following Blackpool's latest defeat echoed the gloom that surrounded me in the stands. That neither the team nor the manager were good enough to ensure survival was the dominant view. Nightmare scenarios were sketched out, whereby Blackpool drop to Division Two, and then into the Conference, at which stage the Oystons wind up the club, and sell Bloomfield Road for housing. "And there's nothing we could do to stop them," was the writer's conclusion.

*

Three days later, I was back at Wigan for another evening game, this time against Sheffield United, probably the 'biggest club' currently in Division One, if you consider their historical profile and current level of support (average home attendance is over 20,000 and only Bradford City comes anywhere near that figure). Blackpool would match them on the first criteria, but definitely not the second.

Because I was due to travel on to Birmingham the next morning, I'd booked myself into an establishment called 'The Coaching Inn' in Ince-in-Makerfield, a mile or so south of Wigan town centre. I'd intended to do a detour to explore Scholes, which is the area where George Orwell stayed, in the notorious lodging house/tripe shop when he was doing research for *The Road to Wigan Pier*. But there was a perishing cold wind, so I decided to postpone that treat until spring. There was a distinct Manchester United flavour about the place names around here: Scholes, Ince… and Gowling (which on a second perusal of the map turned out to be Cowling).

The Coaching Inn turned out to be a nineteenth-century building of rather forbidding appearance, which clearly had once served as a coaching stop, in the times when coaches were the dominant mode of travel. It was close to Wigan cemetery, in a distinctly mundane part of (Lower) Ince. I walked back towards Wigan along the main road, passing over yet another Wigan canal (the town is riddled with them; Wigan – Venice of the North?). Back in the town centre, I passed Galloways, one of the town's many pie outlets where I noted with some incredulity a poster in the window which read "Why not put your favourite pie on a barm?" I would have thought a more relevant question was why on earth would anyone want to, particularly given the excellent quality of their pies!

Further along the High Street was a pub called the Boulevard, announcing itself as featuring "real ale, real music and real people." So where do the unreal people go? I then passed another hostelry, advertising a "ukulele and banjolele night every Thursday." On this evidence, Wigan's cultural life has a distinctly idiosyncratic flavour to it.

Sheffield United, as befitted the town's size and the club's status, were accompanied by a large tranche of visiting supporters, at least 2,000 by my estimate. They made a real contribution to the atmosphere in the ground. Both sides were in attack-minded mood right from kick-off. Wigan's starting line-up included Haris Vuckic, on loan from Newcastle, for a rare appearance up-front, and Chris McCann on the left side of defence for Reece James. The newly-signed Yanic Wildschut was on the subs bench, but would no doubt make an appearance at some stage of the game. United had included the legendary local hero and prolific goalscorer Billy Sharp, recently re-signed by Sheffield after spells elsewhere.

Both sides had created good chances before, 15 minutes into the game, one of them was taken. During a Wigan attack, a clearance from a visiting defender hit the referee, and fell to the feet of a surprised Michael Jacobs who saw Will Grigg in space on the right. His through ball was expertly dispatched past the keeper by Grigg, who is beginning to live up to his goal-scoring reputation whenever he can find a bit of space in or around the penalty area. A fortuitous, if well-taken goal. A minute later, Grigg was put clean through again, and could (and perhaps should) have increased Wigan's lead but didn't.

Sheffield continued to look dangerous on the counter, although a noticeably overweight Billy Sharp was not succeeding in finding space, and was struggling to make an impact; Billy not-so-Sharp on tonight's showing! Shortly before half-time, Wigan increased their lead after a fluent interpassing move down the left, featuring the effervescent David Perkins and Jason Pearce, whose pinpoint cross was headed home emphatically by Haris Vuckic.

Wigan had been playing really well, although Sheffield could reasonably argue that they didn't deserve to be two goals down. In the 60th minute, the home side were three up; good work down the right flank led to a series of blocked goal attempts in the area before McCann found a yard of space that gave him a clear sight of goal, and he shot fiercely past Sheffield's George Long. That appeared to seal the match for Wigan; it was difficult to see the visitors pulling three back. I expected Wigan to fall back and attack on the break. Wildschut came on to an ovation; everyone pleased to see him back and with good reason. We all sat back and waited for a convincing home win against a side on the fringes of the play-offs. Not a great deal of drama to be witnessed this evening, but after the Gillingham game, I guess the home fans would settle for that.

But this turned out to be a premature conclusion. Sheffield pulled a goal back, when a defender found acres of space down the left and crossed for Matt Done to score from close range. Shortly afterwards, more space down the left (where was Leon Barnett?), another cross, and there was Billy Sharp to make it 3-2. The exuberant visiting fans (who, to be fair, had never given up) roared their team on. It was becoming increasingly tense in the West Stand. Had the Wigan players allowed their mindsets to drop?

Shortly before full-time, a mistake in the home defence led to an equaliser from Matt Done, again from close range, but this time from a more difficult angle. In the six minutes of stoppage time, there was only one side that looked likely to win the game, and it wasn't Wigan. Had it not been for two acrobatic saves from Jussi Jaaskelainen, Sheffield would have done to Wigan what Wigan had done to Gillingham the previous week, but with an even bigger deficit to overcome (0-3, as opposed to 0-2). But Wigan held out for a draw, and my 'football as drama' hypothesis was again vindicated.

Had I managed to retain the stance of neutrality with which I started the season, I would have been able to appreciate Sheffield's stirring comeback on its merits, as a rare example of a team pulling back a three-goal deficit in the last half-hour of the game to earn a deserved draw. But given that I hadn't, my appreciation was more than tinged by a sense of disappointment that Wigan had dropped two points in a game which they had looked (almost) certain to win. A win would have put them right up there with three of the four front runners (Burton were still clear at the top with games in hand, and were emerging as promotion favourites). Inconsistent Chesterfield, the visitors next Saturday, may prove less demanding opponents.

The only way back to the town centre which I knew was along the canal towpath; no problem in daylight, but ill-lit and hazardous in the dark. Accessing the path from the nearby car park, I tripped and fell, fortunately not into the canal itself, but onto the puddle-strewn towpath, which was bad enough. Wet, mud-stained, and fed-up, I caught a taxi close to the station to take me to the Coaching House. I told him the result. "Three-all!" he exclaimed. "It was three-nil last time I checked."

We chatted about the town. Wigan was part of Lancashire he thought, nothing to do with Greater Manchester nor Merseyside. I agreed. It didn't have much connection either with Leigh, Atherton and Tyldesley (all part of Wigan Borough Council), which look toward Bolton or Manchester, and should never have been amalgamated with Wigan. Again I concurred. This bloke knew what he was talking about. And why was George Osborne so keen to foist an elected mayor on Greater Manchester, when no-one wanted one? Why indeed?

*

The following Saturday, Blackpool were at home to Scunthorpe United. Usually, I look forward to any game of football I attend, but not on this occasion. It was a bleak day and snow was in the air. The memory of the previous Saturday's dismal 0-1 home defeat to Port Vale was still fresh in my mind. Blackpool were on a losing run – three league defeats in succession – and there was little to suggest that mid-table Scunthorpe would be any easier to overcome than mid-table Port Vale.

An article in the *Blackpool Gazette* by William Watt had reminded me just how unattractive a side Blackpool usually are. They invariably have far fewer shots on target, and much less possession than their opponents, even when they win. Their total of 21 goals in 25 games is the lowest tally in the whole of Division One. When they have won, it has invariably been due to a well-organised defence, defending an early (often streaky) goal. There has been little evidence of creativity in midfield or attack.

The only highlights, on reflection, have been the recent 2-0 win in a downpour against in-form Peterborough, and the plucky 3-4 defeat at Bury, where they actually dominated the game throughout the second half, and nearly managed an unlikely draw. So my expectations, as I joined the Blackpool South-bound train at Preston station were low. But at least that meant, I suppose, that there was a possibility of being pleasantly surprised.

There was no-one playing a round on the famous Royal Lytham & St. Annes Golf Club course as the train trundled past it, although plenty in the clubhouse, on the evidence of the well-filled car park. Nor was there anyone enjoying any of the rides at the Blackpool Pleasure Beach complex; did they actually open it on days like this? Only two tangerine-clad passengers disembarked at Blackpool South station (it had been a dozen or so for the first game of the season). The perishing cold north wind continued to blow, and the sleety snow continued to fall, though not with an intensity that threatened a postponement. Walking to the ground, I passed the familiar assortment of derelicts, hard-faced women, vicious-looking dogs and empty shops.

Inside the stadium, there were perhaps 250 Scunthorpe fans in the visitors' enclosure. What a testament to the loyalty that football clubs inspire that so many had made the tortuous 200 mile round trip from Scunthorpe to Blackpool on a day like this. Part of me hoped it would prove worth their while, but another part of me didn't.

CHAPTER 9

The home supporters were, as ever, thin on the ground, apart from in the rear of the Stanley Matthews stand, which is where my borrowed season ticket was located. Blackpool started brightly, and in the second minute went ahead, when a corner from the right found Tom Aldred totally unmarked, and he placed his header neatly into the top corner. So no repeat of the previous Saturday's 0-1 defeat then, which was a relief; but on the evidence of previous matches, a distinct possibility of a further 88 minutes of a 'defence-in-depth' war of attrition. But no; after a burst of attacking from Scunthorpe, a lovely fluent sequence of interpassing from the home side on the left, in which Jack Redshaw played a central role, led to Brad Potts surging unopposed into the area, where he comfortably slid the ball past the out-rushing keeper. Scunthorpe continued to pass the ball around nicely, but it was Blackpool who looked the more likely to score, which they did (again) on the half-hour mark, when Brad Potts (again) surged through a huge gap in the Scunthorpe defence to score a replica of his first goal.

It was a pleasure to observe the lack of silly dances or indeed any other form of fatuous rehearsed celebrations following the Blackpool goals. All the players were so delighted at this outcome (so far this season, relatively infrequent) that they converged in a delighted huddle around the scorer and provider. This is the way it should be; please take note Wigan Athletic! The downside is that whenever Blackpool do score, the loudspeaker system immediately blasts out The Dave Clark Five's 1960s hit "Glad all over," which the home crowd joins in en masse. We could do without that. The crowd's joyous response doesn't need that kind of artificial augmentation.

Although Blackpool were playing with a degree of fluency and penetration previously absent (or at least rare), it has to be said that Scunthorpe were truly awful, with the most porous defence I have seen all season. How had they ever reached the (relative) safety of 15th place? I wasn't of course party to what was said in the visitors' dressing-room at half-time, but it can't have been pleasant.

During the break, I noticed that many of the advertisement hoardings were for Oyston-owned companies: the *Lancashire and North West* magazine, The Village Hotel Club, the Blackpool FC Hotel, amongst others. Their estate agency business was still featured, although that had been sold some years ago. Was First Stop Loans one of theirs? Probably not; Wonga who sponsor the club kit would no doubt see that as a conflict of loyalties. There remains a small forlorn advert for Belokon Holdings at the back of the main stand, which has survived the onset of the current legal dispute between Valeri Belokon and the Oystons. Little has been heard recently about the possible takeover bid for the club from a Belokon-led consortium, which is a pity because it seemed to offer the one remaining possible way out of the current impasse.

Could Blackpool increase their lead in the second half, or at least keep a clean sheet? Scunthorpe did most of the early attacking, without ever looking likely to pull a goal back. But at least their pressure roused the disconsolate visiting supporters, who began to make more noise than they previously had. At first, I couldn't figure out what they were chanting, and then I realised it was "Iron… Iron…" repeated ad nauseam.

Scunthorpe's industrial identity is rooted in iron and then steel, although the massive steel-making complex there looks increasingly vulnerable, given the way in which cheap Chinese-manufactured steel is currently flooding the market. The club's nickname is 'The Iron' a title it shares with Braintree Town (though I doubt whether many Scunthorpe fans are aware of this). The chanting died down when, after the Scunthorpe defence had missed numerous opportunities to clear the ball in a goalmouth scramble, Blackpool's David Norris put them out of their misery by thumping home Blackpool's fourth. And that wasn't the end of it. After Colin Doyle had made a magnificent save from Scunthorpe's leading scorer Paddy Madden, Blackpool stormed upfield from the resulting corner, and after good play from Jack Redshaw who created an overlap on the right, Danny Philliskirk hit a low cross-shot decisively past the hapless visitors' keeper. And 5-0 was the way it ended.

There was an air of incredulity around me in the Stanley Mathews stand, as we cheered the team off the field. When had Blackpool last scored five goals? (The answer, I later discovered, after extensive research, was August 2012, when they hit six past Ipswich Town.) Neil McDonald was delighted. He'd waited a long time for a result like this: "My best day as manager of Blackpool… we were really sharp in everything we did… we needed a top-class performance from everyone and we got it."

Mark Robins, Scunthorpe's manager was predictably unimpressed. "It was rubbish, absolute rubbish… this is as bad a display away from home as I am prepared to accept," (so it has to be even worse to be unacceptable?). "I can't keep relying on people who are going to let you down." He was right, Scunthorpe were dire, especially in defence, but his reactions were redolent of a manager who had 'lost the dressing-room.'

Was the game a further illustration of 'football as drama'? In a sense it wasn't, in that it was clear after Brad Potts' second goal that it was game over (but that's how it had felt when Wigan had gone 3-0 up against Sheffield!). But then drama is also about the unexpected. For Blackpool to be 3-0 up was indeed unexpected. When, in the second half they increased their lead to 4-0 and then 5-0 it was even more mind-blowing to supporters accustomed to streaky 1-0 wins or frustrating 1-0 defeats. In that sense, the drama was there throughout the match.

The question for Blackpool was whether this was a one-off freak result, or whether it was the start of better times. Certainly some of their football – especially the move leading to the second goal – was in a different class to what we had previously witnessed. But there are some tough fixtures coming up (Walsall away and Sheffield United and Gillingham at home) where Blackpool will be subjected to much sterner tests than that provided by this clueless crew from Scunthorpe.

And the underlying problem remains. Whilst those around me who (whatever their reservations about the Oystons) are continuing to attend home games were understandably ecstatic, the close on 2,000 members of the BST who are choosing not to attend will have had mixed reactions. Yes, great to see the team you support win 5-0. But if that boosts the probability of the Oystons continuing to run the club, that's very bad news.

*

Meanwhile, at the DW Stadium, Wigan were entertaining Chesterfield, who had enjoyed a resurgence of form since Danny Wilson took over from Dean Saunders (will the latter ever work again? His track record is abysmal!). Wigan recovered well from the disappointment of seeing Sheffield United pull back a three-goal deficit the previous Tuesday. Max Power gave them the lead in the sixth minute with a spectacular long-range thunderbolt from well outside the penalty area, a close replica of the goal he'd scored at Oldham. But if his goal was a contender for 'goal of the day,' his celebration left much to be desired. It was a combination of the predictable Wigan silly dance with a series of gestures in the direction of his genitals. I'd strongly advise scrapping that one, Max, it won't endear you to viewers of the *Football League Show,* nor indeed to sensitive female patrons of the DW Stadium.

Towards the end of the first half, Wigan's lead was increased when Reece James scored his first goal for the club, a well-placed lob from the edge of the area. A minute later, the prolific Michael Jacobs made it three with a characteristic cool finish when put through by Haris Vuckic. Chesterfield scored a consolation goal late in the game but never threatened to repeat Sheffield United's comeback heroics four days previously. This win left Wigan in fifth place, but they are gaining on the leaders, and have opened up a seven-point gap over sixth-placed Peterborough. Blackpool had moved out of the relegation zone to 19th place. But for how long?

*

Whether or not Mark Robins had 'lost the dressing room,' he had clearly lost the confidence of the board. Two days after the ignominious defeat at Blackpool he was sacked. Sadly, we'll never know just how bad Scunthorpe would have to be for him to find it unacceptable.

*

The following Saturday, I felt the need for a change of scene, so instead of travelling to Crewe, as I'd originally intended, I went with my friend Harry Pearson (author of the football classic *The Far Corner*) to see Carlisle United's first game back at Brunton Park, which had been under six feet of water in the wake of Storm Desmond on December 6th. The re-laying of the pitch had been completed only a couple of days before.

It was an emotional occasion. The Carlisle squad had voluntarily put in many hours of time in the aftermath of the flooding, helping out in the devastated Warwick Road area adjacent to the ground; a powerful example of the positive relationship between football club and local community which often exists (but not always; contrast with the situation at Blackpool!). They were cheered on and off the field when they emerged for the warm-up, and again when they came out for the game itself by a crowd well in excess of the usual 4,500 average.

Carlisle were playing bottom-placed York City, and a good open game it proved to be, with many chances created at both ends. Carlisle should have been 3-0 up at half-time, instead of their one goal lead, but had to settle for a draw when York snatched an equaliser five minutes from the end. On the evidence of this game, there is little to choose between the quality of football in Divisions One and Two respectively.

But back to Blackpool and Wigan. Both managed one-all draws, an outcome which was as unexpected at Walsall as it was at Crewe, but for different reasons. Blackpool gave a creditable performance at Walsall, creating more chances (nine) than they normally do, and looking the more dangerous side in the first half. In the second half, they soaked up a lot of Walsall pressure, aided by some excellent saves from Colin Doyle, but fell behind half-way through, when Demetriou scored from close range. Blackpool's new signing Uche Ikpeazu, on loan from Watford, was brought on, and it was his free-kick early in added time which found its way through a thicket of legs to Danny Philliskirk, who scored with ease, to the delight of what looked like a sizeable contingent of Blackpool fans behind the goal. Ikpeazu had scored six goals when on loan to Port Vale earlier in the season (including the winner against Wigan), and is a welcome addition to Blackpool's small band of strikers; Mark Cullen (who came on as a substitute), Jack Redshaw, and Danny Philliskirk are all now competing for places with the new signing.

A draw at Walsall was in its way, as impressive as the 5-0 demolition of Scunthorpe the previous week. Walsall are a formidable side, and would have gone top had they held on to their lead. In contrast, Wigan's draw at Crewe was a disappointment. Crewe were bottom of the table and had previously lost eight of their 13 home games. Wigan, undefeated since early December, must have fancied their chances of another three points. Despite dominating the game in terms of possession and chances created, they had to settle for a point.

New signing Reece Wabara (recently released by Barnsley) put Wigan ahead with a well-placed strike from outside the area which Max Power would have been proud of. Crewe hit back against the run of play just before half-time through Brad Inman. After the interval, Wigan piled on the pressure but wasted several chances, including a point-blank header from the otherwise impressive Yanic Wildschut, which he somehow managed to steer over the bar. Despite impressive vocal support from over 2,200 visiting fans, Wigan couldn't translate their dominance into a winning goal. But given Coventry's 3-0 defeat at Southend, the Latics moved up into fourth place. Blackpool remained in 19th place, with a tricky midweek game at home to Sheffield United the following Tuesday.

CHAPTER 9

I did consider driving to Blackpool for this game, but, as so often this winter, the weather was foul: torrential rain, high winds, and the danger of further flooding in Kendal. So I stayed at home and checked the progress of the match on *Gillette Soccer Special* (always highly entertaining; I love the frenzied shrieks of the studio commentators when a goal is scored in the game they are watching!). It was probably a wise decision. Blackpool managed a creditable but not particularly eventful 0-0 draw in the wind and rain against a side on the fringes of the play-offs. Furthermore, they halted Billy Sharp's run of goals in each of the previous seven games.

The statistics indicated an even game, with Sheffield having slightly more of the possession, but the home side having more shots (16 to 11, three on target in each case) Colin Doyle again performed heroics to keep out goal-bound shots from Conor Sammon and others; where would they be without him? (Answer: deep in the relegation zone.) William Watt of the *Gazette* saw the game as an acid test for the Tangerines. Did they pass it? Probably, in his view. "They demonstrated that they could compete regularly in Division One," and could "grind out results," against top sides. He, both managers, and the *Sheffield Star* reporter all thought a draw was a fair result, so it probably was.

*

Earlier in the week, the Blackpool fan who had tried to storm his way into the VIP area during the demonstration during the Huddersfield game in May 2015 was given a 26-month jail sentence. Seemed harsh to me (and to most (though not all) of those commenting online). Another sorry episode in the long-running dispute between Blackpool's owners and supporters.

*

The following Saturday, Blackpool were at home to second-placed Gillingham (another 'acid test'), whilst Wigan entertained Port Vale. Having been to Blackpool twice in recent weeks, I was due a visit to Wigan. A few days earlier, they had made a couple of new signings, shortly before the transfer window was due to close the following Monday: Ryan Colclough, a forward from Crewe Alexandra, who had performed impressively in the previous Saturday's match against Wigan, hitting the crossbar with a ferocious long-range drive, and Sam Morsy, a midfielder from Chesterfield. Both had been regulars with their clubs this season, which is always a good sign. No doubt the two of them will 'strengthen the squad,' but I did have concerns about the timing.

The Wigan team was beginning to develop a more settled look, after months of chopping and changing. Who was going to make way for Morsy? Hopefully not David Perkins, who has been a crucial element in Wigan's success this season. Max Power continues to improve, and Reece Wabara has impressed since coming from Barnsley. And up front, will it be Grigg, Jacobs, Wildschut, or Vuckic who is displaced? Wigan already have a significantly bigger squad (28, before the new arrivals) than most other Division One teams. It would be a pity if the stability of the current settled starting line-up were to be disrupted by the opportunities to experiment with new combinations, and the resulting understandable sense of injustice on the part of those displaced, all of whom are performing well at present.

As I boarded the train at Oxenholme, the sun was shining. A welcome contrast to the weather on all my visits to Blackpool and Wigan since early November. At Wigan, I wandered up the main street (Wallgate) and purchased a meat-and-potato pie at Galloways. "Do you ever get customers asking for their pie to be put in a barm?" I asked, with reference to the notice I'd seen in their window on my previous visit. The woman who served me looked at me with incredulity. Yes, lots of people did. Clearly a stupid outsider's question. What did I know of Wigan? By the time I reached the Henhole for a pre-match pint, the sun had disappeared and I was being bombarded by hailstones. There was the usual lively pre-match atmosphere, with a fair scattering of women and children, as well as men, in their blue-and-white replica shirts (Wigan really does come across as a family-friendly club).

At the DW Stadium, when the teams were announced, it became apparent that my worries about the disruption of the recent stabilised line-up were unfounded. Colclough and Morsy were on the substitutes' bench, from whence they would no doubt emerge later in the game if the circumstances permitted (e.g. a three-goal lead with 25 minutes to go). Michael Jacobs was absent, injured, which meant that Haris Vuckic retained his place. Port Vale had an impressive turn-out of support in the North Stand. They were currently in tenth place, three points from a playoff position, although on the evidence of their recent performance at Blackpool, they didn't look serious playoff contenders to me.

Their noisy fans fell silent after six minutes when Yanic Wildschut found himself in acres of space on the left, and his low cross found its way into the net via a deflection off either a Port Vale defender or Will Grigg. The goal was initially credited to Wildschut (which was clearly wrong). At half-time, on Sky TV, it had been given to Richard Duffy (own-goal). Later that evening it was awarded to Grigg, in line with the referee's view of events (I hadn't realised referees played a role in deciding the identity of goal-scorers).

Port Vale came back strongly, and a header from Mathew Kennedy forced an impressive save from Jaaskelainen. Both sides were creating chances. Wildschut continued to find space down the left and always threatened danger (had Port Vale not done their homework?). Then, five minutes before half-time came the game's decisive moment. Will Grigg had been put through and was bearing down on the goal within the area when he was hauled back by Richard McGovern. It was a clear penalty, and McGovern's subsequent red card was also totally justified (on the 'last man' criterion) although you wouldn't have thought so from the fuss he made. Grigg duly converted the penalty (via the crossbar).

There was no way back for the ten men of Port Vale. Wigan dominated the second half and played some lovely football. They are now operating as a cohesive unit; one senses that they are developing an instinctive feel for where their team-mates are likely to be, which is a key attribute of effective teams. Wildschut was running riot down the left. His pace enabled him to push the ball into space and then easily outpace whoever was supposed to be marking him, race on to the by-line, and put over a series of dangerous crosses. Wigan should have had a bag full of goals, but added only one more, a neat finish, again by Grigg, from a difficult angle, 20 minutes before the end. Neither he nor anyone else seemed to realise that this was his hat-trick; maybe Sky Sports had been in the dressing room at half-time. Ryan Colclough had been introduced ten minutes before and proceeded to impress everyone with his composure, his reading of the game, and his ability to create chances for team-mates. Sam Morsy came on later, and fitted in well, without quite making the same impression.

The other results helped Wigan's cause. Burton, the league leaders, went down 2-1 at Rochdale; Gillingham lost by a single goal at Blackpool; Coventry somehow contrived to lose 2-1 at home to Scunthorpe (who have prospered since Mark Robins was shown the door), and Millwall could only manage a draw at home to lowly Crewe. Wigan are now part of a group of four at the top with only five points between them and Burton. They are playing really well; an eight-match unbeaten run dating from mid-December. Automatic promotion has become a real possibility and a play-off place highly likely.

*

Meanwhile, Blackpool had managed another home win, this time against second-placed Gillingham. It was an uninspiring game, in awful conditions (as at Wigan, most of the second half was played out in driving sleet). The only goal came just before half-time when Mark Yeates was brought down in the area, and Jack Redshaw converted the penalty in his customary confident style. The second half featured the familiar rear-guard action, with the Blackpool defence again proving resolute and well-organised. It was a particularly creditable performance given that, just before kick-off, Hayden White and Craig Robertson had had to pull out, having succumbed to a 'mystery virus' (aren't they all!). Their replacements, Emmerson Boyce and Will Aimson both acquitted themselves well, and Tom Aldred provided another example of his capacity for heroics, flinging himself across the goal-line to keep out a goal-bound effort from Max Ehmer.

The win meant that Blackpool remained in 18th place, but they are now on 33 points, five clear of the relegation zone. They are unbeaten in four games (three of them against leading clubs) and have kept successive clean sheets in the last three home games. "The tide is turning for the Tangerines," was the headline in the match report in *The Football League Paper*. Maybe it is on the field, but little sign that it is doing so off it.

Ten days previously, Blackpool Supporters Trust had addressed the local council, asking it to intervene in the stalemate between owners and supporters, which, in their view is endangering the club's future, and indeed its very existence. The initiative received short shrift from the council's Labour leader, who argued that it was "not his problem."

Later, the leader of the Conservative opposition did express the view that some kind of action was needed. He advocated a truce between the owners and the disgruntled alienated supporters, of which BST are the main representative organisation. In the view of William Watt, the football correspondent of the *Blackpool Gazette*, the idea of a truce is unhelpful. He prefers the idea of change: "It's change which all the powers that be should be calling for at Bloomfield Road, on and off the pitch." The process should begin, he thinks, with an end to the Chairman's policy of taking legal action against supporters. "Once all that nonsense has ended, Blackpool's owners need to make genuine attempts to build bridges with the supporters and the media." In principle, I'm sure that's the right way forward, but I have an uneasy suspicion that

BST may feel that the opportunity for 'building bridges' has long since passed.

CHAPTER 10

FEBRUARY: LATICS GO FROM STRENGTH TO STRENGTH; POOL FROM BAD TO WORSE

On the first Saturday of February, I'd planned to re-visit Oldham to watch Blackpool try to pull themselves further out of danger (they would have had a good chance; Oldham have won only one home game all season). But there was the customary Saturday deluge, and the game was abandoned late in the morning. Wigan's game at Sheffield was still on, but there was no way I was going to drive over a hundred miles (and back) on rain-drenched and wind-battered motorways. So I stayed at home and watched *Gillette Soccer Special*.

In the event, Wigan emerged worthy winners. In a first half of few chances, they concentrated on retaining possession, with plenty of familiar passing to and fro across the back line, which is tedious to watch, but which does have the effect of frustrating the opposition.

In the second half, they were much more positive, and went ahead, when Yanic Wildschut bustled his way into the penalty area, where he was brought down unceremoniously by the appropriately-named Chris Basham. Will Grigg scored confidently from the resulting penalty, which he usually does. Two minutes later, Wigan increased their lead. Wildschut again made progress down the left and squared the ball to Max Power, who in turn found debutant loan signing Conor McAleny in space to his right. McAleny let the ball run on to his right foot, before firing in a low shot from the edge of the area.

Wigan could and should have extended their lead when they were awarded a second penalty after Chris McCann was tripped in the area, but this time, Sheffield's George Long guessed right and palmed Grigg's attempt away. But it mattered little; Wigan played out time and returned to Lancashire third in the table, their highest position yet, helped by Walsall's 0-3 defeat at home to Millwall and Gillingham's scoreless draw at home to Swindon.

*

On the same Saturday, there was an unexpected but long overdue development at Blackpool. Karl Oyston issued an invitation, via the club website, to representatives of five supporters' organisations, including BST, to attend a meeting on March 10th to try to find ways of improving relations between the owners and the fans. The meeting would be chaired by Blackpool Community Trust (represented by the Reverend Michael Ward).

The BST leadership are consulting their members as to whether or not they should respond positively to this 'olive branch.' I think there's a good case for doing so, not least because it would confirm their 'reasonable and responsible' reputation; and they can always walk out if they think they aren't getting a fair hearing.

*

The following Saturday, I went to Bloomfield Road to watch the first of Blackpool's two home games against fellow relegation candidates. They were up against Shrewsbury Town, and the following Tuesday, Oldham Athletic were the visitors. If the Tangerines were to take maximum points from these two fixtures, they would be firmly entrenched in mid-table, with fears of relegation fast diminishing. The problem is that both opponents have been much more successful on the road than at home. Shrewsbury have accumulated nearly twice as many points away than at the Greenhouse Meadow, and Oldham have only lost twice on their travels (although they have drawn most of the rest).

BST were in their usual position outside the main entrance, so clearly were not yet convinced by Karl Oyston's apparent change of heart. When I talked to vice-chair Christine Seddon, I understood why. The invitees to the March 10th meeting include only one from the BST, but five representatives from the Fans Parliament, the 'official' fans forum set up by Karl about a year ago, when BSA

(Blackpool Supporters Association) detached itself from the club. Five is the full extent of the current membership! So is the meeting an attempt to legitimise the role of the Fans Parliament?

Christine was also not encouraged by the content of a recent Radio Lancashire interview with Karl Oyston, in which, although he admitted past mistakes, there was little awareness of the legitimate concerns of the BST. It may be that there is an element of games-playing involved in the olive branch! But she will abide by the majority view of BST members as to whether they should be represented at the meeting. The London and Yorkshire supporters' groups who have also been invited (one member each), will follow the lead of the BST. If all three groups decide not to attend, the stance of the BSA would become crucial. If they were also absent, the March 10th meeting would have zero legitimacy.

There was a large and noisy contingent of Shrewsbury supporters present (as there had been at Wigan). They were delighted, when, after five minutes, Nathaniel Knight-Percival scored with a deftly executed overhead kick, following a right-wing corner. No stopping that one; a real goal-of-the-month contender. They were even more delighted two minutes later when Shaun Whalley took advantage of a costly misunderstanding between Tom Aldred and David Ferguson in the penalty area to force home a second. And joy was unconfined when, on the half-hour mark, Andy Mangan (a former Blackpool player) hit an unstoppable power-drive from the edge of the area.

Blackpool had threatened little and looked completely out of it, and a handful of departures from the main stand ensued. There were several below-par performances. Ferguson was struggling in the back four, with some uncertain defending and poor distribution, which had been the case for much of the season. The fans around me had no time for him, and were not slow to tell him so! Mark Yeates kept running into blind alleys and was replaced by Jim McAllister shortly after Shrewsbury's third goal. Brad Potts gave a passable impersonation of a lumbering carthorse in midfield; recently he seems to have lost the creative spark and energy which proved so valuable earlier in the season. For the visitors, Shaun Whalley looked dangerous every time he had the ball. I remember him from my Conference Season visits in 2012-13 when he was playing for Southport. He then moved to Luton Town, for whom he made only a handful of appearances, and then on to Shrewsbury. A late developer perhaps?

So poor were Blackpool that it came as something of a surprise when they pulled a goal back shortly before half-time. A loose ball found Tom Aldred in the penalty area, with his back to goal, and he cleverly swivelled and hooked the ball into the net. That's his third goal in the past ten games; not bad for a central defender. There followed another unnecessary blast of 'Glad all over' (I must let the management know what a pain this practice is).

Ten minutes into the second half, Blackpool scored again; a really well-worked goal this time. Breaking from a Shrewsbury corner, Jim McAllister raced upfield and played a lovely through ball to Danny Philliskirk, who controlled the ball neatly, moved forward and placed the ball expertly beyond the advancing keeper into the far corner. As at Bury, Blackpool were demonstrating a capacity to fight back from seemingly impossible positions, which had been totally lacking earlier in the season. Could they do what Sheffield United had done at Wigan and come from 3-0 down to 3-3?

The answer was 'nearly but not quite.' The home side exerted an intense spell of pressure half-way through the second half when Shrewsbury keeper Jayson Leutwiler performed heroics in keeping out a series of close-range shots, not least a goal-bound header from Brad Potts which he palmed onto the bar. But they couldn't sustain the momentum, and the game petered out in a series of long-range shots and free-kicks, all well off target to the dismay of the (increasingly critical) home supporters.

In the post-match press conference, Neil McDonald was his usual phlegmatic self, expressing disappointment, but focusing on the positives. He thought Blackpool responded well to the three-goal deficit, "Earlier on in the season, we might have folded and got beaten by more; it shows how much we've come on." This view involved, I thought, an unmerited degree of positive gloss, although to be fair, two of Shrewsbury's three goals were of the unstoppable variety, which they would find difficult to replicate on a regular basis. However, there was a worrying lack of quality in Blackpool's performance, which raises concerns about their capacity to pull themselves clear of danger. They remain 18th, only three points clear of the relegation zone.

*

Meanwhile, Wigan were entertaining Oldham at the DW Stadium. Given the 18 places that separated them, the odds were on another home win for the Latics. But that's not the way it turned out. In a lacklustre encounter, Oldham came close to snatching an unlikely away win. Wigan's veteran keeper Jussi Jaaskelainen pulled off a couple of spectacular saves to deny the visitors, and although Oldham's keeper Joel Coleman produced an equally impressive effort to frustrate Will Grigg in the closing stages, a Wigan victory would have been an injustice, as Wigan manager Gary Caldwell was quick to acknowledge after the game. "We were maybe a bit lucky to come away with a point," he said. "We got the very most we deserved." Good to hear a manager recognising that his side had been fortunate. It's not something you tend to hear from Blackpool's Neil McDonald, even after the palpable injustice of the home win against Fleetwood.

*

The next Tuesday, Oldham were at Blackpool. Had I not been visiting relatives in Scotland, I would probably have been there, despite the bitter cold. Fortunately, as it turned out, I wasn't present to witness what was a mind-numbingly tedious nil-all draw. "Definitely a night best forgotten quickly," was the headline of William Watt's match report. "In a season of dull and uninspiring games, last night's 0-0 draw against struggling Oldham was the worst by far. At half-time, the talk in the press box was how the gathered media were going to fill the column inches in the morning."

The home side managed a mere three shots on target (not that Oldham were any more productive). So Blackpool had to settle for a single point from their two encounters with fellow relegation contenders, which probably isn't going to improve the prospects of undisturbed nights' sleep for Neil McDonald. The advantage is that it will help sustain interest over the next month or so. Blackpool in a safe mid-table position by March would not be good news for this book. What I need is uncertainty and drama right up to the last Saturday of the season, with Wigan needing a result at home to Barnsley to clinch an automatic promotion place, and Blackpool likewise at Peterborough to avoid relegation. On the basis of Blackpool's last two games, I wouldn't, in that eventuality, fancy their chances!

*

The following Saturday, Wigan were away to Walsall, and Blackpool away to Swindon. The Walsall/Wigan game was definitely Division One's match of the day. Leaders Burton were playing on Monday and second-placed Gillingham were at boring Oldham. If Blackpool failed to return with anything from the trip to mid-table Swindon, they would be right back amongst the relegation-threatened squad.

On yet another day of incessant rain and blustery winds, Wigan came away with a 2-1 win from Walsall's Bescot Stadium. They really are on a roll at the moment. It's now 11 consecutive games without defeat (including seven wins) and 12 away games undefeated. Indeed, since the 12th of September, their only defeats have been at home to Burton Albion (understandable) and Blackpool (totally incomprehensible).

Gary Caldwell's batch of recent signings, which I was worried would disrupt the camaraderie of the established first team, have proved astute. Conor McAleny, a recent loan signing from Everton, opened the scoring shortly before half-time with a viciously dipping long-range strike. Against the run of play, mid-way through the second half, Walsall equalised through an equally impressive effort from Sam Manton, and could well have gone into the lead were it not for a couple of spectacular saves from Jussi Jaaskelainen. Wigan then began to dominate again and clinched the victory shortly after the onset of stoppage time, when Yanic Wildschut, who had been brought on as a substitute late in the second half, hit a superb winner from the edge of the area.

"Yanic's not happy at being a sub," commented Gary Caldwell after the game. I bet he isn't, and with good reason. He's a class player in a mediocre division and has scored or created numerous vital goals since coming to the club. What's the problem about playing him from the start every week, Gary? Wigan's starting line-up included three relative newcomers – Morsy, Colclough, and McAleny – but they all seem to have blended in quickly. I was pleased to see that, whoever else gets left out, David Perkins is always there in midfield, the indispensable (in my view) focus of the team.

As a consequence of Gillingham's unexpected defeat at struggling Oldham, Wigan ended the day in second place. Given Walsall's dodgy home form, and Gillingham's equally unimpressive away performances, there's no reason why Wigan shouldn't stay there and bounce straight back into the Championship without having to endure the play-off lottery.

For a while, it looked like Blackpool would have an equally profitable afternoon at Swindon. After two minutes, Tom Aldred (again) powered a header past Lawrence Vigouroux, following a left-side corner. On only one occasion this season have Blackpool lost a game in which they have taken the lead and almost always they have gone on to win. But on 15 minutes, the usually reliable Colin Doyle inexplicably allowed a tame cross from the right to bounce off his chest, into the path of Nicky Ajose, who couldn't miss (and didn't). Soon after the interval, the same player scored again from close range. But Blackpool soon retaliated, when Clark Robertson was pushed over in the penalty area, and Danny Philliskirk converted the resulting penalty with aplomb. Just when it looked like Blackpool would come away with a much-needed point, up popped Nicky Ajose again to score a late winner after bustling his way into the box.

The match statistics indicated that Swindon deserved their win: 63% possession and 17 shots (ten on target) to Blackpool's six (four). Neil McDonald again sought to make the best of it, "It is frustrating knowing that we have had a decent performance with two goals away from home, but we come home with nothing." This perhaps over-complacent verdict on the game led to a sharp exchange between the manager and the *Gazette*'s William Watt. The journalist suggested, not unreasonably, that Blackpool must start winning games, following good victories from the sides beneath them. This was the manager's response, "You've always got the negative side. You always go for the difficult questions. You never ask me nice questions, or talk nice about the players when we win." I always thought it was the job of a good journalist to ask the difficult questions, but apparently McDonald doesn't agree! There's a degree of over-sensitivity displayed here; perhaps he's feeling more beleaguered than his usual placid demeanour suggests?

As so often with Blackpool, the post-match analysis was soon overtaken by events off the field. On the Tuesday after the Swindon defeat, BST members voted by a 60% to 40% majority not to attend the March 10th meeting. The turnout was over 1,000 an impressive 60% of the total membership. Initially, the BST leadership had been open to the idea of the meeting, and wrote to the appointed chairperson, Rev Michael Ward of the club's Community Trust, with some queries and suggestions about the meeting, all of which were rejected by the club. Steve Rowland, BST's chairman, gave the following verdict on the result: "When the meeting was proposed, I suspected the vote could have gone the other way, but our suggestions were point-blank rejected. We asked for a level playing field and that was rejected out of hand. I believe it was that that made peoples' minds up to vote no."

I think the BST membership made the right choice; the meeting was increasingly looking like a device for legitimising the Fans Progress Group. Again, the BST have behaved in a responsible (and democratic) way. It will be interesting to see whether the club comes forward with a revised proposal. But don't hold your breath!

*

A fine Saturday at last! I have developed a routine on Saturday visits to Wigan, which starts with a visit to Galloways, where I purchase a meat-and-potato pie (not, I hasten to add, encased in a bap!). This succulent offering scored 58/70 in Martin Tarbuck's *Life of Pies*, and finished in 16th position in the league table of the 314 pies he sampled. I then make my way to the Henhole, eating my pie en route. My mum and dad would have been appalled at the idea of their young lad walking along a road in Wigan, munching a pie, in broad daylight. But I'm 73 now, and I'll do as I please! The Henhole (I can't be bothered typing out its full name) always has a lively pre-match atmosphere, and there's real ale available. There's plenty of blue-and-white striped replica shirts in evidence, in which, I have to say the women look particularly fetching. I then complete the short journey to the DW Stadium over a couple of old bridges and purchase my over-65s ticket in the West Stand.

Today's opponents were Bury, who have proved something of a bogey side for Wigan this season, having won 2-1 in the Carling Cup at the DW and then thrashing Wigan 4-0 at Gigg Lane in the first round of the FA Cup. However, the Latics did manage a two-all draw there in October in the league, thanks to a last-minute rocket from Captain Morgan.

Bury, promoted from Division Two at the end of last season, had a hugely impressive start; they recorded seven consecutive wins and had reached the lofty heights of third position by early October. Since then, their form has been erratic, and they are currently settled in a mid-table position, safe from relegation, but unlikely to make the playoffs. Wigan started with Yanic Wildschut (quite right too), and Reece Wabara replaced the injured Donervon Daniels on the right of the back four.

Wigan started fluently, and took the lead on five minutes, when Bury's Tom Soares was dispossessed on the left, leaving Wildschut free to surge forward and send over a perfect cross for Will Grigg to nip in front of the keeper and score with a glancing header. Two minutes later it was two-nil, when Ryan Colclough cut in from the right and dispatched a powerful left-foot shot into the far corner – another contender for Division One goal of the month, together with Conor McAleny and Yanic Wildschut's strikes at Walsall the previous week.

Wigan were playing superbly, and it was no surprise when they went three up. An excellent through ball from David Perkins (who doesn't always get the credit he deserves for the creative side of his play) found Will Grigg racing to beat the keeper to the ball. Having (just) managed to do so, he was brought down and coolly slotted home the resulting penalty. Then Chris McCann, who was having an impressive game (but weren't they all) cleverly worked his way into the area, but couldn't quite finish it off to make it four.

After 27 minutes, a ripple of applause began to echo around the ground, in which almost everyone joined. At first, I thought it was a spontaneous tribute to the quality of Wigan's football, in which case it would have been thoroughly deserved. But then I recalled a news item I'd seen on the web earlier in the week: 93-year-old Wigan-born Jimmy France had passed away. Apparently, Jimmy had been watching the Latics since 1932, when they were reformed after Wigan Borough folded the previous season. He would have been nine at the time, and having then had to settle for 45 years of watching them play in the Lancashire Combination and Cheshire County League, must have been overjoyed when, at the age of 56, he finally saw them elected to the Football League. He was still attending matches up to the time of his death, and his family had asked that in the 27th minute (the 27th being the date of his birthday), there should be a minute's applause in his memory. As indeed there was. It's totally fitting that such dedication should be recognised in this way. Football fans everywhere would understand and appreciate this kind of loyalty.

Wigan continued to dominate, but shortly before half-time, Bury would have pulled a goal back, had it not been for a remarkable double save ('world-class' according to *The Football League Paper*) from Jussi Jaaskelainen, who managed to keep out close range shots from Danny Mayor and Craig Jones, with incredible instinctive reactions. The response from the home crowd was similar to that which greets a goal, which is a rare outcome for goalkeeping heroics, but was thoroughly deserved. A similar outburst of cheering greeted the Wigan players as they left the field at half-time. 'Best we've seen them play all season' was the consensus amongst the fans around me in the West Stand.

Just before play resumed in the second half, the Wigan players, supervised by one of the training staff, performed their customary warm-up routine close to the touch-line, accompanied by the music of the classic 'Just can't get enough.' This takes the form of a coordinated sequence of jumps, lunges, and body shakes alternating with muscle-stretching exercises, the overall impression being one of a synchronised disco performance. I don't know what difference it makes, but the players seemed to enjoy it!

The second half was always going to be an anti-climax. Wigan sat back for a while and allowed Bury, who managed to string together some neat interpassing sequences, to make the running. Jaaskelainen again did brilliantly to keep out a close-range header from Ryan Lowe. But the visitors were never going to do a

Sheffield United, and Wigan soon began to look menacing going forward. Will Grigg hit the bar, having engineered himself a good opportunity on the break, and Max Power did likewise with a characteristic long-range power-drive.

The home side brought on Craig Davies, Conor McAleny, and Haris Vuckic in place of Wildschut, Grigg, and Colclough respectively, which rather disrupted the fluency of their play. In particular, Craig Davies struggled to make an impression up front; the youngster Jordan Flores might have been a more imaginative choice of substitute. The game petered out, only to flicker briefly back into life, when a poor tackle by Jones on Max Power resulted in a late flurry of mutual aggro, with several yellow cards being brandished. The industrious Sam Morsy was given the man-of-the-match award, but Chris McCann, David Perkins, or Yanic Wildschut would have been equally worthy winners. Wigan remained in second place. With Burton and Walsall playing out a goalless stalemate, and Gillingham managing to lose at home to struggling Chesterfield, could it be that Wigan might just finish as champions?

*

February had so far proved an unproductive month for Blackpool; a solitary point from three games. There was a chance to improve matters in the home game against Bradford City. Sadly, the opportunity was not taken. The visitors went away with a deserved one-nil win, having created 18 chances to Blackpool's eight, in another uninspiring Bloomfield Road game.

The first half was evenly contested, and Mark Yeates was unlucky when his angled shot rebounded from the underside of the bar just before half-time. But once Kyle Reid had put Bradford ahead ten minutes into the second half with a well-placed shot following a good run from Stephen Darby, Blackpool's fragile self-belief evaporated, and they rarely looked likely to salvage anything. To make matters worse, defender Will Aimson, who has impressed in recent weeks, was sent off in stoppage time for pushing James

Hanson. And Brad Potts' recent slump in form must have continued with a vengeance. He was awarded a 3 in *The Football League Paper*, when most of the other players were scoring 6s and 7s. What has happened to the two-goal hero of the Scunthorpe game?

The size of the visiting contingent of fans was officially registered at over 3,000, which means that if you make the normal deduction of 2,000 (non-attending season ticket holders) from the official attendance of 8,800, there were nearly as many visiting supporters as Blackpool fans in the stadium. So much for home advantage! The Bradford contingent developed an inspired chant late in the game: "You've got more Seagulls than Fans."

Neil McDonald presented his usual self-effacing stoical persona in the post-match interview. He lamented a "lack of clinical finishing," (a concern presumably shared by his Bradford counterpart, whose team had delivered ten more shots). "We've had a few good chances," he said, "and we didn't take them, so we keep trying and that's all we can do." It's all becoming a bit too predictable.

William Watt in a recent *Gazette* column compiled a list of McDonald's most used phrases, entering all of the manager's post-match quotes into a 'word cloud' which highlighted the words he uses most. "Chances" comes top of the list. "Whether bemoaning the lack of goal-scoring opportunities, or claiming that they should have won the game, 'created a lot of chances' is something you will often hear McDonald saying," wrote Watt. The reality is that compared with most other teams in the Division, they create very few chances. "Disappointing," "outplayed," and "frustrating," all appear in the top ten list of words. Together they just about sum up Blackpool's season so far.

Recently, I've been watching the DVDs of the 2009-10 season, when Blackpool won promotion to the Premiership, and the 2010-11 season, when they almost managed to stay up, after delighting supporters and neutrals alike with their positive attack-focused attitude. The contrast between the flamboyant way the team played then and the dour defensive tactics deployed this season couldn't be more stark.

Blackpool are now in real trouble. Although still just outside the relegation zone (on goal difference) they have played three more games at home than away. That balance will be redressed over the next three weeks, when they face Chesterfield, Millwall, Oldham and Crewe away, interspersed with a solitary home game against Coventry. Anything less than six or seven points and the writing will be on the wall!

BST have issued their own plan for a meeting during the second week in March, now that Karl Oyston's proposal has collapsed (he's presumably not going to go ahead with a session with the five remaining members of the so-called Fans Progress Group). Their plan involves each supporters group (excluding the Tangerine Knights), the club, and the Community Trust sending two delegates to a meeting chaired by Councillor Williams, the leader of the Conservative opposition on Blackpool Council, who, unlike the Labour leader, does believe that sport and politics mix (he's right, of course; just think of the significance of a successful Blackpool FC to the local economy and its importance to the local community identity of the town). Karl Oyston and a colleague will also, of course, be invited. But the action will now be played out on a much more level playing field. BST have gained control of the agenda (and the moral high ground). But will Karl agree to attend?

CHAPTER 11
MARCH: BEWARE THE IDES

Just as each football match constitutes a two-act drama in itself, so the fortunes of each club over the whole season can be seen in the same dramatic way, a slowly-unfolding epic, full of twists and turns with the denouement typically postponed until the late stages.

There are exceptions.

In the 2014-15 season, Blackpool's story was one of relentless decline, with the outcome predictable by the end of 2014, and confirmed several weeks before the end of the season. But that is unusual. In 2015-16, by contrast, there has been a striking difference in the thematic development of the two season-long dramas of Wigan and Blackpool respectively.

In Wigan's case, there was an initial mismatch between the high expectations (Wigan as a 'big club'?) and early performances, which were erratic, with three of the first four away games ending in defeat. Then came the revival; 11 league games undefeated and a gradual climb up the table from tenth in mid-September to fourth by mid-November. A brief slump then occurred; two home defeats in succession (the second to Blackpool) and a goalless draw at Southend. Alarm bells began to ring, and Gary Caldwell's managerial credentials began to be questioned in some quarters.

But then a 2-0 win at Barnsley set in motion a run of 12 league games without defeat, and Wigan moved up from sixth to second in the table by the end of February. A real sense of momentum developed, a realisation that unless there was a sudden slump in form (which is always a possibility, but doesn't feel very likely at present), the club is destined to return to the Championship at the first attempt.

Blackpool started as everyone's favourite for relegation, and nine games into the season, that prediction looked well-founded, as Blackpool propped up the table with four points. Then came the first of the mini-revivals: five games undefeated (including three wins) and a move up to 19th. Five games and five defeats later, the club was back down to 23rd and relegation loomed. There followed a second mini-revival; three wins in succession and back up to 17th. Could it last? No it couldn't; three straight defeats followed and Blackpool were back in the relegation zone.

But just as despair was setting in, they had an unbeaten run, this time of four games (two wins and two draws), and the club rose to 18th, with the security of mid-table beckoning. Then it all fell apart (again) and with one point from the next four games, Blackpool were back in real trouble. So the dramatic theme of Blackpool's season (so far) has been one of alternating barren and fruitful sequences; times of hope followed by times of despair.

*

Blackpool badly needed to kick-start a fourth mini-revival as they made their way across the Pennines to fellow-strugglers Chesterfield on March 1st. Wigan had a difficult away fixture at play-off contenders Millwall, which would be a real challenge to the continuation of their 12 match unbeaten run.

Blackpool came away from Chesterfield with a one-all draw, which was less than they deserved. They dominated the game, outclassing poor opponents and creating over 20 goal-scoring opportunities to the home side's paltry eight.

Three of their efforts hit the woodwork in the first half, including a powerful drive from the rejuvenated Brad Potts. It was Potts who put Blackpool ahead early in the second half when another long-range shot took a deflection, which wrong-footed the keeper (but weren't Blackpool due a bit of luck?). Four minutes later, Chesterfield's Jay O'Shea equalised with a stunning 25-yard drive.

Potts could have won it for the Tangerines when put clear in the box by Danny Philliskirk, but pulled his shot wide, and the visitors held out for a much-needed point. Unfortunately, a rare home win for Shrewsbury against Rochdale moved them ahead of Blackpool, who returned (after a long absence) to the relegation zone. Both Neil McDonald and William Watt made Brad Potts man of the match, so there's no arguing with that. And both the manager and (more importantly) the journalist thought it was a much-improved display. Maybe it is the start of mini-revival number four, but there's a tough game coming up on Saturday at Millwall.

*

At the New Den, Wigan continued their unbeaten run (now 13 games in the league since December, and 13 away games since September), but in uncharacteristic fashion. Shortly before half-time, after a relatively even half, Sam Morsy was sent off when he received a second yellow card, which meant that Wigan had to survive for over 45 minutes with ten men. But survive they did, thanks to some inspired goalkeeping by Jaaskelainen (again) and some resolute defensive work from everyone else.

Millwall peppered the Wigan goal with shots in the second half, and their manager Neil Harris said after the match that his team had been "brilliant." But not brilliant enough to take advantage of the extra man, it would seem! This was a crucial result for Wigan, who would probably have settled for a point before the match (Millwall were currently fifth in the table and on a good run). Momentum had been maintained, and Peterborough United (five successive defeats) shouldn't pose too much of a problem at the DW Stadium next Saturday.

Another pre-match wander around Wigan town centre made me realise (again) how much pleasanter an environment it presents than the centres of most industrial towns and cities in the north and indeed elsewhere in the country. The quality that makes it special is the almost total absence of modern concrete and glass atrocities.

There are two major new developments containing the familiar high street chain stores, but they're tucked away behind the street frontages, from whence they emerge as arcades. As a result, the shops you pass as you walk around are small-scale businesses: tobacconist, barbers, confectioners (including two Galloways outlets which provide my lunch), and small general stores, plus a range of pubs and eating places. The architectural highlight is probably Wigan Wallgate station, fronted by an ornate glass canopy. The parish church looks impressive too; unfortunately, it's hidden behind the main shopping streets, from which you only get the occasional glimpse of it. So Bryson and Engel were right: Wigan town centre is an unexpected delight.

It was Spurs versus Arsenal on the big screen at the Henhole, where I dropped in for my usual pre-match pint. It made for compulsive viewing. Arsenal were 1-0 up when I arrived but then had a man sent off and quickly conceded two goals, the second a wonderful long-range cross-shot from Harry Kane. I always find it fascinating observing Arsene Wenger's face on such occasions. Worry and tension are built into its fabric at the best of times but faced with setbacks such as Tottenham's two successive goals, it registers deeper levels of agony and despair in a variety of different contortions. It's a shame his talented side puts him through the emotional wringer so often. Like most neutrals, I'd love to see low-budget provincial Leicester City win the Premiership this season, but failing that, I'd settle for Arsenal. Anyway, ten-man Arsenal managed an equaliser shortly before the end, which means that if Leicester could win at Watford in the evening kick-off, they'd have a five-point lead over their challengers (which they duly did).

Onwards (and upwards?) to the DW Stadium, to see if Wigan could gain the three points which everyone was expecting. Struggling Peterborough emerged from the tunnel in a hideous strip that can best be described as a darker shade of pink. Their kit consultant should be dispatched at once to the nearest job centre! But despite the strip and the form-book, the visitors proceeded to dominate play for the first 20 minutes, creating space on both flanks, and creating several chances.

It appeared they would take the lead when a shot from Martin Smith looked on its way into the net. However, it was inadvertently deflected over the bar by team-mate Jon Taylor who – in the process – collided with Wigan's keeper Jussi Jaaskelainen, who was led from the field in a dazed state. He was replaced by debutant Lee Nicholls, a former youth international who has come through the ranks at Wigan. Latics fans would no doubt have been reassured to discover in the match programme that Lee featured as substitute keeper in Max Power's line-up of the best players he has played with during his career.

Wigan then came back into the game and began to create chances themselves. Wildschut should have scored shortly before half-time, but sliced a close-range shot wide. The football wasn't flowing quite as smoothly as it had against Bury the previous week, but Wigan finished the half well on top, and it felt like it would only be a matter of time before they found the net.

The home side continued to dominate in the second half, although Peterborough continued to look dangerous on the break. At least there remained a level of uncertainty and drama in the game, unlike the previous week, when it was in effect all over after 20 minutes. Yanic Wildschut was turning in one of his more erratic performances. In some games, he has been consistently menacing, in others intermittently so. This was one of the latter occasions. For every surging run down the left followed by a cross, there would be a turn into a cul-de-sac and subsequent dispossession. He should certainly have scored in the 70th minute after a characteristic run down the left. Meanwhile, David Perkins was proving outstanding again in midfield, always at the centre of things, always using the ball well, and putting in some crucial tackles.

Shortly after Wildschut's miss, Wigan went ahead when Donervon Daniels retrieved the ball on the right and sent a through ball to Will Grigg who ran unchallenged into the area and finished clinically. The regulars in the West Stand were ecstatic. It had been a long wait. A 1-0 win would do just fine. But Peterborough had other ideas. Ten minutes later, Marcus Maddison hit a stunning free-kick from way out on the left, which evaded the keeper's despairing lunge, hit the post and went in. At last, the 200 or so away fans in the North Stand had something to shout about, and shout they did.

In the remaining minutes, Wigan had several opportunities to regain the lead, but didn't quite manage to do so, with near misses, blocked shots, and some inspired keeping from Ben Alnwick frustrating them. So one-all it ended; two points unexpectedly dropped, but with the unbeaten league run extended to 14 games. David Perkins was deservedly adjudged man of the match.

It wasn't that Wigan had played badly; just not as well as in recent weeks (Walsall and Sheffield United away and Port Vale and Bury at home). On another occasion, one or more of the many chances they created would have been taken.

Wigan's challengers for promotion all did them a favour. Burton drew at Crewe, Gillingham likewise at Scunthorpe, and Walsall obligingly lost 3-1 at home to a resurgent Barnsley. Of the front runners, only Millwall managed to win, at home to an increasingly beleaguered Blackpool side.

*

"Roaring Lions are Ruthless" was the headline of the report in *The Football League Paper* on the Millwall/Blackpool game, which the hosts won decisively and comfortably 3-0. It might have been different if Uche Ikpeazu had put away an easy headed opportunity in the second minute but Blackpool's season has been full of 'might have beens', and by all accounts, they were outclassed at the New Den.

To add to their woes, they had a player sent off for the third game in succession, Haydn White this time, for a second yellow card offence involving some blatant shirt-pulling. What did Neil McDonald have to say? For once he offered no excuses, and lambasted his players for "Not putting their bodies on the line." (Millwall's second goal was a free kick which went straight through a gap which developed in Blackpool's defensive wall, when John Herron (or was it Ikpeazu?) turned his back as the ball came through). "We conceded two of the softest goals I've ever seen," McDonald added, but he also claimed that "the team spirit is still there." But he has to, hasn't he! We'll see next week.

Earlier in the week, Blackpool favourite Brett Ormerod turned down an offer to play his testimonial at Bloomfield Road, "Because of the toxic atmosphere there," preferring to hold the event at AFC Fylde's new stadium at Wesham. What a telling comment on the current plight of Blackpool FC!

*

At this stage of the season (11 games to go) the results of fellow promotion or relegation candidates are just as important as what Wigan and Blackpool manage to achieve. If the results of Wigan's nearest rivals were good news, Blackpool's fellow-strugglers did them no favours at all. Chesterfield won 1-0 at Southend and Shrewsbury 1-0 at Doncaster. There is now a two-point gap between Blackpool in 21st position and Doncaster in 20th, with Fleetwood Town and Shrewsbury Town both five points ahead of the Tangerines. If Blackpool can't muster at least four points from the next two games (at home to declining Coventry and away to erratic Crewe), then the writing really will be on the wall.

Hope springs eternal, or to be more precise it wells up before each new game. Okay, Blackpool are on a bad run, but today may be different. Remember Scunthorpe? It's the same squad of players who scored five that day. Why can't they do it again? Coventry have lost their last four games. Maybe today is the 'new start' we've all been waiting for. It is with such misplaced optimism and clutching of straws that fans of relegation-threatened clubs, like Blackpool, all over the country must be consoling themselves, as the end of the season (and nemesis) draws ever closer.

I made a detour from Blackpool South station to have a look at the South Shore promenade. Bill Bryson is right; it's most impressive, with its sinuous curvaceous lines distinguishing it from the typical 'straight-up-and-down' variety you find in most other resorts. He's also right in his observation that looking out to sea from the prom is fine, but turning to face the buildings is less inspiring. This is the downmarket part of the town's seafront.

There have been some interesting developments in the 'peace initiative' saga. Both the Football Association and the Football League (and indeed the Minister for Sport) have said that they are prepared to come to a meeting to try to help sort out the Blackpool FC problem (but is there any chance they'll be able to agree on a definition of 'the problem'?). It looked like Karl Oyston had been backed into a corner; no allies left (except for the so-called Fans Parliament) and some major national players coming on to the scene. He is no longer in control of the agenda; indeed, his status at the proposed meeting was to be that of invitee. BST were understandably happy about these developments but concerned that there are now signs of a reversion to the original, more limited concept of a meeting which its members had already voted to reject.

Before entering the ground, I watched the customary pre-match demonstration outside the main entrance. Groups of Coventry fans, on their way to the North Stand, walked past the BST contingent and applauded them as they did so. It was a powerful example of the brotherhood which exists between football supporters (Coventry were exiled from the Ricoh Arena for most of the 2013-14 season, playing 'home' games at Northampton Town's Sixfields stadium, before crowds of 2,000/3,000, because of the bizarre behaviour of their absentee middle-eastern owners).

Now that Coventry are back at the Ricoh Arena, their home crowds average around 13,000 (third highest in Division One), and they have a formidable away following. Their travelling fans filled not only their allotted space in the North Stand but almost half the 'temporary' stand as well. It was by far the largest contingent of visiting fans I'd seen at Bloomfield Road this season; there must have been at least 3,000 of them. Again, given the 2,000 or so Blackpool absentees, who are nevertheless included in the official attendance (8,869), there must have been nearly as many away fans as home fans in the ground. As usual, they made a lot more noise; you'd have thought it was Coventry who were at home. There was a spirited rendition of "In our Coventry home" (based on the Liverpool original; apparently there are also two cathedrals in Coventry). They mercifully refrained from "You're supposed to be at home," which would have been eminently justified.

Blackpool had made several changes, some of them necessitated by suspensions, but others no doubt inspired by the manner of the defeat at Millwall. Luke Higham, Emmerson Boyce, Liam Smith and Lloyd Jones were all in the starting line-up; Robertson, Ferguson, Cullen and White were notable absentees. Blackpool started well, and Liam Smith hit a superb 25-yard strike, which was well-saved by the Coventry keeper. The visitors looked as unimpressive as their recent record suggested. At this stage, a rare Blackpool win looked a real possibility.

Then it all went wrong (again).

Coventry forced a couple of corners on the right. From the second, Colin Doyle was clearly (in my view, and in Neil McDonald's) impeded by two visiting players, who looked like they'd been positioned to do just that. The ball then fell kindly for Marc Antoine-Fortune, who scored with ease. *The Football League Paper* thought Doyle had "made a hash of claiming a dropping ball," but that's not how it looked from where I was sitting. He has good grounds for appeal against his post-match rating of 3!

Half-way through the first half, the Coventry fans broke into a resounding chant of "Oyston out" with which many of the fans around me in the main stand joined in, and indeed stood up to applaud the visiting contingent. Another example of the solidarity of supporters of mismanaged clubs. There must be times when Karl feels that no-one loves him.

The second half was awful. Football can be a great spectacle, but it can also be tedious. Blackpool relied on long balls in the general direction of Redshaw and Philliskirk, neither of whom managed to do anything on the rare occasions they gained possession. Mark Cullen came on for Redshaw, but that made little difference. Bright-Samuel replaced Luke Smith, and had one individual burst down the left which promised better things, but hardly saw the ball subsequently. Emmerson Boyce was having an off day; one feels that, at 36, he may be coming to the end of his long and distinguished career. There was no width in Blackpool's attacking strategy (such as it was); there were too many players crowded in midfield and hardly any options down the flanks. They seemed incapable of stringing together a coherent inter-passing movement.

Not that Coventry were much better. They rarely looked like adding to their one-goal lead, but probably felt that they didn't need to. A balding and portly Joe Cole (yes, that Joe Cole) came on as a substitute, and after one excellent through ball to Adam Armstrong, proceeded to misplace passes all over the field. The playing surface was uneven with patches of sand in both penalty areas which didn't facilitate constructive football, but you felt that both sides could have overcome this obstacle better than they managed to do. The game petered out, punctuated by a late ping-pong session of head tennis in the Coventry penalty area, from which nothing productive emerged.

Just before the seven minutes of injury time commenced, there was an invasion of seagulls. Dozens of them flew into Bloomfield Road, circulating the stadium as if seeking inspiration, before departing, disappointed, for a more promising location. It all seemed symbolic, although of 'what' was not apparent. If they had been vultures, the symbolism would have been crystal clear.

*

Meanwhile, Wigan were at Colchester, who had been propping up Division One for some time. An away win looked, if not a foregone conclusion, at least highly likely. Certainly, when Yanic Wildschut (who as usual was causing havoc down the left side) scored neatly ten minutes before half-time, that expectation was strengthened. But Colchester, despite their precarious position, do score a lot of goals (their problem is that they concede them even more prolifically) and two minutes later they equalised through a magnificent 25-yard strike from Alex Gilbey.

Undeterred, Wigan soon took the lead again, when Wildschut found Ryan Colclough in space, and he slid the ball past the keeper. Colchester's manager Kevin Keen described Wigan's performance, especially in the first half, as the best he'd seen since he arrived at the club before Christmas. But his team were acquitting themselves well, and Elliot Lee, on loan from West Ham, equalised with an impressive long-range strike (something he'd never managed to do in a brief and unproductive loan spell with Blackpool earlier in the season).

Then George Moncur put Colchester ahead from the spot after he'd been fouled by Reece Wabara. It looked like a major upset was on the cards, and more importantly a blow to Wigan's prospects of automatic promotion. But, at the end of the 90 minutes, Will Grigg was in the right place at the right time to convert Craig Davies' deflected pass. In what was a thoroughly entertaining game (5 stars in *The Football League Paper*) Wigan deserved at least a point on the evidence of possession (64%) and shots (17 to Colchester's 13), and the unbeaten run has extended to 16. But four of the last six games have ended in draws, and with Walsall (4-1 winners at Chesterfield) snapping at Wigan's heels, a couple of wins in the games against Bradford and Swindon would help restore momentum.

*

The following Tuesday, Blackpool had a vital rearranged game at Oldham, who were a point behind Blackpool, but with two games in hand: one of a series of cup finals, as Neil McDonald predictably described it.

Oldham had improved since the appointment of John Sheridan in January and had managed 0-0 draws at both Blackpool and Wigan earlier in the month (the first a game of unremitting tedium, and the second one in which Wigan were fortunate to emerge with a point). In another undistinguised game of few chances, Oldham ended up winners, thanks to a goal from Tom Palmer, following one of the few fluent attacking moves of the match. Blackpool had matched their opponents in the first half, but once they'd conceded a goal, never looked like getting back in the game. "We were rubbish," admitted Neil McDonald afterwards. They must have been… the manager rarely makes comments as damning as this! As a result, Blackpool dropped to 22nd place, two points from safety. A win at Crewe was essential if the circling vultures are to be dispersed.

*

The Crewe game was the crunchiest of crunch matches, not just for Blackpool, but also for Crewe. Blackpool had managed a meagre couple of points from the last eight games, and confidence was at a low ebb. Crewe had managed three from the last seven matches, and no doubt had a similar problem. Neil McDonald thought his side needed five wins from the last nine games (and even that might not be enough; clubs with 50 points have been relegated in recent years). Crewe, next to bottom, had to win today to have any realistic chance of staying up. A draw would be of little use to either team.

It was a nostalgia-seeped return to Gresty Road for me. The last time I'd been there was in the early 1960s, to witness Stockport County's exit from the FA Cup (Crewe went on to hold the mighty Spurs to a 2-2 draw there in the next round, but lost the replay 8-2). I remember the bank of cinders which constituted the Railway End (a 'collector's item' matched only by Wigan's grass-covered Shevington End in their Springfield Park days). The rest of Gresty Road was then in a ramshackle state, but not so now. There's an impressively large main stand in which I was seated, which totally dwarfs the other three, each of which has at most nine or ten rows of seats.

There was a reasonable number of Blackpool supporters in the stand opposite where I was positioned (518 of them, it later transpired). They were making a lot of noise, which continued throughout the game, providing a level of support for the Tangerines which contrasted sharply with to the lukewarm climate in the Main Stand at Bloomfield Road. I suspect that a fair proportion of them were people who are boycotting home games but are prepared to turn out when Blackpool are playing away.

Blackpool started with three strikers (Cullen, Redshaw and Philliskirk) and dominated play from the start, managing more shots on target in the first 20 minutes than they had done in several entire games recently. Crewe were unimpressive, although they had a couple of good chances, including one when Brad Inman had only Colin Doyle to beat. The keeper smothered the shot well.

It turned out to be a crucial save. Ten minutes before half-time, Blackpool went ahead, when a header from Jim McAllister hit the crossbar, and Jack Redshaw was well-positioned to head in the rebound. In the rush to celebrate in front of the delighted Blackpool fans, Redshaw was booked, although as far as I could see, he'd done nothing more than slide along the turf on his knees, a commonplace occurrence nowadays. But how costly that celebration proved to be! Two minutes later Redshaw accidently caught David Fox on the head with a high boot and received a second yellow followed by the inevitable red. It all seemed so unjust; a standard form of celebration followed by an accident, as a result of which Blackpool were down to ten men. As half-time approached, the scale of the visitors' task in holding on to their lead became apparent, as Crewe began to dominate the game.

The Blackpool fans had, of course, made their views about Karl Oyston clear, and must have been gratified to hear Crewe supporters joining in with the "Oyston out" chant. There is clearly a good deal of sympathy for their situation around the football grounds of the country. There were also some expressions of disdain for Neil McDonald. But what was really refreshing was the way they had supported and encouraged their team throughout the half. Could they now inspire them to an unlikely, against-the-odds victory?

Well, over the next 35 minutes, the chances of victory moved from possible to probable. Crewe had the bulk of possession, and several near misses, including shots which hit bar and post respectively. But they were not playing well, and the long-suffering home crowd was becoming increasingly restive. Blackpool looked just as likely to score, in their frequent breakaways, typically featuring Brad Potts, now back to his best. On two occasions, he received the ball just outside his penalty area and ran the length of the pitch, in one case hitting the post and in another setting up Danny Philliskirk with an opportunity he should have taken.

This was a rejuvenated attack-minded Blackpool, who managed 16 shots (nine on target). When did that last happen? But just when it looked likely that the ten men would gain a deserved victory, a mazy run down the right by Oliver Turton set up Marcus Haber, who back-heeled the ball for Crewe into the net from close-range.

Despair turned to joy a couple of minutes later when, following another breakaway, Tom Aldred found space in the Crewe penalty area (what was he doing there!) and his shot was deflected by a defender and looped over the despairing leap of keeper Ben

Garrett. There followed another mutual celebration between players and fans, some of whom spilt on to the pitch. But no yellow cards this time.

But this compelling drama of a football match was not yet over. In the last minute of normal time, substitute Emmerson Boyce tripped Crewe's Tom Hitchcock to concede an undisputed penalty. Up stepped Brad Inman… to balloon the ball over the bar. There followed one of the loudest and most heartfelt renditions of "You're a load of rubbish," from the home supporters that I've ever heard. And they were right.

Even then, the drama was not over. In the very last minute of injury time, a goal-bound header was headed off the line by Hayden White. Then, at last, the final whistle, and more (wholly justified) celebrations. The Blackpool ten; heroes all!

The Football League Paper awarded the match five stars for entertainment value, a rare accolade on their part. They were right to do so; it was a game full of the drama which makes football, at its best, such a nerve-shredding, but rewarding experience. It's not that either team was particularly talented. I overheard a conversation between two Crewe regulars at half- time. "Two poor teams," one of them said. "No. One poor team and one very poor team," the other replied. But two poor teams managed to create a spectacle which was gripping from start to finish. Comedy, tragedy, pathos, injustice, heroes and villains were all there in abundance.

As a result, Blackpool ended the day outside the bottom four (all their fellow-strugglers conveniently lost). They still have a long way to go, but there is now a glimmer of hope that was not apparent after the Oldham game.

*

Meanwhile, Wigan were up against Bradford City, a team in a playoff position who don't score many goals, but who concede even fewer. It was not likely to be a high-scoring game, and that's the way it turned out. In a game of few chances, Wigan clinched a priceless win in the 80th minute, when Haris Vuckic, a second-half substitute, took the ball to the by-line, rounded the outrushing keeper, and steered the ball into the net from a very tight angle. Walsall also won, though they left it very late at home to bottom club Colchester, coming from behind to secure a 2-1 win with goals in the 89th and 94th minutes. Both clubs are on 68 points, but Wigan have a greatly superior goal difference. It's as tight at the top as it is at the bottom.

*

It was Good Friday. Blackpool were at home to Bury and Wigan away to Swindon. There are times when some promotion and relegation issues are settled over the Easter weekend, but not this year. We were still in March, and Blackpool had eight games left to play; Wigan nine. I could have gone to Bloomfield Road but decided against it. It was a sunny day, and day-trippers would be pouring into the resort by road and rail.

I also feared an anti-climactic follow-up to the stirring scenes the previous Saturday at Gresty Road. Besides, Wigan were making a rare appearance live on Sky Sports in a 5.30 kick-off, which I wouldn't have wanted to miss. So I followed Blackpool's progress on *Saturday Soccer Special*.

It turned out I had made a wise choice. Ian Dowie was the commentator allocated to the game, and he could find little to say whenever he was brought on air. Bury dominated the first half, and Blackpool were booed off the field at half-time. They started with yet another on loan striker (Jacob Blyth from Leicester City) although he'd never actually played for their first team. He had, however, scored five goals for Burton Albion in a loan spell the previous season when they were on their promotion run. Apparently, he had been formidable in pre-match training sessions, although I'm not sure I'd read too much into that.

Blackpool improved in the second half, and went ahead 15 minutes from the end when Danny Philliskirk was tripped in the area, and then coolly despatched the resulting penalty. The lead lasted two minutes. Following a break down the right, Ryan Lowe crossed for Danny Mayor to sweep the ball home from close range. It's a pity Blackpool can't reproduce the inventiveness and commitment to attack which they showed against Crewe on a more consistent basis. But then Crewe were a very poor side, and middle-of-the-table Bury proved much better-organised.

In BST's weekly column in the *Gazette*, there were some interesting statistics about Blackpool's crowd figures. Having been informed of an accurate method for working out actual, as opposed to recorded, attendances at Bloomfield Road, BST revealed that the number of non-attending season ticket-holders had averaged at around 2,700 in three recent home games. As there are 4,600 who have season tickets, this means that over half of them are choosing, for one reason or another, not to use them. This research also helps to explain the discrepancy between the large numbers of vacant seats in the home supporters stands and the published attendance.

To take one example, the published attendance figure was 8,790 for the recent game against Bradford City. But the actual number of home supporters present totalled 3,047 excluding the 2,680 absent season-ticket holders. The actual attendance figure was 6,100, of whom over half (3,063) were visiting fans. Thus the away fans actually outnumbered the home fans, an outcome which was repeated in the next game against Coventry City. It shows how far interest has fallen; even in the calamitous 20014-15 season, the average home attendance was close to 11,000.

At 5.30 p.m. there were three customers, including me, in the White Hart in Kendal. Neither of the others were interested in watching Wigan take on Swindon, but the landlady obligingly turned up the volume for my personal benefit, so that I could savour the 'big match' atmosphere.

Wigan were playing in their usual composed fashion but were jolted out of any emergent sense of complacency when Swindon's Nathan Thompson embarked on a solo run which ended with a powerful shot scudding close to the post (but just the wrong side from his point of view).

Wigan soon got back into a rhythm and began to dominate the game. Recent loan signing Steve Warnock from Derby County (previously with Liverpool and Aston Villa) had replaced Jason Pearce and was blending in seamlessly. The breakthrough came midway through the first half when Chris McCann made ground down the left and crossed for Will Grigg to volley the ball home; an impressive strike given that McCann's cross was miscued. Swindon were making little impression, and Wigan should have added to their lead when a free-kick from Max Power somehow evaded the unmarked head of Craig Morgan and the unmarked feet of Will Grigg in quick succession.

Five minutes into the second half there was an inspired burst of attacking football from Wigan which ended the game as a contest. First Max Power cut in from the left and unleashed a superb right-footed drive into the far corner. A definite goal-of-the-month contender. I noticed in the replay how well-balanced his body posture was as he made contact; maybe that's the secret behind his succession of memorable long-range strikes this season. The 1,400 Wigan fans who'd made the long trip and who were positioned right behind the goal were in raptures.

Then, a minute later, Will Grigg scored his second, courtesy of a wicked deflection which left the keeper helpless. Two further minutes had passed before a cross from Yanic Wildschut found Sam Morsy on the edge of the area, and he scored with a well-placed daisy-cutter. Game over.

Wigan went close soon afterwards through Chris McCann, and could well have notched another two or three, had Gary Caldwell not decided to take off three of the players who had been so effective – Power, Wildschut and Grigg – and replaced them with

Tim Chow, Craig Davies (who rarely scores nowadays) and Andy Kellett. Fair enough, I suppose, when the game is clearly won, but it would have been nice to see a rare five or six goal away victory.

Ajose pulled a goal back for Swindon near the end, and Nathan Thompson was sent off for a nasty foul on Chris McCann before the Wigan players celebrated a vital and hugely impressive win with their delighted supporters. That makes it 17 games unbeaten in the league and 15 successive undefeated games away from home. They deserve to make it back to the Championship with a record like this, and for the quality of football they have been playing.

*

Three days later Wigan were at home to in-form Rochdale who had won five of their previous six games and who now had a real possibility of reaching the playoffs. Their manager Keith Hill, in a pre-match interview, persisted with his 'How can little Rochdale compete with a big club like Wigan, but we'll give it our best shot' theme, familiar from Wigan's visit there in November.

I really think this 'big club' perspective is overdone.

Okay, it's the third year of the parachute payments, but Wigan's average home gate is only 8,000/9,000, far fewer than those of Bradford City, Coventry City and Sheffield United, and less than Barnsley and Millwall. Before their unexpected rise to fame in the mid-2000s, Wigan were widely seen as a little club, and may well become so again, especially if the Whelan dynasty were to lose interest. So Keith, give it a rest, will you!

Rochdale brought a large and noisy contingent of supporters, which always helps the atmosphere in the stadium. The early exchanges were evenly contested; both sides demonstrating some neat approach work, but neither creating much in the way of chances. Wigan were enjoying more of the play, but the final ball invariably lacked precision.

Colclough was struggling to make an impression on the right, although Wildschut, as usual, looked threatening on the left whenever he got the ball. Then, in the 35th minute, came a potentially game-changing moment. Wigan's Jason Pearce put in a bad tackle on Rochdale's leading scorer Ian Henderson, directly in front of the two managers. From where I was sitting, high up in the East Stand, it looked like it merited a yellow card (which is what it eventually received), rather than a straight red, although some referees would have disagreed (and Keith Hill certainly did).

Henderson then kicked out at Pearce, who was slumped in a heap next to him, with the fourth official looking on. Following a consultation between the latter and the referee, the Rochdale player received his marching orders (I hadn't realised that fourth officials could intervene in such a decisive way). For the rest of the half Wigan piled on the pressure. Perkins made a storming run down the left, but his tempting low cross managed to evade everyone. At half-time, the game was still goalless.

For the second half, Wigan brought on Conor McAleny for the ineffective Colclough, which quickly turned out to be a good move; there was now penetration down the right flank as well as the left. Wave upon wave of attack battered the Rochdale defence. Wigan was like a remorseless machine. They would pass the ball around at the back until someone spotted an opening up front, typically inside the flanking defenders for Wildschut or McAleny to run on to and then produce dangerous crosses. But still a goal wouldn't come.

Haris Vuckic came on for Jason Pearce and then Chris McCann for Sam Morsy, both of whom provided additional options in attack. Still no breakthrough, as a result of a combination of some inspired goalkeeping from Rochdale's Josh Lillis and a series of crosses which somehow evaded outstretched feet or heads.

Wigan were playing really well. It can be frustrating playing against ten men all spending most of their time in their own half, but the home side were frequently carving open Rochdale's defence. Just when it was beginning to look as if the visitors would hold out for a valiant goalless draw, the goal came at last. It was the scruffiest of goals; a Wildschut header rebounded off the bar to Vuckic, who couldn't squeeze the ball in. But in the confusion which followed, McAleny stepped forward to poke the ball home from close range.

Rochdale then had to push forward and began to look dangerous from set-pieces. In doing so, they left a good deal of space at the back, on which Wigan failed to capitalise. The last few minutes were purgatory for the home supporters. Shouts for penalties were turned down. Surely Wigan wouldn't drop two valuable points by conceding a late goal? To widespread relief, they didn't. It would have been a blatant injustice if they hadn't won, but they certainly kept the agony going until the very end.

As soon as I returned home, I checked the Doncaster/Blackpool result. A 1-0 win for the Tangerines, lifting them to 19th place, although both Oldham and Fleetwood are only one point behind, with games in hand. I read the match reports the next day. As I'd expected, it had been an undistinguished scrappy game; too much at stake to expect anything different.

Neil McDonald had opted for a defensive formation, but even so, Blackpool had created the better chances. They were fortunate when half-way through the second half Tommy Rowe (once with Stockport County) hit the bar, and even more so when, in the 87th minute Mark Cullen was put clear on the left, courtesy of an astute through ball from David Norris, and his shot deflected off a defender and spiralled into the net. A close replica of Tom Aldred's equally fortuitous winner at Crewe.

All the bad luck that McDonald has been moaning about throughout the season has now been amply compensated for by two strokes of good fortune within eight days. The outcome is that Blackpool have recorded two of the five wins which, two weeks ago, McDonald felt they needed to stay up. Three more are required from their final six games, which include Colchester at home and Fleetwood away. The fight for survival is clearly going right to the wire. Maybe I should book my ticket for the final game at Peterborough on May 8th.

CHAPTER 12
APRIL: THE CRUELLEST MONTH

Six games to go. At least three more wins needed. The first of Blackpool's games was at home to Southend United, who, having hovered within sight of the play-off places for a few months, were currently six points adrift of them. It is always tempting in such circumstances to think that their motivation and commitment may have diminished and that three points will be there for the taking. But that is rarely the way it works. There was no questioning Bury's commitment at Bloomfield Road on Good Friday, and they arrived firmly anchored in mid-table with no prospect of either promotion or relegation.

Blackpool started with the 11 that had just about managed to overcome a dismal Doncaster side on Easter Monday. It was my first chance to see Jacob Blyth, yet another on-loan striker, who has apparently proved so impressive in training, but has yet to make much impression in the real world. Blackpool got off to a lively start (they often do; the problem is that they rarely sustain it). Blyth and Cullen both had powerful shots saved within the first three minutes. Then a typical Brad Potts pile-driver rebounded off the Southend keeper but unfortunately, not into the path of a team-mate. So far, so good.

Southend came more into the game, and their Congolese international Jamar Loza should have put them ahead, when the ball was deflected into his path, two yards from goal, with Colin Doyle scrambling across his line. He hit the post, and the rebound was ballooned over the bar by Will Atkinson. Back came the home side after this let-off, and another Potts scorcher went narrowly wide, after what was an untypically excellent passing movement. Southend were producing the slicker approach play, but Blackpool were creating the better chances. At half-time, you felt that the match could go either way, or indeed finish goalless, which would be of little use to either side.

Three minutes into the second half, Blackpool went ahead. In a crowded penalty area, a diverted shot from David Norris found its way through to Mark Cullen, at head height on the edge of the six-yard box. His well-placed header evaded Daniel Bentley, and the home side had a precious lead. The Southend players made it clear that they thought Cullen was off-side, and it certainly looked close, but the linesman obligingly kept his flag down, and the goal stood. Sadly, Blackpool have finally succumbed to the choreographed goal celebration bug, after months of managing without it. Cullen ran to the edge of the pitch, dived into a prone position, and soon found nine bodies piled on top of him, which must have been extremely uncomfortable for him. And of course the banal lyrics of "Glad all over" resonated around the sparsely filled stadium.

Predictably, Blackpool then fell back into defensive mode, and Southend piled on the pressure. Defending a one-goal lead in depth for the best part of 40 minutes is always a high-risk strategy, but it had worked for Blackpool on previous occasions (Swindon, Fleetwood, Gillingham) and no doubt reflected the caution inherent in McDonald's approach. Luke Smith came on for Brad Potts, who received a warm ovation, despite a rather erratic performance. On their rare breakaways, Blackpool looked threatening, and ten minutes before the end increased their lead. Mark Cullen made an excellent run down the right, and his cross found Jacob Blyth who had space to switch the ball from left to right foot and smash it high into the net from close range. Cue a replica of the previous celebration!

Southend continued to play some pretty football, but their finishing was abysmal, and Blackpool comfortably played out the last few minutes. So, at last, a home victory, the first since Gillingham were defeated at the end of January. It was one of Blackpool's better performances. The defence was solid throughout with Luke Higham, on the left, a big improvement on the displaced David Ferguson. Mark Cullen had worked tirelessly, scoring one goal and creating the other, and deservedly received a standing ovation when he was substituted just before the end of normal time.

And what of Jacob Blyth? He certainly used his height to his advantage, winning aerial battles with defenders in a way the diminutive Jack Redshaw could never have hoped to do. Some of his headed flicks found Mark Cullen, but others landed in the middle of nowhere. He scored a crucial goal, but otherwise, showed little ability to read the game and often appeared clumsy. In my view, he represented little improvement on Elliot Lee, Uche Ikpeazu, Adam Little, and the rest. But what do I know! Neil McDonald thought he was "terrific" and *The Football League Paper* gave him a nine and included him in the Division One 'team of the day'.

"A massive win" was the view of the *Gazette*, and with ten points from the last four games, Blackpool's fourth mini-run of good results has come at just the right time. But there is still plenty to do. The fourth relegation place now looks likely to be contested between Blackpool, Oldham, Fleetwood, Chesterfield and Shrewsbury, all of whom have one or more games in hand over the Tangerines. In 2004, Peterborough were relegated from the Championship with 54 points. Blackpool may need another three wins, rather than the two that were in the manager's original calculations.

*

Meanwhile, after their game at Shrewsbury, Wigan found themselves at the top of Division One for the first time this season, displacing Burton Albion who could only manage a one-all draw at home to Bury. The Latics are now the bookies' clear favourite to take the title. It was another hugely impressive performance. Finding themselves one-nil down halfway through the first half, they soon equalised through a lethal dipping long-range strike from Conor McAleny, which Max Power could not have bettered. Then in the second half, Wigan ran riot. First, another powerful strike from McAleny hit the post, and the rebound was turned in by Yanic Wildschut from a difficult angle. Then a precision corner from Max Power was met by a decisive header from Jason Pearce to make it three-one. Will Grigg was then brought down in the area by Zak Whitbread, who received a straight red for his pains. Grigg coolly converted the penalty and added a fifth in added time, converting Power's cross from close-range.

Wigan look unstoppable. That's now four wins in succession. Nine goals have been scored in two away games, whilst there have been two hard-fought one-nil victories at home. At both Swindon and Shrewsbury, they hit a purple patch early in the second half, scoring three goals in the space of ten minutes (or to be precise, six minutes at Swindon). The quality of their football is currently in a class of its own in Division One.

*

The following Saturday, Blackpool were at home again, this time to Colchester who look highly likely to be relegated (they're currently ten points behind Blackpool, but have struck a late run of form – seven points from the last three games). The mid-week results had not gone well for the Tangerines, with both Oldham and Fleetwood recording home wins. But if Blackpool could continue their run of success and win, they would be on 48 points, and although still by no means safe, in with a strong chance of survival.

Sadly, they couldn't and didn't and aren't. In a rare display of solidarity, both Neil McDonald and William Watt agreed that they were awful. "Worst display of the season," reckoned the manager, which is indeed a condemnation (remember Shrewsbury and Millwall away, and Doncaster and Port Vale at home, Neil?). Colchester managed 18 shots (seven on target) to Blackpool's six (three) and scored in the 60th minute, following a goalmouth scramble. Before that, they'd hit a post and had a goal-bound shot diverted by Tom Aldred's outstretched leg. Blackpool were outplayed and rarely threatened.

So the question is, where are the next points coming from? The one remaining home game is against Wigan Athletic, the likely champions. Blackpool can only hope that they have clinched the title the previous Saturday and spent most of the following week celebrating. The away games are at Rochdale (inconsistent, but with an outside chance of making the playoffs), Fleetwood (fellow relegation candidates) and Peterborough (mid-table). Blackpool need at least two wins, to reach 51 points, but even that may not be enough. The alternation of hope and despair continues.

*

But it was a good weekend for Wigan. At the DW Stadium, they faced an obdurate Coventry side, who even though out of the promotion race themselves, were clearly not inclined to do Wigan any favours. In an even game of few clear-cut chances, Wigan clinched it with the game's only goal early in the second half. Stephen Warnock made progress down the left and crossed for Will Grigg to get in front of his marker and score from close-range.

That makes it 20 league goals for the Northern Ireland striker, equalling his total with MK Dons the previous season. He should have made it 21 a few minutes later when Conor McAleny was judged to have been fouled in the box, but uncharacteristically his penalty was too close to the keeper and was saved. Another uneasy last few minutes ensued, but Wigan held on, to make it 20 league games without defeat, including 13 wins. The last three home games have all been 1-0 wins (in contrast with their prolific scoring record away from home – 12 goals in the last three games). But no-one will be too bothered about that; Leicester City are continuing their march to the Premiership title with a similar sequence of one-nils (home and away in their case). With Burton losing at Scunthorpe and Walsall at Oldham, Wigan are now four points clear of Burton and ten ahead of third-in-the-table Bradford. The game at Burton in ten days could well decide the title.

*

The home defeat to Colchester had cranked up the pressure on Blackpool to get something out of their visit to Spotland to take on Rochdale. Rochdale still had an outside chance of making the playoffs, and were enjoying a good run; their only defeat in the last six games had been the 1-0 reverse at Wigan. I'd first been to Spotland in the early 1960s to watch a dismal relegation battle with Stockport County (Stockport won, but both teams were ultimately relegated to Division Four). I remember it as a decrepit venue, totally lacking in atmosphere, in part due to the lack of height of the stands, and the space between them and the pitch. Some grounds tower above the terraced streets in which they are set (Grimsby Town, Leyton Orient, and Liverpool are good examples), but not Spotland. If it weren't for the floodlight pylons, the ground would be hard to locate; the stands were little higher than the surrounding houses. When I returned in the early 1990s, there had been significant improvements. The timber-and-cinder terracing of the Pearl Street Terrace (reminiscent of the old Railway End at Crewe's Gresty Road) had been concreted over and given a roof, and the Main Stand had been refurbished.

In 2016, Spotland has a neat, compact, unpretentious feel about it, as befits a club of modest means (and attendances). All four sides are now covered, but one of the end terraces is unseated, which I always feel is appropriate for smaller, lower division clubs. Looking through the attendance statistics in the programme, and allowing for the hugely variable levels of visiting fans, it is clear that around 2,500 local supporters regularly turn up for home games. Rochdale have never graced either of the two higher divisions, so what an achievement it would be if they made it to the Championship this year; a heart-warming example of 'little club makes good.' There was a friendly atmosphere in the Main Stand; very different from the drink-fuelled tensions and foul language of nearby Boundary Park, which I had visited in October.

But none of this would be of any interest to Blackpool, a big club fallen on hard times, who were in desperate need of points. They started well (as usual), encouraged perhaps by a noisy contingent of around 500 supporters. Support at away games is often better than that displayed in the chilly atmosphere of Bloomfield Road, presumably reflecting the attendance of significant numbers of BST members who are not prepared to attend home matches but will travel to away grounds. Chants of "C'mon the Pool" alternated with the inevitable "Oyston Out." It was looking like a game from which Blackpool might come away with something. Rochdale had more of the ball, and their approach play was more inventive, but most of their moves were petering out and the visitors looked dangerous on the break. Mark Cullen was finding space on the flanks and had a couple of reasonable efforts on goal, and Jacob Blyth saw a cross-shot go narrowly wide. But just when it looked as if they would reach the interval on level terms, they conceded a free-kick, which resulted in a goal. Donal McDermott's lofted cross found Ashley Eastham in space close to goal, and he headed Rochdale in front. As the half-time whistle blew, a hailstorm moved in from the West Pennine Moors, symbolising the end of the road for Blackpool (or so it felt).

Five minutes into the second half, Colin Doyle produced an impressive finger-tip save to deny Rochdale a second goal. But from the resulting corner, Blackpool spurned several opportunities to clear the ball, before it fell kindly for Joe Bunney, who smashed it home. Ten minutes later the impressive Nathaniel Mendez-Lang ran onto a through ball and poked it past the helpless Doyle. The hail continued to fall. There was now no way back for Blackpool.

For the final 30 minutes, Rochdale provided a football lesson, carving through the visitors' defence (or what passed for it) at will. They could and should have doubled their lead. Blackpool played without a vestige of self-belief. Redshaw, Smith, and Paterson came on as substitutes but made not an iota of difference. The Blackpool fans continued to sing their way through the now inevitable defeat, including an appropriate rendition of the Beach Boys' classic "Sloop John B" – "I want to go home… this is the worst trip we've ever been on!" They paid tribute to favourites from the recent past ("One Charlie Adam, there's only one Charlie Adam"), and also chanted 'Dino, Dino, give us a wave" (I assume Dino is the name they've given to Neil McDonald), which was followed by an (ironic?) outburst of booing, when he failed to respond. In one corner of the ground, a huge inflatable snowman, decked in a Rochdale scarf, swayed in the wind. And still, the hail came down.

I checked the other Division One results on the car journey home. The crucial game between Fleetwood and Oldham had ended in a one-all draw. Fleetwood's game in hand, the following Tuesday, was at Millwall. If they lost that (which was not unlikely) and if Blackpool won the local derby at Fleetwood a few days later, then the Tangerines would be one point ahead of their local fellow-strugglers, with two games left to play. But after this lamentable display, it was hard to imagine Blackpool beating anyone. William Watt had a similar view. Writing in the *Gazette* the next day, he expressed his concerns thus:

"After watching total capitulation, lack of effort, lack of commitment and a ridiculously poor second half display, I'm starting to wonder if some of this Blackpool squad could care less. Not once did anyone storm into a tackle to set the tone, there appeared to be no arguments amongst the players, and the manager hardly moved from the inside of his dug-out. Blackpool were shaky, spineless carefree, inept, lacking passion and ultimately poor."

William has always striven to be fair and balanced in his columns on Blackpool. He has supported the club since young adulthood and has made it clear that he wants them to avoid relegation. But this must have seemed to him the last straw, to inspire such an emotional outburst. I had every sympathy with him.

I had checked the half-time score at Doncaster, where Wigan were playing, whilst queuing for a cup of much-needed hot Bovril. Wigan were leading one-nil, and on the way to yet another away win, or so I assumed. Imagine my surprise when the final score came through: Doncaster 3 Wigan 1. This was Doncaster's first win since January 2nd, and Wigan's first defeat in the league since December 12th, and the first on the road since September 12th. All good runs have to come to an end sometime, but at Doncaster!!

The reports the next day suggested that it was a well-deserved win. Wigan had gone ahead in the first half when Will Grigg headed home from close range following a typical marauding run down the left by Yanic Wildschut. But early in the second half, Doncaster defender Andy Butler scored twice within five minutes. Wigan then fought back, but couldn't manage a breakthrough, and fell further behind when David Perkins fouled Gary McSheffrey in the area, and Andy Williams scored the resulting penalty, whilst red-carded Perkins left the field for an early bath. Wigan remain top of the table, but the game against second-placed Burton the following Tuesday now takes on an enhanced significance, especially with Walsall, one-nil winners today at home to Southend, lurking in third place, with a game in hand over both clubs.

*

Burton: a town built on beer. You can smell the malty aromas of the brewing process as soon as you exit the station. And you can see the evidence of the town's economic base as you walk through its centre; a mixture of lovely, often ornate old brewery buildings and groups of vast shiny metallic cylindrical tanks. I made a detour to admire the impressive Gothic town hall (well it may not have been a priority for you, but my career had been centred on local government!). Then I checked the map and made my way to the Three Queens Hotel, where I was to stay the night.

It was a less straightforward journey than I'd expected. First I had to cross two roads on the edge of a roundabout; one of those roundabouts where cars are perpetually edging forward, seeking to take advantage of momentary gaps in the traffic. Having risked life and limb in doing so, I then found myself needing to cross a busy road bridge, with no pavements on either side. After a perplexing five minutes, I managed to locate a decrepit pedestrian bridge, running alongside the road bridge but with a very obscure access point. Burton was not proving a pedestrian-friendly town! When I finally located my hotel on Bridge Street, the entrance was locked, and there was no intercom. I checked my reservation document. Registration from 3.00 p.m. It was 4 o'clock. A warm welcome awaits you in Burton! I began to wonder whether the proprietors had done a moonlight flit since I'd made the booking, and retraced my steps to a nearby pub to consider my options.

When I returned, I walked round to the back of the hotel, which turned out to be where the main entrance was, adjacent to a spacious car park. Anyone coming by car would have no problem gaining access, but for the odd stray pedestrian like myself, a sign on Bridge Street suggesting that you should go around the back would have been helpful. Once I'd got in, the hotel was fine; highly recommended in the unlikely event of you ever needing to stop overnight in Burton.

I'd arranged to meet *Mudhutter*-editor Martin Tarbuck and a group of fellow Wigan supporters in the Burton Bridge Brewery hostelry, conveniently situated just across the road from the Three Queens. It proved to be a lovely traditional pub, which brewed its own beer somewhere around the back of the premises; a much better bet than the Coors ales which seem dominant in Burton nowadays. We then made our way to the Pirelli Stadium, via a chippie where I was surprised to see that the author of *Life of Pies* opted for a battered sausage and chips, rather than one of the many varieties of pie on sale there.

The Pirelli Stadium, sponsored by the well-known tyre firm whose premises are close by, was built as recently as 2005 when Burton were still in the Conference, from which they were promoted as champions in 2009. It may interest you to know that Burton Albion were established as late as 1950, and have absolutely no connection with either Burton United, who played in the Football League (Division Two) between 1892 and 1907, before disbanding, nor with

Burton Wanderers who played in the same division between 1894 and 1897, before meeting a similarly untimely end. So for three successive seasons, there were two Burton clubs in the same division, at a time when there were only 32 clubs in the entire league. Not many people know this!

The Pirelli Stadium is a compact, well-designed arena with a main stand, and three standing terraces; 1,500 Wigan fans were packed into the East Terrace, with another 200 or so seated in one end of the main stand. The atmosphere was electric, as would be expected in a clash between leaders Wigan (on 80 points) and second-placed Burton (on 77 points) with four games to go before the end of the season. It had been a long time since I found myself standing on a packed terrace in a full stadium, watching a Division One fixture, and it was exhilarating. The Wigan fans were in good voice, as they had been all season at away matches. "Your ground's too small for us," they sang, with a degree of justification; the allocation of tickets to Wigan had sold out in a matter of days. Perhaps to counter possible accusations of arrogance, they followed this with "Our ground's too big for us," a self-deprecatory reference to the fact that the DW Stadium has been around one-third full for most of this season's games.

Within eight minutes they were at full volume. Michael Jacobs, starting for the first time after a long absence through injury, cut in from the right. His cross-shot evaded the in-rushing Will Grigg, and, more importantly, also evaded the Burton keeper, to nestle snugly in the corner of the net. Shortly afterwards Jacobs set up another chance for Grigg, which he couldn't quite reach. Things were going well for the visitors.

As the game progressed, the sunset and the colour of the sky changed from light blue to dark blue with successive tints of yellow and azure on the horizon. It had been a lovely warm spring day; the hailstorm at Rochdale seemed light years ago, although in reality it was only three days earlier. Burton came back into the game and might have had a penalty when Lucas Akins appeared to be impeded on the edge of the area. Rightly (as far as I could judge) the referee ignored the appeals and booked Akins for diving. It was proving an evenly-balanced competitive game of few chances. But ten minutes before half time, Burton created one and took it. A free kick on the left was floated into the box by Matty Palmer, and there was Tom Naylor, towering above his marker, to plant a well-directed header into the net.

Burton were beginning to dominate the game, a situation which continued in the second half. As in the game in November at the DW Stadium, they were proving adept at closing down Wigan's options in midfield, whilst at the same time looking dangerous in attack, though still not creating many chances. It was turning into a rear-guard action for the visitors, who were losing out in midfield, where they were missing the suspended David Perkins. If any side was going to win the game, it was Burton. But Wigan were holding out, despite an over-zealous referee who was minded to blow for a free kick every time a Burton player tumbled to the ground. There were several nail-biting moments for the visiting fans, not least when Jaaskelainen had to clear the ball from the toes of an advancing Burton forward with his feet, after a defensive misunderstanding.

At the final whistle the fans' relief was tangible; holding on for a draw had seemed the best that could be hoped for from half-time onwards. We all departed contentedly into the Burton night. Walsall had also drawn, so Wigan's three-point advantage (and much better goal difference) over their two closest rivals had been maintained. If Wigan beat Southend on Saturday, and either Burton or Walsall lose, the Latics will be promoted.

*

And so to Fleetwood, for what promised to be another tense affair before a capacity crowd, this time at the other end of the table. Fleetwood had indeed lost at Millwall in midweek (unluckily, it would appear) and were on 47 points, two ahead of Blackpool.

Both clubs had three games left to play. A Blackpool win would give them a fighting chance of avoiding the drop. But anything less and they looked doomed.

Fleetwood is an interesting town, stuck out on a limb, topographically-speaking (rather like Barrow in this respect). It is the creation of a nineteenth-century entrepreneur, Peter Hesketh, who owned most of the land in the area and had a vision of establishing a fishing port-cum-holiday resort on the site. In 1831 he changed his name to Hesketh-Fleetwood and proceeded to name the embryonic town after himself (prone to a degree of self-aggrandisement, were some of those Victorians!). It became the first 'planned town' of the Victorian era, with a grid-iron street pattern which is still in place today. His ambitious venture succeeded; in time, Fleetwood became a thriving fishing port (third largest in the country in the early 1900s) and a modest but viable seaside resort for 'those who found the brashness of nearby Blackpool too daunting.' As a child, John Lennon spent his summer holidays there. All was fine until the mid-twentieth century, when the bottom fell out of the holiday trade, as the overseas package holiday boom developed. Very few people now take holidays in Fleetwood. Then the Cod Wars of the 1970s destroyed its fishing industry. The last deep-sea trawler left the port in 1982.

Fleetwood is now a shadow of its former self. Its largest commercial employer is the firm of Lofthouses, who manufacture Fisherman's Friend throat lozenges (now available in a vast number of different flavours). So at least there is still a tenuous economic connection with its fishing past. Their surprisingly large factory is situated close to the football ground. The town has all the hallmarks of deprivation: high unemployment, low average household income, and lots of charity shops and money lenders in the town centre. But it remains a fascinating place steeped in distinctive history. I recommend a visit.

But if the town is in a state of decline, the football club is on the up. Nine years ago they were playing the likes of Kendal Town, as they progressed from the lower levels of the non-league pyramid to the Conference, which they won in 2012, helped considerably by the 31 league goals scored by a certain James Vardy. Two seasons later, they made it to Division One, after defeating Burton Albion in the play-off final. Last season they finished in mid-table, but as late as April were in contention for a play-off place. The generative force behind this remarkable rise to fame is Andrew Pilley, a likeable local businessman, and long-term Blackpool supporter. At one time he expressed interest in buying a stake in his hometown club but was turned down by the Oystons. How Blackpool could do with him now! The two clubs provide a stark contrast. One is an ambitious well-run club with a popular owner and an impressive new training facility, recently opened by Sir Alex Ferguson. The other is Blackpool.

As I made my way to the ground, I passed a house with the sign 'For Sale: Oystons' outside it. If only! The Highbury Stadium (good to see the name of Arsenal's iconic previous ground resurrected in Fleetwood) is an attractive venue of modest scale, which is appropriate for a town with a population of little more than 25,000 (the smallest town to currently host a Football League club). I'd been there once before, in the previous season, to watch an action packed 0-0 draw with Chesterfield. My ticket was for the Percy Ronson Stand (whoever he was), which is a traditional standing terrace. Initially, my access to the ground was denied because I was carrying a pie, purchased from the chippie across the road for £1.50. Did they think I intended it as a missile? When I did manage to get in, I quickly realised the thinking behind this regulation. Pies in the kiosk sold for £3.50. It would have its business decimated if alien pies were allowed in.

The Percy Ronson Stand was full of Blackpool fans, who as usual at away games, were making a lot of noise. There was an Oyston-directed chant I'd not heard before (to the tune of "Sloop John

B")… "You greedy bastards – get out of our club." There were also references to the disparate sizes of the two towns, "You're just a tram stop in Blackpool," being my favourite. To the right was the Main Stand, shaped imaginatively as a semi-circle, with a convex roof. Opposite was a terrace, housing the less affluent home fans, many of whom were waving St George's flags, distributed by the club to mark not just the saint's day, but (more importantly) the Queen's 90th birthday. I opened my programme, which was priced £1, the cheapest by far that I've recently come across. It looked like a throwback to the time they were in the Conference (Northern Section) and took about three minutes to read. Then out came the teams, and the battle commenced.

Fleetwood had the best of the early exchanges, with Amari Bell causing Luke Higham all sorts of problems. But they created little in the way of clear-cut chances, and Blackpool began to come back into the game, with a similar outcome. It was, in all honesty, proving to be a scrappy encounter, but I guess we were never going to get attractive attacking football in this situation (and would Blackpool have been capable of it anyway?).

Hayden White made a couple of good breaks down the right, one of which resulted in an opening for the lively Mark Cullen, but nothing came of it. At the other end, Colin Doyle made a couple of competent, but not overly difficult saves. Then, just before half-time, came what proved to be the game's defining moment. Blackpool's Jim McAllister broke clear on the left, and his cross-shot had the Fleetwood keeper beaten. It looked like it would find the net, but in rushed Danny Philliskirk to make sure, by side-footing the ball home. Delirium ensued in the Percy Ronson Stand. But the linesman had raised his flag for offside, and the post-match video indicated that he was probably right to do so. If Philliskirk had not intervened and the ball had gone in, then offside would not have applied. On the basis of such nuances do clubs stay up or go down.

CHAPTER 12

Blackpool proved more dominant in the second half. They passed
the ball around in midfield to a much greater extent than usual and
created several reasonable chances, including a header from
substitute Martin Paterson, which was tipped over the bar by
Fleetwood's Chris Maxwell. But the elusive goal just would not
come. In one of the home side's increasingly rare attacks, Jimmy
Ryan rattled the angle of post and crossbar, but otherwise, Doyle
had little to do. Shola Ameobi, on loan from Newcastle, came on
and produced a few nice touches, but as the game neared its end,
neither side looked capable of breaking the deadlock. It finished 0-
0. Fleetwood remain two points clear of Blackpool, who are
themselves now only one point above Doncaster, who beat a fading
Coventry City 2-0. So the Tangerines still have it all to do, starting
with next Saturday's home game against Wigan Athletic.

*

Meanwhile, at the DW Stadium, Wigan were seeing off visitors
Southend United in convincing fashion. Chris McCann gave the
Latics an early lead, side-footing the ball home after good work
from Max Power and Michael Jacobs. A few minutes later, a shot
from the resurgent Yanic Wildschut cannoned back off the post and
fell conveniently for Will Grigg to tap the ball past a prone
goalkeeper. Ten minutes before the break Grigg scored again,
lifting the ball over Southend's Ted Smith after an inch-perfect
through ball from Michael Jacobs. Wigan were proving
unstoppable, and early in the second half, Jacobs himself hit the
target, after a shrewd pass from Wildschut. Southend pulled one
back when Craig Morgan inadvertently diverted a stray ball into
his own net, which was probably the only way they were going to
score (two shots, neither on target, compared with Wigan's 18 and
eight respectively).

It was a fitting way for Wigan to clinch promotion back to the
Championship at the first attempt. Walsall lost 4-0 at Bradford, and
although in theory they could still catch Wigan, they would have to
overcome a goal difference of 22 goals to do so. That wasn't going

to happen (or so I would confidently predict). So well done Wigan; your success is thoroughly deserved.

*

Saturday 30th April. Blackpool at home to Wigan Athletic. Barring a couple of highly unlikely goal bonanzas from Walsall, the Latics had already secured promotion. A win (or draw) today would confirm this outcome. Blackpool remained desperate for points. Even if they won today, they could still go down. The kick-off had been switched to 12.30 at the request of the police, ostensibly because of the large number (up to 4,000) of travelling fans expected. But the fact that a large pre-match demonstration, organised by BST, was scheduled to take place may have been a more important consideration for the police. This was Blackpool's last home game of the season, and the parallel occasion in 2015 had seen the infamous pitch-invasion and sit-in by angry supporters, and the subsequent abandonment of the match.

Having long since discarded any vestige of neutrality concerning the BST/Oystons dispute, I joined the march with my friend Phil Hartley, who had been present at the abandoned game (but had not taken part in the pitch invasion, he hastened to assure me). That was the last time he had watched Blackpool. Despite having two season tickets (the second was for the use of one of his three sons) that were valid for the current season, he and they had joined with around 2,000 other supporters and BST members in deciding not to use them until the Oystons withdrew from the club, or experienced a (highly unlikely) change of heart. I had been the beneficiary of this abstention, gratefully accepting the loan of the season ticket for all the games at Bloomfield Road which I attended.

The march started appropriately at the Stanley Arms, which is where the club was formed in 1887. It moved on past the town hall, where someone (presumably from BST) had fixed a facsimile of a 'blue plaque' – the kind that records birthplaces or residences of famous artists or writers – recording the decline of Blackpool FC under the ownership of the Oyston family. Then it progressed on to the Golden Mile and paused at what is known as the celebrity pavement, which records the names of all the famous entertainers who have appeared in Blackpool over the years (as you can imagine, it is a large area of pavement). Several celebrities, most notably James Corden had issued statements of support for BST and the march, as had a number of Blackpool's former players (including Trevor Sinclair and Brett Ormerod).

It was a sunny day, with a cold north-westerly wind. There were as yet no takers for the legendary donkeys, lined up on the deserted beach. The march was good-humoured, even if the content of the chanting wasn't. All ages and both sexes were well-represented (although there was little sign of an ethnic minority presence). Mobility scooters were also in evidence. A burst of applause swelled up from a group of Wigan fans sitting outside a seafront pub. We applauded them in return. I found myself quite moved by this display of solidarity from Blackpool's opponents. (By no means the first time this has happened this season). You sense a deep-felt sympathy for the Blackpool fans' predicament. There but for fortune…

The march finally reached Bloomfield Road about an hour before kick-off. There was a slight sense of anti-climax, although a lot more chanting, a flurry of tangerine smoke bombs, and one or two short speeches. If it had been a political rally, we'd have heard a series of inspiring addresses. But it wasn't and we didn't. However, BST can be well pleased with the way things worked out. It was later estimated that there were 3,000 on the demonstration, a thousand more than last year, and it was well-organised, law-abiding and crystal-clear in its message to the club's owners and the outside world.

After Phil had driven back to Kendal, I made my way into the ground for the last time. Final purchase of a (typically uninspiring) Blackpool programme. Final purchase of an over-priced Holland's meat-and-potato pie. Final walk up to my seat at the back of the

Stanley Matthews Stand. The Wigan fans not only filled the half of the South Stand allocated to visiting fans but half of the 'Temporary' Stand as well. The club had clearly sold out its allocation. A sense of excitement and anticipation simmered throughout the stadium. The Wigan contingent not only joined in with the 'Oyston out' chants, they initiated some of their own. We in the main stand rose to applaud them. Well, most of us did; there must still be a small minority who think that continuing Oyston ownership is the right way forward. We'll see just how small, when the season ticket sales figures are announced at the start of next season. Before kickoff, a plane flew over the ground, trailing a banner which read, "Oyston: club killers: get out now."

In the early stages of the game, it was Blackpool who dominated. As at the DW Stadium in November, they succeeded in stifling the visitors' patient midfield build-up and soon began to create chances. There was no questioning their commitment. Jack Redshaw brought out a good save from Jaaskelainen. Mark Cullen dragged a promising opportunity wide when put clear. And then the best chance of the game fell to Redshaw, following an uncharacteristic bout of hesitancy from David Perkins. With an empty net facing him (but, to be fair, a difficult angle to contend with) his shot cleared the crossbar. Wigan were on the back foot, and must have been expecting a half-time roasting from Gary Caldwell. Blackpool came off to a deserved ovation, but without the lead that their dominance justified.

A similar pattern continued into the second half, although Wigan were beginning to create chances of their own. Then Mark Cullen, as he raced on to a promising through ball on the right, suddenly stumbled and fell, clutching his right thigh. The curse of the pulled hamstring again! That was a blow; Cullen had proved a lively and disruptive presence going forward. I had no such hopes for his replacement, the lumbering Jacob Blyth. And sure enough, with Blackpool's attacking options now more limited, things soon fell apart for the home side. The breakthrough came in the 60th minute.

CHAPTER 12

Chris McCann found himself with time and space, on the edge of the area, to try a shot. Taking a slight deflection from Tom Aldred, it flew into the corner of the net, leaving Colin Doyle helpless. The two banks of Wigan fans erupted, as the whole team (Jaaskelainen apart) descended on McCann, who has been playing an increasingly influential part recently in Wigan's progress. No silly dances, this time, just a euphoric collective embrace.

That goal opened the floodgates. Ten minutes later, Yanic Wildschut, who had replaced Sam Morsy late in the first half, found space on the left of the area and neatly steered the ball past Doyle. Two minutes later, in a similar position, he cut back inside and side-footed the ball into the near corner. For someone whose shooting prowess had come in for criticism recently, he was doing pretty well today. Wigan were now passing the ball around confidently, and tearing holes in Blackpool's shattered defences. Max Power's corner on the right found Craig Morgan, whose header across the face of the goal was neatly nodded in by Will Grigg, his 24th league goal of the season (how could we ever have doubted him?). His goal was greeted by a joyous rendition from the Wigan fans of a recently-composed (not sure by whom) tribute song, which starts "Will Grigg's on fire; your defence is terrified."

By now, many Blackpool regulars had departed. The odd scarf and season ticket had been thrown on to the pitch, and a group of 30 or so disgruntled fans had assembled at the base of the main stand and were gesticulating menacingly in the direction of the directors' box. But mercifully, there was no pitch invasion this time. The final whistle was blown, the Blackpool players trooped disconsolately from the pitch, and the Wigan team, including unused substitutes and those who had been substituted, ran over to the corner of the ground where their supporters were located, for protracted celebrations, in which 80-year-old club owner Dave Whelan joined.

Next week they will be at home to Barnsley, still in contention for a play-off place. Whatever the result, assuming Burton can't manage to score 15 or more goals at Doncaster, Wigan will be champions.

Blackpool go to Peterborough, knowing that if Fleetwood lose at Walsall next Tuesday (likely) and then lose at home to Crewe the following Sunday (highly unlikely), then they will stay up, if they beat Peterborough. Too many ifs, one would have thought, but you never know. The fat lady has yet to sing!

Endgame

Fleetwood did indeed lose at Walsall, so Blackpool, on the last day of the season, were still in with a remote chance of survival. And when Jacob Blyth scored with a header after 16 minutes, that glimmer of hope began to grow. But not for long! The euphoria lasted only five minutes until Fleetwood went ahead against Crewe. Three minutes later they were two up. That effectively meant the end of the road for Blackpool. Fleetwood only had to draw to stay up, and the possibility of Crewe's goal-shy attack scoring three times against the best defence in the bottom half of the table seemed highly unlikely. Such speculation became irrelevant three minutes into the second half when Peterborough equalised from a penalty. As was the case the previous week, Blackpool, whose players must have known the situation at Fleetwood, then fell apart and conceded a further four goals, three of them scored by substitute Jon Taylor in the space of 12 minutes. Blackpool's relegation meant that they had dropped from the Premiership to the fourth tier over a mere six years, which may well be a record.

I was at the DW Stadium, for Wigan's final game. It felt like the season had come full circle. I had driven to Wigan for their first home game, against Doncaster Rovers on a sunny August day. That too had been a 12.30 Sunday kick-off, against a team from a town once the centre of a coal-mining area (as Wigan had been). And here I was on a sunny Sunday in early May to watch them play Barnsley, which also had a strong mining tradition.

But what a contrast in the ambience in the stadium. In August, the sunshine had engendered a degree of lethargy in both teams, who played out an uninspiring nil-nil draw in front of an unenthusiastic crowd of 8,800. Today, the stadium was fuller than I had ever seen it (attendance 18,730 including 4,770 visiting supporters), and there was a carnival atmosphere. This was not just because Wigan would be presented with the Division One champions trophy at the end of the match (their goal difference made them uncatchable), it was also because Barnsley were sitting in the final playoff position, equal on points with Scunthorpe United, but with a marginally bigger goal difference. Their red-and-white-bedecked fans filled the whole of the South Stand. Both the West and East Stands were close to capacity, with vast numbers of blue and white shirts in evidence (had they been brought out especially for the occasion, or purchased the previous week, I wondered?). I was delighted that my final game had real significance, not for Wigan (apart, no doubt, from a wish to delight their fans with a stunning victory) but certainly for Barnsley.

Wigan started with their strongest line-up, with one notable exception. Reserve keeper Lee Nicholls was given a chance to show what he could do, with Jaaskelainen enjoying (or perhaps not) a seat on the substitutes' bench. I was pleased to see that during the previous week, David Perkins had received not just one but three 'Wigan Player of the Year' awards ('Away Player of the Year,' 'Players' Player of the Year' and' Player of the Season' (voted for by supporters)). It's reassuring to discover that my views about the crucial role he has played are widely-shared.

The champions-elect started in confident style, with Yanic Wildschut (as usual) making penetrating runs down the left. In the tenth minute, his cross found Will Grigg, who stabbed home his 25th league goal of the season from close range, thereby probably saving Barnsley's Alfie Mawson (who looked like he'd handled it before it reached Grigg) from a red card. Wigan continued to dominate play, and had further chances, whilst Barnsley were creating very little. But ten minutes before half-time Stephen Warnock upended Barnsley's Ashley Fletcher, and Sam Winnall coolly converted the resulting penalty. Was this a temporary blip in Wigan's progress to another home victory? Barnsley were growing in confidence, and shortly before the interval, the same player scored again, slotting the ball home from close range after a goalmouth scramble.

Two-one down at half-time was certainly not in the Wigan script. Gary Caldwell replaced Donervon Daniels and Yanic Wildschut with Reece Wabara and Ryan Colclough respectively. But things went from bad to worse. Ten minutes after the interval, Lee Nicholls made a horrible mess of a high cross from the right, and when the ball came back to Conor Hourihane on the edge of the area, his astutely-placed curling shot found the net. There was now no way back for Wigan. The home fans' celebrations became muted, and some of the moaners in the West Stand began to find their voices, particularly when Wigan's intricate passing movements found their way back to the keeper, rather than forward to a striker. I began to recollect how annoying I'd found this practice earlier in the season. Barnsley's Josh Brownhill added a fourth with a superb free-kick 15 minutes before the end. And then to cap a miserable afternoon, Chris McCann was guilty of a stupidly reckless tackle on Adam Hamill and was rightly sent off.

Thus Wigan ended the season conceding four goals in a league match for the first time, whilst slumping to their heaviest defeat of the season. In a way, it didn't matter, given that the title had already been won. But it was something of an anti-climax, and I decided not to stay for the formulaic celebrations, which in a way seemed incongruous after the result and the sending-off. Had I been a long-term Wigan fan, I'm sure I would have stayed. But even though I have warmed to the club and its supporters (and indeed the town itself) over the season, and was clear that the title had been won on merit, I was still really an outsider. I made my solitary way back to the carpark.

CHAPTER 13
RETROSPECTIVE

Wigan's title was well-deserved. After an erratic August and September, they had slowly climbed the table, moving into a playoff position by late October, and then progressed steadily upward: second place by mid-February, and first by April 2nd, a position which they never subsequently relinquished. They lost only twice in 2016, amassing 47 points from 23 games. They were well-organised defensively (with occasional evidence of vulnerability) and played some superb attacking football, scoring prolifically (although there were several hard-fought one-nil wins at the DW in the run-in).

Although at the start of the season, several pundits predicted that Wigan would be promoted (often on the basis of their continuing access to parachute payments following their relegation from the Premier League in 2013), I wasn't, at the time, at all convinced. The new manager was young and inexperienced. Sometimes this kind of choice works out, but often it doesn't. The squad assembled for the start of the campaign had almost all been brought in during the close season; only Barnett, McCann, Pearce, and Cowie (plus a few untried youngsters) had been retained from 2014-15, and of these, only McCann and Pearce became regulars. The new signings comprised a mixture of youth and experience, but only Will Grigg had involved a substantial transfer fee. The track records of most of the newcomers hadn't, on the face of it, looked particularly outstanding: Max Power was signed from Conference-bound Tranmere, Donervon Daniels and Michael Jacobs had experienced loan spells the previous season with an abject Blackpool side (for whom David Perkins had been a regular). Craig Davies, signed from Bolton, had found goals hard to come by in recent years. At the start of the season, the question was whether Gary Caldwell could transform this disparate group into a team capable of challenging for promotion.

He could, and he did. After an uncertain start, the Wigan team began to develop an impressive cohesiveness. It was becoming clear that everyone knew what they were supposed to be doing, and were acquiring an instinctive sense of where their teammates would be (or the spaces they would be moving into) at any point in time. There developed a machine-like quality to their play (and the term is not meant critically). Week after week, the team dominated possession and managed more shots than their opponents (I've checked the evidence in *The Football League Paper* statistics!).

In October, a new face appeared at the DW, someone who was to prove crucial in Wigan's continued progress. Yanic Wildschut had cost Middlesbrough over a million pounds when signed from the Dutch club Heerenveen in the summer of 2014. But he hadn't managed to hold down a regular place; during the 2014-15 season, he made only three starts and eight appearances as a substitute. 2015-16 was proving no more fruitful for him, and Middlesbrough had little or no compunction about releasing him to Wigan on loan. It soon became clear that he was able to provide a new dimension to Wigan's approach; a combination of pace, ball-control, and vision which enabled him to embark on marauding runs down the left and create numerous chances for colleagues with his dangerous crosses.

When his loan spell expired in January, the Wigan management wisely decided to seek to make the move permanent, which they succeeded in doing within a week. Wildschut became Wigan's second million pound signing and continued to play a decisive role in the club's inexorable progress to the title. Soon afterwards, the squad was further strengthened when Ryan Colclough was signed from Crewe, Reece Wabara from Barnsley, and Sam Morsy from Chesterfield. All played a part in sustaining the momentum and look good long-term prospects. Conor McAleny was brought in on loan from Everton and scored some vital goals. The experienced Stephen Warnock arrived, also on loan, from Derby County in mid-March and became a regular.

Wildschut apart, the key player, in my view (and that of most of the Wigan fans, given his multiple 'player of the year' awards) has been David Perkins. I doubt whether much was expected of him when he was signed on a free transfer from Blackpool in the close season; probably a 'useful journeyman to have in the squad'. But what a revelation he has been, even to me, who has fond memories of his time with Morecambe in the Conference in the early 2000s. In the 1960s and 70s, there used to be a chant from the terraces of 'He's here, he's there, he's every bloody where... Colin Bell' (or whoever). They should be singing it for David Perkins! He has been at the centre of so much of the midfield play, passing the ball around intelligently (and rarely giving it away), until he (or someone else) has seen an opening develop up-field. His number of completed passes over the season must have been astronomical. As Martin Tarbuck eloquently puts it in *Mudhutter 57*, "The style of play we have adopted requires an engine room terrier, and the 'Albino Iniesta' has been absolutely essential to this role and controlling the whole tempo of the team." Perkins will be 34 in June, and might be seen as 'entering the twilight of his career', but if he can maintain his current prodigious energy levels, I can imagine him playing a key role for Wigan for another couple of seasons.

Of the other regulars, Jussi Jaaskelainen has also belied his advancing years (40 in his case) and put in some class performances in goal, with numerous memorable saves (I recall the Bury game in particular) which have had the fans responding in the same way that they would to a goal. Max Power has improved as the season has progressed, scored some spectacular goals, and exudes an infectious enthusiasm. Michael Jacobs has a touch of class about him and has scored some crucial goals (had he not had a lengthy mid-season break through injury, he could well have doubled his ten-goal tally). Chris McCann has displayed his versatility in a variety of different positions and became increasingly influential in the latter part of the season. Will Grigg didn't impress me at first and was not always in the starting line-up in the autumn months. But from January onwards his goal-scoring record was phenomenal (19 goals in 21 appearances), and he contributed substantively to Wigan's success. Few of his goals have been spectacular, but he developed a happy knack of moving into the right place at the right time and then taking advantage of his foresight.

In defence, Craig Morgan, Jason Pearce and, for a time, Reece James, all played their part. But the important point to stress is the coherence of the whole team and the fluency with which they often played, sometimes hitting a groove where they would score three or more goals within 15-20 minutes (Colchester, Bury, and Southend at home; Swindon, Shrewsbury, and Blackpool away). The sum was more, much more, than the parts.

Wigan had prepared well for their brief sojourn in Division One. They planned ahead. Early in 2015, when relegation was looking increasingly likely, they continued to shed players on high salaries from the Premier League era, and began to identify younger replacements who they felt would help them regain their Championship status. The misjudgement in appointing Malky Mackay was recognised, and in April a new manager was appointed who shared the philosophy of the re-constituted board. When the team hit a brief bad patch before Christmas, the need to strengthen the squad was recognised, and acted upon in the transfer window early in the New Year. By the end of the season, the fans who had criticised decisions made during the 2014-15 season had been won back, and have been rewarded by a decision to significantly reduce all season ticket prices to below £200 for the 2016-17 season, further evidence that this is a club which really cares about its supporters. Wigan's recovery has been impressive, but it has not happened by chance, but rather by foresight and astute planning.

My feeling is that Wigan are well-equipped to survive in the Championship, and may even be capable of challenging for another promotion. No doubt Gary Caldwell will want to strengthen the squad, but I hope he doesn't do so to the extent that the current first team regulars don't have the chance to show what they can do at a higher level. Over the season, and particularly from January onwards (played 23, won 13, drawn 8, lost 2, goals for 48, goals against 24, points 47), they've surely earned the right to do so. Encouragingly, Jonathan Jackson told me that he didn't think major investment in new players was likely.

I look forward to continuing to visit the DW Stadium (even though I no longer have a book to write) to see how they get on. Watching Wigan over the 2015-16 season has been an invigorating and satisfying experience. I particularly relished the one occasion I stood with the Wigan fans at an away match, the crucial game at Burton, late in the season. Having previously admired the passion of their support from elsewhere in the ground (or on TV), it was exhilarating to be in the midst of it. I almost felt like I belonged!

*

Although at various stages in the season Blackpool looked like they had just about enough quality (and certainly enough grit and determination) to survive, in the disastrous final run of matches (played 5, drawn 1, lost 4, goals for 1, goals against 13) it became apparent, that they hadn't, something William Watt had for a long time suspected. In the final analysis, they didn't deserve to stay up.

Although they possessed a well-drilled defence, which on its day could protect a one or two-goal lead, and often did, there was a palpable lack of quality in midfield and a parallel lack of effective striking power up front. The match statistics usually revealed less possession (often much less), and fewer shots on or off target (sometimes a derisorily small number) than their opponents. A meagre total of 40 goals were scored in the 46 league games, less than one per game, and less than any other team in Division One. And of these goals, a significant number were deflected shots, penalties, or own goals. I would estimate that little more than half this total came from well-struck shots or headers.

CHAPTER 13

It would have been much more enjoyable if Blackpool had followed the example of fellow strugglers Colchester, who may have conceded 99 goals, but who managed to score 57. But that was never Neil McDonald's style. It was apparent from early in the season that a defensive strategy, with a reliance on breakaway goals, was the order of the day. In McDonald's defence, it was clear that he had to start from scratch. When training started there were only eight players on the books (one of whom was the legendary Nile Ranger!) and most of them played little part in the subsequent campaign. And at least, unlike its predecessor, his team managed to acquire enough points throughout the season to maintain interest until the final day. But, as far as positives are concerned, that is about as much as can be said.

Of the disparate bunch of players McDonald recruited (or in one or two cases inherited) there were a handful who could look back on the season and feel that they had a made at least a reasonably positive contribution. Tom Aldred had not only performed heroics in defence on numerous occasions – it was invariably his body which was thrown in the path of a goal-bound shot – but he also contributed some decisive goals, including the winners at Wigan and Crewe. If Blackpool had bothered to organise a 'player of the season' event, he would have got my vote.

Mark Cullen worked tirelessly up front, typically with precious little support, and ended up as leading scorer (albeit with a paltry nine goals). Brad Potts, at his best, came across as a determined midfielder, prepared to run at defenders (who can forget the run from his own penalty area to the edge of Crewe's, culminating in a powerful shot which hit the post?) but, unfortunately, at his worst, he provided a passable impersonation of a lumbering carthorse. Jack Redshaw was also prepared to run at defenders, and often managed to find space in attacking positions when others couldn't. But his finishing was disappointing, after a reasonable goal-scoring record with Morecambe. Clark Robertson was reliable in central defence. Hayden White was the best of the loanees, showing a preparedness to overlap on the right and a degree of attacking flair. The youngster Bright Osayi-Samuel showed a lot of pace and promise earlier in the season, and should perhaps have been used more often than he was. The loss of the equally-promising Henry Cameron to injury early in the season was a blow.

But the rest of the squad proved far from satisfactory. David Ferguson, who started the season as club captain struggled from the start and disappeared from the scene from mid-February onwards. Striker Martin Paterson, who was a Northern Ireland international, was regularly brought on as a substitute by McDonald midway through the second half, but never managed a single goal. The two mid-season signings from Oldham, Danny Philliskirk and Mark Yeates, made little impression. None of the loan signings apart from White made significant contributions, including the gawky Uche Ikpeazu, and the homesick Elliot Lee.

In the aftermath of Blackpool's defeat at Peterborough and relegation, the *Blackpool Gazette* was awash with responses to this outcome from the manager, players, former players, the Blackpool board, Owen Oyston, and BST, to name but several. But earlier that week, there had been a significant and well-publicised statement from Councillor Tony Williams, who had, during the previous three months, been attempting to arrange a meeting between Karl Oyston and the fans (which at one time was also scheduled to involve the Football League, the FA, and even the Minister for Sport) to try to sort out the future of Blackpool FC., 'for the good of the town'. Councillor Williams had now abandoned his attempt to negotiate a peace deal and was calling for the owners to leave, for the following reasons.

"I had a lengthy meeting and a subsequent telephone conversation with Karl Oyston, and also discussions with the fans associations... I have to sadly conclude that it would be highly unlikely that the differences between the club and the fans could be resolved around the negotiating table. In my opinion, the distrust runs deep, and it could be that Blackpool FC's only hope for a return to glory would be, as many fans have already confirmed, for the Oyston family to walk away.

"I did originally believe Karl's father, Owen, when he claimed to be a passionate supporter of the club… however I cannot understand why he has allowed the situation to continue to fester and grow, eating into the very heart of the club he claims to love so much.

"I would suggest that Owen Oyston needs to intervene with immediate effect, starting meaningful and positive dialogue with BST. He should also appoint someone new to take over the helm at the club, and try to salvage any last-minute opportunity to save both the integrity and future of Blackpool FC."

This was a significant development, which leaves the Oystons even more isolated than before. Councillor Williams had made a genuine attempt to act as peacemaker but had clearly come to realise the futility of persuading the Oystons to come to the negotiating table.

So how would the owners react in the aftermath of relegation? The statement issued the following Monday acknowledged that "The Board takes full responsibility for the position we are in. Mistakes have been made in the last few years, and we continue to pay for some of them, whilst learning from others."

The crucial question was what sort of mistakes did they think they had made? A few days later, Owen Oyston, in a rare interview provided more detail. "We haven't done a thing right in football terms for four years," he claimed. "We've certainly been wrong about managers; they didn't fit in." He went on to mention the fact that the pre-season changes to longer-term contracts for players hadn't worked either (though the previous use of short-term contracts had resulted in the premature loss of some valuable players and promising youngsters).

It is clear that the perception of 'mistakes' was limited to errors of judgement about managers and players. There was no concern expressed about the financial management of the club nor the hugely problematic relationship with the fans. Indeed, in relation to the former, Owen claimed that "Financially, we've been a huge success. The net value of the club has risen from a minus figure in 1987 to £38.7 million, at cost, in 2016." I'm no accountant, and can't judge whether this is a healthy financial position for a club of the size and status of Blackpool, but any sensible evaluation would surely have to compare financial performance with success on the field. Over six seasons, the club has descended from the Premiership to Division Two, which (Portsmouth apart) is probably a record for 'speed of descent'.

The content of Owen Oyston's emotional interview contains some inconsistencies. "The club is not for sale. It's never been for sale. I don't want to sell it. I love it too much to want to sell it." In which case why did the Oystons spend three months seriously considering the leverage bid from BST in the autumn of 2015? And as one social media response aptly put it, "If you love the club so much, set it free!" His comments about the fans might also raise an eyebrow. "The fans are amazing. I love their passion (has he actually watched a game at Bloomfield Road recently?). I'm asking the fans to come back and give us a chance to prove we can get it right." Later, he claimed, "I'm not sure what the fans want."

In commenting on what he described as a "somewhat surreal interview," BST chair Steve Rowland pointed out that BST have been trying to initiate a dialogue with the Oystons for three years, in which they could have made it crystal clear what the fans wanted. In any case, I can't imagine that the Oystons aren't aware of their position; the BST column in the *Gazette* has regularly set out their concerns and objectives.

Maybe the best way for Owen to inform himself would be to listen to BST vice-chair Christine Seddon's BBC Radio Lancashire interview on April 8th. In it, she passionately articulates the love which Blackpool fans in general, and BST members in particular, have for the club, and the sadness with which they have witnessed the club's spiral of decline over the past four years. She has no doubts as to where the blame lies. The opinion column in the *Gazette* on May 9th echoed her sentiments:

"A club is nothing without its fans and this marriage is utterly doomed… sadly, the bitterness and hatred is so deeply entwined, there can be only one outcome, if we are to prevent the seemingly relentless march to oblivion. It's time to do the decent thing, Karl, before any more damage can be done."

The Board's statement of May 9th claimed that "fan representation on the Board had already been initiated" (a reference to the now almost moribund Fans Progress Group). It promised that "a democratic process for fan Board membership will be implemented in the coming season, with fans having a large say in shaping policy" which sounds encouraging until the statement adds that "areas of control will be devolved to the Fans Progress Group."

If the Oystons are serious about involving the supporters (and I have yet to be convinced of this) that involvement has to focus on BST. Throughout their history, they have been the de facto voice of the fans. They have behaved imaginatively and responsibly. They have a high level of credibility everywhere, except within the enclosed world of the Oyston family. Any initiative which bypasses or marginalises them is doomed to failure.

And what of Blackpool's beleaguered manager? Neil McDonald admitted to being "embarrassed" by the team's performance at Peterborough. He said afterwards, "It's been an impossible job. I don't think the club has been shown in a good light by anybody, and I mean anybody," which I take to be a thinly-veiled reference to the Oystons. It was widely expected that he would be sacked, but after a meeting with Karl Oyston the following weekend, it was reported that he would remain (maybe the costs of cancelling his contract were an obstacle?), unless of course he decides that he's had enough. This may well be the case; he is reported as being less than happy about proposed cuts to his staff, budget, and wages. Apparently, doubts have been raised about the future of the goalkeeping coach and kitman as full-time members of staff. Consideration is being given to ending the funding of players' meals before and after training sessions, and to cutting back the practice of overnight hotel stops before away games. If these ideas are implemented, it suggests that there is little hope for a revival of the club's fortunes. A meanness of spirit is apparent here, which is at odds with Owen Oyston's claim that he "wants to see the club strong."

Steve Rowland, on behalf of BST, is clear that McDonald should be replaced. "McDonald is not the man to take us forward," he argues. "He's probably a nice guy, but he hasn't got the ability to get the best out of players. Tactically, he's not of an attacking mind, which we've always been when we've been successful." I think he's right. The prospect of a further series of streaky 1-0 wins or dismal 1-0 defeats does not appeal. It's just not the Blackpool way!

Three days later, the uncertainty was ended. McDonald was deemed to have failed in the 'impossible job', and was relieved of his duties. He claimed that he had left the team in a stronger position than he had inherited it, which is arguably true, in a limited sense. 16 players have been retained, several of whom – Redshaw, Cullen and Potts for example – may find Division Two, where they have performed well in the past, an environment to which they are more suited than Division One. At least next season will start with a degree of continuity. We shall see.

As noted earlier, Wigan had foreseen the probability of relegation halfway through the 2014-15 season, and taken early steps to deal with its implications. Sadly, the same cannot be said of Blackpool. William Watt is clear that there was a missed opportunity at the end of the 2014-15 season. If Karl Oyston had been prepared to acknowledge that the season had been a disaster, admit the contribution of his own misjudgements, and made a serious offer to BST to become involved in the running of the club, then it may have been possible to at least mitigate the conflict and bad blood that had developed between owners and fans, and perhaps also to halt the decline of fortunes on the pitch. But the opportunity was missed, and the toxic atmosphere surrounding the club has worsened. Until the Oystons are prepared to invest in the club, and show a degree of appreciation of, and respect for, its fan base, it is hard to see any prospect of improvement. All football clubs, including Blackpool, are only viable if they can generate the support necessary to sustain them as going concerns. The *Gazette* is right, "A club is nothing without its fans."

My outstanding memory of watching Wigan is being in the midst of their passionate fans at Burton Albion, witnessing the one-all draw which took them a step nearer to the title. For Blackpool, it is being part of the protest on the penultimate Saturday of the season, when I joined 3,000 or more Blackpool supporters in marching through the town, to express our concern about was has happened to a once-proud and successful club, and to demand action to halt its decline. Whilst I will certainly return to watch Wigan at the DW Stadium next season, I will delay any return to Bloomfield Road until the time when BST have achieved their aims, or enough of them to be prepared to end their own principled boycott. It may take a long time, and things may have to get worse before they get better, but that day will surely come.

There's a passage in Bobby Robson's book *Newcastle: My Kind of Toon*, which seems apposite to the very different climates which currently prevail at Blackpool and Wigan:

"What is a club, in any case? Not the buildings or the directors or the people who are paid to represent it. It's not the television contracts, get-out clauses, marketing departments or executive boxes. It's the noise, the passion, the feeling of belonging, the pride in your city. It's a small boy clambering up stadium steps for the very first time, gripping his father's hand, gawping at the hallowed stretch of turf beneath him, and without being able to do a thing about it, falling in love."

OTHER BOOKS FROM BENNION KEARNY

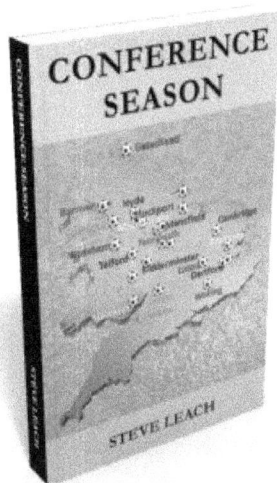

Conference Season by Steve Leach

Disillusioned with the corporate ownership, mega-bucks culture, and overpaid prima donnas, of the Premiership, Steve Leach embarked on a journey to rediscover the soul of professional football. His journey, over the 2012/13 season, took him to twenty-four different Football Conference towns and fixtures, visiting venues as diverse as the Impact Arena in Alfreton, Stonebridge Road in Ebbsfleet, and Luton's Kenilworth Road.

Encountering dancing bears at Nuneaton, demented screamers at Barrow, and 'badger pasties' at rural Forest Green – Steve unearthed the stories behind the places and people – it was a journey that showed just how football and communities intertwine, and mean something.

As the season progressed Steve relished how unfancied teams of part-timers, such as Braintree Town and Dartford, could defeat higher status opponents, and watched 'big name' clubs such as Luton Town and Lincoln City struggle to make an impact. Throughout all this, his anguish grew at the prospect of his beloved Stockport County getting relegated.

Conference Season is a warm and discerning celebration of the diversity of towns and clubs which feature in the Conference, and of the supporters who turn up week-after-week to cheer their teams on.

Bennion Kearny publishes a lot of books on football.

You can see all our soccer books at:
www.BennionKearny.com/football

<< Or click on the QR code to the right >>

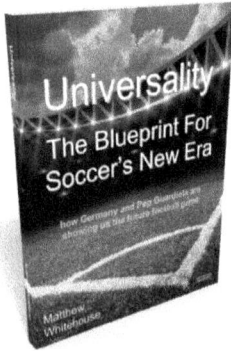

Universality | The Blueprint for Soccer's New Era: How Germany and Pep Guardiola are showing us the Future Football Game | Matthew Whitehouse

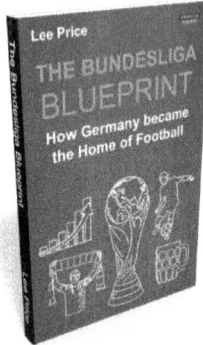

The Bundesliga Blueprint: How Germany became the Home of Football | Lee Price

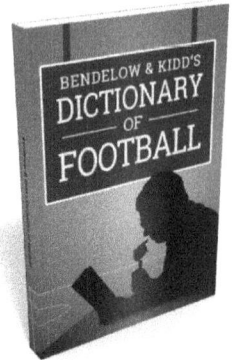

Bendelow and Kidd's Dictionary of Football | Ian Bendelow & Jamie Kidd

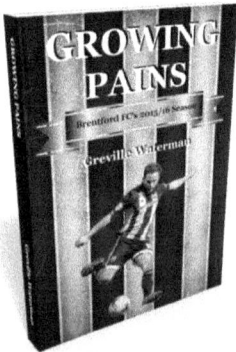

Growing Pains: Brentford FC's 2015/16 Season | Greville Waterman

Worst in the World: International Football at the bottom of the FIFA Rankings | Aidan Williams

Saturday Afternoon Fever: A Year on the Road for Soccer Saturday | Johnny Phillips

And non-football books:

The Hidden Motor: The Psychology of Cycling | Martijn Veltkamp

I've Got a Stat for You: My Life with Autism | Andrew Edwards

Plus many more!

www.ingramcontent.com/pod-product-compliance
Ingram Content Group UK Ltd.
Pitfield, Milton Keynes, MK11 3LW, UK
UKHW021354121125

8927UKWH00010B/109

9 781910 515556